T0219689

Lecture Notes in Computer Science 9277

Commenced Publication in 1973
Founding and Former Series Editors:
Gerhard Goos, Juris Hartmanis, and Jan van Leeuwen

More information about this series at http://www.springer.com/series/7412

Albert Ali Salah · Ben J.A. Kröse
Diane J. Cook (Eds.)

Human Behavior Understanding

6th International Workshop, HBU 2015
Osaka, Japan, September 8, 2015
Proceedings

 Springer

Editors
Albert Ali Salah
Computer Engineering Dept
Bogazici University
Bebek, Istanbul
Turkey

Diane J. Cook
Washington State University
Pullman, WA
USA

Ben J.A. Kröse
HvA University of Applied Sciences
Amsterdam, Noord-Holland
The Netherlands

ISSN 0302-9743   ISSN 1611-3349 (electronic)
Lecture Notes in Computer Science
ISBN 978-3-319-24194-4   ISBN 978-3-319-24195-1 (eBook)
DOI 10.1007/978-3-319-24195-1

Library of Congress Control Number: 2015948852

LNCS Sublibrary: SL6 – Image Processing, Computer Vision, Pattern Recognition, and Graphics

Springer International Publishing AG Switzerland is part of Springer Science+Business Media
(www.springer.com)

Preface

Domains where human behavior understanding is a crucial need (e.g., robotics, human-computer interaction, affective computing, and social signal processing) rely on advanced pattern recognition techniques to automatically interpret complex behavioral patterns generated when humans interact with machines or with other humans. This is a challenging problem where many issues are still open, including the joint modeling of behavioral cues taking place on different time scales, the inherent uncertainty of machine detectable evidences of human behavior, the mutual influence of people involved in interactions, the presence of long term dependencies in observations extracted from human behavior, and the important role of dynamics in human behavior understanding.

The Sixth Workshop on Human Behavior Understanding (HBU), organized as a satellite to the 2015 ACM International Joint Conference on Pervasive and Ubiquitous Computing (UBICOMP 2015, Osaka), gathered researchers dealing with the problem of modeling human behavior under its multiple facets (expression of emotions, display of relational attitudes, performance of individual or joint actions, imitation, etc.). The HBU workshops, previously organized jointly with the International Conference on Pattern Recognition (ICPR 2010, Istanbul), the International Joint Conference on Ambient Intelligence (AMI 2011, Amsterdam), the IEEE/RSJ International Conference on Intelligent Robots and Systems (IROS 2012, Algarve), ACM Multimedia (ACM MM 2013, Barcelona), and the European Conference on Computer Vision (ECCV 2014, Zürich), have highlighted different aspects of this problem since their inception.

The 6th HBU workshop focused on behavior analysis for the elderly. A better life for the aging population requires facilitating technologies, digital assistance, smart and multimodal monitoring, and technologies for health assessment and intervention. While different aspects of mobile platforms and ubiquitous computing are tackled in several venues, the HBU workshop specifically solicited human behavior analysis solutions that clearly advance the field, and chart the future of behavior-sensing for the elderly, which brings its own issues and challenges.

The two keynote speakers of the workshop were Dr. Tanzeem Choudhury (Cornell University) and Jakob E. Bardram (IT University of Copenhagen). In the first keynote talk, entitled "Tracking Behavioral Symptoms of Mental Illness and Delivering Personalized Interventions Using Smartphones and Wearables," Dr. Choudhury argued that continuous and unobtrusive sensing of behaviors has tremendous potential to support the lifelong management of mental illnesses by: (1) acting as an early warning system to detect changes in mental well-being, (2) delivering context-aware, personalized micro-interventions to patients when and where they need them, and (3) by significantly accelerating patient understanding of their illness. She discussed her group's work on turning sensor-enabled mobile devices into well-being monitors and instruments for administering real-time/real-place interventions.

It is obvious that there is much to learn from behavior traits collected in a semi-automatic fashion from ordinary smartphones. These traces can be used for analysis, as well as prediction. In his keynote talk, entitled "What is the Role of Personal Health Technology in Mental Health for the Elderly?" Dr. Bardram shared his experiences in designing and evaluating personal health technology for mental disorders (like depression) with a focus on elderly users. Based on their results from smartphone-based behavior sampling and mood forecasting, he discussed how to design personal health technology for mental health, with a specific focus on the design space of the elderly population.

This proceedings volume contains the papers presented at the workshop and an overview contribution of the focus theme by the co-chairs. We have received 15 submissions. Each paper was peer-reviewed by at least two members of the Technical Program Committee, with three reviews per paper on the average. Eleven papers were accepted, revised for the proceedings in accordance with reviewer comments, and presented at the workshop. The papers have been organized into thematic sections on Interacting with the Elderly, Learning Behavior Patterns, and Mobile Solutions. Together with the invited talks, the focus theme was covered broadly and extensively by the workshop.

We would like to take the opportunity to thank our Program Committee members and reviewers for their rigorous feedback, our authors and our invited speakers for their contributions, and our media sponsor Noldus for the help in disseminating news about the workshop.

September 2015   Albert Ali Salah
                                                                 Ben J.A. Kröse
                                                                 Diane J. Cook

Organization

Conference Co-chairs

Albert Ali Salah	Boğaziçi University, Turkey
Ben J.A. Kröse	HvA University of Applied Sciences and University of Amsterdam, The Netherlands
Diane J. Cook	Washington State University, USA

Technical Program Committee

Gilles Adda	CNRS LIMSI, France
Elisabeth André	Universität Augsburg, Germany
Juan Augusto	Middlesex University, UK
Lynne Baillie	Glasgow Caledonian University, UK
Jakob Bardram	IT University of Copenhagen, Denmark
Nadia Berthouze	University College London, UK
Özlem Durmaz İncel	Galatasaray University, Turkey
Gwenn Englebienne	University of Twente, The Netherlands
Cem Ersoy	Boğaziçi University, Turkey
Parisa Eslambolchilar	Swansea University, UK
Jesus Favela	CICESE, Mexico
Kaori Fujinami	Tokyo University of Agriculture and Technology, Japan
Stefan Göbel	Technische Universität Darmstadt, Germany
Dilek Hakkani-Tür	Microsoft Research, USA
Ahmed Helmy	University of Florida, USA
Tristan Henderson	University of St. Andrews, UK
Jesse Hoey	University of Waterloo, Canada
Larry Holder	Washington State University, USA
Hayley Hung	Delft University of Technology, The Netherlands
Alexandro Jaimes	Yahoo New York City, USA
Michel Klein	Vrije Universiteit Amsterdam, The Netherlands
Tsvika Kuflik	University of Haifa, Israel
Bruno Lepri	Fondazione Bruno Kessler, Italy
Janne Lindqvist	Rutgers University, USA
Paul Lukowicz	DFKI, Germany
Nuria Oliver	Telefonica, Spain
Francis Quek	Texas A&M University, USA
Elisa Ricci	Fondazione Bruno Kessler, Italy
Parisa Rashidi	University of Florida, USA

Stephan Sigg	University of Göttingen, Germany
Enrique Vidal	Universitat Politècnica de València, Spain
Katarzyna Wac	University of Geneva, Switzerland

Additional Reviewers

F. Serhan Daniş
Dean Kramer
Can Tunca
Remzi Yavuz

Contents

Learning Behavior Patterns

Behavior Analysis for Elderly

Albert Ali Salah[1]([✉]), Ben J.A. Kröse[2,3], and Diane J. Cook[4]

[1] Department of Computer Engineering, Boğaziçi University, Istanbul, Turkey
salah@boun.edu.tr
[2] HvA University of Applied Sciences, Amsterdam, The Netherlands
b.j.a.krose@hva.nl
[3] University of Amsterdam, Amsterdam, The Netherlands
[4] School of Electrical Engineering and Computer Science,
Washington State University, Pullman, WA 99164-2752, USA
cook@eecs.wsu.edu

Abstract. Ubiquitous computing, new sensor technologies, and increasingly available and accessible algorithms for pattern recognition and machine learning enable automatic analysis and modeling of human behavior in many novel ways. In this introductory paper of the 6th International Workshop on Human Behavior Understanding (HBU'15), we seek to critically assess how HBU technology can be used for elderly. We describe and exemplify some of the challenges that come with the involvement of aging subjects, but we also point out to the great potential for expanding the use of ICT to create many applications to provide a better life for elderly.

1 Introduction

The aging population of the world calls for new applications, systems, and technologies, to be used by older adults, or for them. By elderly, we typically mean people of age 65 and above, although, of course, "old" is a fuzzy concept. In this overview paper, we focus on technology for people whose physical and cognitive skills are declining or impaired due to ageing, and particularly look at human behavior understanding for elderly.

Information and communication technology (ICT) serves a number of critical roles for elderly. The present volume primarily deals with analysis of older people's behaviors via systems and applications that ultimately target new services for elderly or their caretakers. But ICT is also conceived as a way of connecting the elder people to social life, as more and more people spend time in virtual worlds, and use them as a surrogate social life [43]. This function, however, requires not so much an invention of new sets of applications, but a re-thinking of the interfaces of existing applications so that elderly can be included. Indeed, it is reported by Selwyn and colleagues that age is a highly significant factor when it comes to the individual's ability to access and make use of ICT [35,36]. Subsequently, several issues are important in this context:

– How should technology interfaces be designed so that the elder people can have as much access to technology as possible?

A.A. Salah et al. (Eds.): HBU 2015, LNCS 9277, pp. 1–10, 2015.
DOI: 10.1007/978-3-319-24195-1_1

– What special technologies or applications should be implemented to improve the life of elderly?
– What guidelines, safeguards, and considerations should the development of new technology for elderly follow?

This overview is not an exhaustive attempt to answer all these questions, but rather an introduction for setting the stage and for describing recent research in this area. In Sect. 2, we describe the interaction and interface aspects, and also discuss some common applications for elderly. Section 3 deals with approaches of machine learning (and pattern recognition) for creating systems that adapt to elderly. Section 4 is on mobile solutions, where applications are ported to (or created for) smart phones. We conclude in Sect. 5 with a few observations about this rapidly developing field.

2   Interactions with Elderly

ICT effort for elderly focused in the last decade on the Ambient Assisted Living (AAL) vision, where smart environments provide services to elderly, especially in health monitoring and assistance [8]. AAL seeks to enable healthy and independent ageing of elderly, preferably in their home environment, where caregiving costs are reduced. In Europe, this is an important area of research, and the Ambient Assisted Living Association (AALA) is organizing the Ambient Assisted Living Joint Programme (AAL JP)[1] to strenghten the ICT base for AAL. The recently completed "Support Action Aimed at Promoting Standards and Interoperability in the Field of AAL," within the auspices of AAL JP, promoted several representative use cases, which illustrate the focus of AAL research[2]:

– Behavior Monitoring
– Calendar Service
– Social Interaction with Smart TV
– Shopping and Nutrition Planner
– Mobility Assistant
– Personal Trainer
– Environmental Health Monitoring and Alarms at Work

As will be obvious from this list, behavior understanding is a crucial part of the AAL vision, and finds applications from monitoring to personal trainers.

Jaschinski and Ben Allouch list the three general domains of AAL as ageing well at home, in the community, and at work, respectively [16]. Their work is conducted under the SONOPA (SOcial Networks for Older adults to Promote an Active life) project, which is a part of the 5th AAL JP Call termed 'ICT-based Solutions for (Self-)Management of Daily Life Activities of Older Adults at Home'. This project combines smart home technology and a social network

---

[1] http://www.aal-europe.eu/.
[2] The final report available from http://www.aal-europe.eu/wp-content/uploads/2015/02/AAL_JP_Interop_D5_Final_Report.pdf.

environment to create an integrated system which empowers applications like activity recognition or social matchmaking (for exchanging knowledge and services). SONOPA is one of the many AAL projects conducted in the last decade, and goes beyond the implementation of the individual technologies, which is a major theme in the earlier projects of the domain.

Among the many challenges of AAL, Jaschinski and Ben Allouch list the intrusiveness of the systems, protection and control issues over the collected data, the constant involvement of caregivers and family members (as a social burden), and the difficulty of replacing solutions in use with novel, more technology-dependent solutions [16]. As can be seen from their analysis, these challenges are more social and cultural hurdles for the realization of AAL systems, as opposed to technological barriers (such as imperfect activity recognition systems), and require a strong design component.

This emphasis in interaction design is also apparent in the number of user studies devoted to measuring the quality of interaction of proposed smart systems for elderly. Sensor-based monitoring of the elderly, for instance the continuous detection of Activities of Daily Living (ADL) over long periods implies that a great amount of data should be collected, stored, processed and served to various applications. The creation of the ground truth for the training of learning systems is a costly process.

In another work performed under the SONOPA project, Eldib et al. propose the use of a network of visual sensors installed in an AAL environment to monitor the activities of an elderly over a long time [10]. The system is used to detect sleep patterns and bathroom visits, and subsequently can be used to find out about sleeping disorders. They use low-resolution visual sensors as opposed to a high-resolution camera (e.g. [14]), as a consideration for privacy concerns. They observe a single subject over ten months, and against a ground truth where the subject noted his sleep and wake up times in a diary, obtain good results for detecting the sleep patterns.

Such ground truth collection may not be possible for each observed subject and for every application scenario. While jotting down sleeping and waking times is not too much of an effort, other application scenarios may look at a broader set of activities, and thus require much more detailed ground truth annotation. Kanis et al. draw attention to the fact that the elderly needs to be empowered in terms of technology use, when it comes to applications and systems that fulfill the needs and respect the abilities of elderly [18]. They should know what kind of data are being collected, how they are used, and in general, "actively participate and contribute to sensing outcomes". Their approach is to record the data from a Living Lab, which is typically expensive to set up and operate, but allows much more realistic data collection over longer periods of time. These labs are equipped with various sensors, and allow a control center to select (and inspect) the data streams that are collected and stored at any given period. The people inhabiting the Living Lab for the duration of the experiment lead their normal lives (or a close approximation of it), and their daily activities are recorded.

Ranjan and Whitehouse divide activities of daily living (ADL) into two broad categories, those that are performed in a home environment, and those that are performed in a community, respectively [29]. They continue listing a number of indices that can be used to measure an elderly persons ability to live and function within a home or a community. These measures are used in clinical settings, and while their terminology and extent sometimes differ, they all measure the frequency and the ability level in the assessed activities. Ranjan and Whitehouse remark that "Every state in US has its own set of ADLs, which is then applied uniformly to all elderly within the state," pointing out to the need for creating a dictionary of ADL labels that can be used widely. Because the performance of the elderly over ADLs has legal and clinical implications (including decisions to commit a person to a care facility, and insurance related consequences) the measurement of these sometimes require controlled conditions and involvement of certified experts. The behavior sensing technology, if to be used in such situations, should create reliable measurements for the experts' use.

On the other hand, depending on the purpose, monitoring the behavior of the elderly is sometimes performed in a very simple and straightforward way. In Japan, for instance, a special tea-kettle is sold, which can connect to the Internet and send a message everytime it is used, thus signalling the well-being or routine-adherence of the elderly who uses it[3]. The specific cultural conditions lead to different technologies and solutions, making the design and the user interaction aspects essential. The assumptions under which behavior-sensing technology is presented to the elder should be different from those created for the contemporaries of the technology, and as such, should be validated via extensive user testing.

The cultural values shape the design, no matter how advanced the technology. An example that readily comes to mind is the SnowGlobe, designed by Visser et al., which can be placed in the house of the elder and its twin in the house of the loved ones [42]. The SnowGlobe displays movement of a remote user by glowing brighter, and users can exchange nudges by shaking their SnowGlobes, making the remote SnowGlobe blink. Subsequently, the device can increase the social connectedness of the elder by indicating presence and by displaying a visible call for attention only very briefly, so as not to disturb the daily life of the loved ones. This kind of concern is factored in by observing the cultural values and needs. Other forms of adaptation are achieved by designing systems that can learn over time.

3   Learning Behavior Patterns

Learning activities and behaviors is essential for pervasive systems, yet it is a challenging problem, because of the broadness of the domain, the possibilities of interleaving behaviors, and the inherent ambiguity in labeling the boundaries of behaviors [19].

---

[3] Internet-Connected Tea Kettle, http://www.mimamori.net/index.html.

Simple behavior monitoring systems may be built on rules and fixed thresholds. In [24], a smarthome system is proposed to assist caregivers of dementia patients. Video cameras, motion sensors (and their combinations to detect postures and fall), contact sensors (for the doors and the beds), and inexpensive smart carpets are used to detect presence and track the people in the environment. The detection of anomalies (including falls and too long time spent in bathroom) follows a set of manually designed rules with adjustable thresholds. The availability of cheap sensors enables off-the-shelf solutions for simple activity detection, with little need for incorporating machine learning for adaptation.

Learning is useful when the analyzed activities are rich enough to exhibit idiosyncratic variations, and when the detection of an activity is not trivial with the available sensor configuration. In such cases, learning is used to improve detection and prediction rates.

In the work of Derungs et al., stroke patients' activity patterns and habits during their residence in a day-care center was learned based on motion data recordings from wearable inertial measurement units [9]. For such patients, it is very useful to quantify the amount of motion primitives like sitting, standing and walking, over a defined period of therapy, as the therapist will be able to see periods of positive and negative trends. In their study, Derungs et al. suggest extending the motion sensors with contextual information encoded by light, temperature, acoustic and vital sign sensors. This would not only help automatic classification, but also allow greater insight into activities performed by the patient in different contexts.

The effect of context can be incorporated into different approaches in different ways. Selecting sensors that can use such information and feeding additional data streams to the classifiers is but one way. In the contribution of Lago et al., the notion of a contextualized sequential pattern is introduced. This approach extends prefix trees for event-based sequential behavior mining [20].

In sequential pattern mining, frequently co-occuring patterns are detected from a sequence of events [23]. In an AAL context, these may be behaviors of an elder, recorded and classified into discrete events, like eating, working, washing, and such. Traditional sequence mining approaches like the Apriori algorithm [1] look at groups of events (or items) that occur together. Markov model based approaches, on the other hand, try to predict the next activity in the sequence, and require that the temporal dimension should also be discretized [19]. To alleviate the problem of detecting interleaved or concurrent events, conditional random fields can be used [39], but the temporal discretization is still a problem. The T-pattern approach, and its extensions, model the arrival times of events based on other, related events, and construct behavior dictionaries [22,33], thus allowing for flexible event intervals.

These approaches enable the discovery of behavior patterns that occur frequently, but also the detection of deviations from expected behaviors. Taking the temporal dimension into account makes it possible to investigate the durations of behaviors, and can be relevant for observing progress or deterioration for health-related issues.

Soto-Mendoza et al. propose to mine the manually kept logs of geriatric centers for patient monitoring, to derive observations that go beyond the simple content of the logs and to detect anomalies [38]. Some of these annotations can be automatically generated by environmental sensors, or even wearables, but if they are kept by caregivers, they tend to be complex, with temporal gaps, replete with inconsistencies and noise. In their work, about 20.000 activity records were considered for 15 residents of the geriatric center, with 8–9 activities per day per resident. The activities were clustered in an unsupervised fashion, and then each cluster was labeled. A sequential pattern mining approach is used on the labeled events to determine abnormal events.

Sensor activations (or events) collected in an AAL environment are used to detect activities, which require some assumptions to be made [20]. As the semantic level of the description is increased, the labeling and segmentation of the elements of behavior becomes more difficult. For instance, when does *idling* end, and *working* begin? This is one difficulty in the assessment of the automatic behavior mining approaches; the labeling inaccuracy reflects both on the quality of the training data, and the specification of the ground truth.

Another major difficulty involves the requirements of testing. Behavior analysis for the elder may require long periods of testing for reliable and robust assessment of performance. For instance in [10], the camera-based classification of sleep patterns shows distinct seasonal trends, as the amount of light in the home environment is different during winter and summer. Shorter amounts of testing, or testing in lab-conditions may produce over-confident estimates of the system's accuracy.

In recent years, the number of mobile applications designed to monitor and maintain elderly has increased sharply. We give a few examples of these in the next section.

4   Mobile Solutions

For detecting activities of daily living, phones carry several advantages (and disadvantages) over the more traditional static sensor-based smart environment solutions. Hernández and Favela propose an approach to detect the fatigue of a user with a mobile phone carried in the hip area [15]. The idea is that the accelerometer data can be used for predicting breathing, which is correlated with oxygen consumption and with fatigue. Such an approach removes the need to be in the visual field of a camera for the detection of a certain property or activity. The energy requirement of the phone remains a disadvantage, especially if sensors are supposed to be sampled in a high-frequency, as dictated by the application demands.

Another issue is the cost of installing a dedicated monitoring system in the living environment of the elder, and the maintenance of such a system. Mobile phone based solutions are also sought to minimize the extra hardware cost [15].

In [4], a method is proposed for predicting the next location of an individual based on the observations of his mobility habits. While this problem can be cast into a framework of detecting frequent patterns (see Sect. 3), most learning approaches do not quickly adapt to habit changes, for instance due to location changes. Boukhechba et al. propose an incrementally updated tree structure to store the habits of the subject [4]. The association rules derived from the habit tree make prediction possible. Since GPS coordinates are stored continuously on the phone itself, reducing the storage and computation requirements is essential for the usability of such applications.

One should not forget that the evaluation of the interaction itself is not straightforward for elderly. Some difficulties are reported in Hernández and Favela, such as the inconvenience for a subject to attend a lab or similar measurement facility, and the unreliability of self-report measures [15]. Unobtrusive and reliable observation of the subjects is a major issue. Mobile applications can achieve this easily, through the installation or a single application that uses the numerous sensors on the phone. Another benefit is that the application, while monitoring the elder, can take actions and provide notifications, for instance to induce behavior change [32].

In smartphone notifications, different interrupt response patterns are observed depending on the context. In the work of Turner et al., a 6-month in-the-wild case study with over ten thousand to-do list reminders sent to close to a hundred users was performed [40]. The authors propose a four-step model of interrupting the user, where first the device seeks to gain the user's attention by sound, vibration, or visual cues. If the user chooses to react, a summary of the notification is provided to allow the user to either continue the previous activity, or to dedicate some time to the notification. The mobile phone, compared to a smart environment, more readily allows for discrete notifications, and they are handled over a very familiar interface.

5   Conclusions

ICT for the elderly has traditionally focused on healthcare aspects, and made extensive use of the rich sensor technology that allows monitoring and engaging subjects in smart environment scenarios [2,26,41]. High-impact applications in these scenarios include fall detection systems [7,25], tools for combatting cognitive decline [3,17,28], and serious games for exercising, rehabilitation and for socializing [6,11,12,21,30,31,37]. While we did not tackle them here, robotics research is also active in developing applications usable for the aging population [5,13,27,34].

Recent approaches, as exemplified in this overview paper, focus more on the interaction issues, and take the basic capabilities for granted. Off-the-shelf solutions exist for the building blocks of assistive systems, both in terms of hardware (i.e. inexpensive sensors), middleware, and analysis software [24]. More elaborate scenarios are now being considered, where behavior learning and adaptation is used to solve challenges of noise, idiosyncratic behaviors, and changes over time.

Mobile applications play an increasingly important role in this domain, and offer unobtrusive, interactive and flexible solutions. While issues like power consumption for continuously running applications and compatibility issues remain as open challenges, long-term studies produce promising results, with high acceptability and usability.

Acknowledgments. This publication was supported by the Dutch national program COMMIT, project VIEWW.

References

1. Agrawal, R., Srikant, R., et al.: Fast algorithms for mining association rules. In: Proceedings of the 20th International Conference Very Large Data Bases (VLDB), vol. 1215, pp. 487–499 (1994)
2. Alemdar, H., Ersoy, C.: Wireless sensor networks for healthcare: a survey. Comput. Netw. **54**(15), 2688–2710 (2010)
3. Bharucha, A.J., Anand, V., Forlizzi, J., Dew, M.A., Reynolds, C.F., Stevens, S., Wactlar, H.: Intelligent assistive technology applications to dementia care: current capabilities, limitations, and future challenges. Am. J. Geriatr. Psychiatry **17**(2), 88–104 (2009)
4. Boukhechba, M., Bouzouane, A., Bouchard, B., Gouin-Vallerand, C., Giroux, S.: Online prediction of people's next point-of-interest: concept drift support. In: Salah, A.A., et al. (eds.) HBU 2015. LNCS, vol. 9277, pp. 97–116. Springer, Heidelberg (2015)
5. Broekens, J., Heerink, M., Rosendal, H.: Assistive social robots in elderly care: a review. Gerontechnology **8**(2), 94–103 (2009)
6. Brown, J.A.: Let's play: understanding the role and meaning of digital games in the lives of older adults. In: Proceedings of the International Conference on the Foundations of Digital Games, pp. 273–275. ACM (2012)
7. Chaudhuri, S., Thompson, H., Demiris, G.: Fall detection devices and their use with older adults: a systematic review. J. Geriatr. Phys. Ther. **37**(4), 178–196 (2014)
8. Cook, D.J., Das, S.K.: How smart are our environments? an updated look at the state of the art. Pervasive Mobile Comput. **3**(2), 53–73 (2007)
9. Derungs, A., Seiter, J., Schuster-Amf, C.: Activity patterns in stroke patients - is there a trend in behaviour during rehabilitation? In: Salah, A.A., et al. (eds.) HBU 2015. LNCS, vol. 9277, pp. 146–159. Springer, Heidelberg (2015)
10. Eldib, M., Deboeverie, F., Philips, W., Aghajan, H.: Sleep analysis for elderly care using a low-resolution visual sensor network. In: In: Salah, A.A., et al. (eds.) HBU 2015. LNCS, vol. 9277, pp. 26–38. Springer, Heidelberg (2015)
11. Gerling, K., Livingston, I., Nacke, L., Mandryk, R.: Full-body motion-based game interaction for older adults. In: Proceedings of the SIGCHI Conference on Human Factors in Computing Systems, pp. 1873–1882. ACM (2012)
12. Gerling, K.M., Schild, J., Masuch, M.: Exergame design for elderly users: the case study of silverbalance. In: Proceedings of the 7th International Conference on Advances in Computer Entertainment Technology, pp. 66–69. ACM (2010)
13. Görer, B., Salah, A.A., Akın, H.L.: A robotic fitness coach for the elderly. In: Augusto, J.C., Wichert, R., Collier, R., Keyson, D., Salah, A.A., Tan, A.-H. (eds.) AmI 2013. LNCS, vol. 8309, pp. 124–139. Springer, Heidelberg (2013)
14. Heinrich, A., Geng, D., Znamenskiy, D., Vink, J., de Haan, G.: Robust and sensitive video motion detection for sleep analysis. IEEE J. Biomed. Health Inform. **18**(3), 790–798 (2014)
15. Hernández, N., Favela, J.: Estimating the perception of physical fatigue among older adults using mobile phones. In: In: Salah, A.A., et al. (eds.) HBU 2015. LNCS, vol. 9277, pp. 84–96. Springer, Heidelberg (2015)

16. Jaschinski, C., Ben Allouch, S.: Understanding the user's acceptance of a sensor-based ambient assisted living application. In: In: Salah, A.A., et al. (eds.) HBU 2015. LNCS, vol. 9277, pp. 13–25. Springer, Heidelberg (2015)
17. Jorge, J.A.: Adaptive tools for the elderly: new devices to cope with age-induced cognitive disabilities. In: Proceedings of the 2001 EC/NSF Workshop on Universal Accessibility of Ubiquitous Computing: Providing for the Elderly, pp. 66–70. ACM (2001)
18. Kanis, M., Robben, S., Kröse, B.J.: How are you doing? enabling older adults to enrich sensor data with subjective input. In: In: Salah, A.A., et al. (eds.) HBU 2015. LNCS, vol. 9277, pp. 39–51. Springer, Heidelberg (2015)
19. Kim, E., Helal, S., Cook, D.: Human activity recognition and pattern discovery. IEEE Pervasive Comput. **9**(1), 48–53 (2010)
20. Lago, P., Jiménez-Guarín, C., Roncancio, C.: Contextualized behavior patterns for ambient assisted living. In: In: Salah, A.A., et al. (eds.) HBU 2015. LNCS, vol. 9277, pp. 132–145. Springer, Heidelberg (2015)
21. Larsen, L.H., Schou, L., Lund, H.H., Langberg, H.: The physical effect of exergames in healthy elderly - a systematic review. Games Health Res. Dev. Clin. Appl. **2**(4), 205–212 (2013)
22. Magnusson, M.S.: Discovering hidden time patterns in behavior: T-patterns and their detection. Behav. Res. Methods Instrum. Comput. **32**(1), 93–110 (2000)
23. Mooney, C., Roddick, J.: Sequential pattern mining - approaches and algorithms. ACM Comput. Surv. **45**, 19 (2013)
24. Moshnyaga, V., Osamu, T., Ryu, T., Hashimoto, K.: Identification of basic behavioral activities by heterogeneous sensors of in-home monitoring system. In: Salah, A.A., Kröse, B.J., Cook, D.J. (eds.) In: Salah, A.A., et al. (eds.) HBU 2015. LNCS, vol. 9277, pp. 160–174. Springer, Heidelberg (2015)
25. Mubashir, M., Shao, L., Seed, L.: A survey on fall detection: principles and approaches. Neurocomputing **100**, 144–152 (2013)
26. Osmani, V., Balasubramaniam, S., Botvich, D.: Human activity recognition in pervasive health-care: supporting efficient remote collaboration. J. Netw. Comput. Appl. **31**(4), 628–655 (2008). http://www.sciencedirect.com/science/article/pii/S1084804507000719
27. Pineau, J., Montemerlo, M., Pollack, M., Roy, N., Thrun, S.: Towards robotic assistants in nursing homes: challenges and results. Robot. Auton. Sys. **42**(3), 271–281 (2003)
28. Pollack, M.E.: Intelligent technology for an aging population: the use of ai to assist elders with cognitive impairment. AI Mag. **26**(2), 9 (2005)
29. Ranjan, J., Whitehouse, K.: Rethinking the fusion of technology and clinical practices in functional behavior analysis for the elderly. In: In: Salah, A.A., et al. (eds.) HBU 2015. LNCS, vol. 9277, pp. 52–65. Springer, Heidelberg (2015)
30. Rego, P., Moreira, P.M., Reis, L.P.: Serious games for rehabilitation: a survey and a classification towards a taxonomy. In: 2010 5th Iberian Conference on Information Systems and Technologies (CISTI), pp. 1–6. IEEE (2010)
31. Rice, M., Wan, M., Foo, M.H., Ng, J., Wai, Z., Kwok, J., Lee, S., Teo, L.: Evaluating gesture-based games with older adults on a large screen display. In: Proceedings of the 2011 ACM SIGGRAPH Symposium on Video Games, pp. 17–24. ACM (2011)
32. Salah, A.A., Lepri, B., Pianesi, F., Pentland, A.S.: Human behavior understanding for inducing behavioral change: application perspectives. In: Salah, A.A., Lepri, B. (eds.) HBU 2011. LNCS, vol. 7065, pp. 1–15. Springer, Heidelberg (2011)
33. Salah, A.A., Pauwels, E., Tavenard, R., Gevers, T.: T-patterns revisited: mining for temporal patterns in sensor data. Sensors **10**(8), 7496–7513 (2010)

34. Schulz, R., Wahl, H.W., Matthews, J.T., Dabbs, A.D.V., Beach, S.R., Czaja, S.J.: Advancing the aging and technology agenda in gerontology. The Gerontologist p. gnu071 (2014)

35. Selwyn, N.: The information aged: a qualitative study of older adults' use of information and communications technology. J. Aging Stud. **18**(4), 369–384 (2004)

36. Selwyn, N., Gorard, S., Furlong, J., Madden, L.: Older adults' use of information and communications technology in everyday life. Ageing Soc. **23**(05), 561–582 (2003)

37. Shim, N., Baecker, R., Birnholtz, J., Moffatt, K.: Tabletalk poker: an online social gaming environment for seniors. In: Proceedings of the International Academic Conference on the Future of Game Design and Technology, pp. 98–104. ACM (2010)

38. Soto-Mendoza, V., Beltrán, J., Chávez, E., Hernández, J., García-Macías, J.A.: Abnormal behavioral patterns detection from activity records of institutionalized older adults. In: In: Salah, A.A., et al. (eds.) HBU 2015. LNCS, vol. 9277, pp. 119–131. Springer, Heidelberg (2015)

39. Sutton, C., McCallum, A.: An introduction to conditional random fields for relational learning. In: Introduction to Statistical Relational Learning, pp. 93–128 (2006)

40. Turner, L.D., Allen, S.M., Whitaker, R.M.: Push or delay? decomposing smartphone notification response behaviour. In: In: Salah, A.A., et al. (eds.) HBU 2015. LNCS, vol. 9277, pp. 69–83. Springer, Heidelberg (2015)

41. Varshney, U.: Pervasive healthcare and wireless health monitoring. Mobile Netw. Appl. **12**(2–3), 113–127 (2007)

42. Visser, T., Vastenburg, M.H., Keyson, D.V.: Designing to support social connectedness: the case of snowglobe. Int. J. Des. **5**(3), 129–142 (2011)

43. White, H., McConnell, E., Clipp, E., Bynum, L., Teague, C., Navas, L., Craven, S., Halbrecht, H.: Surfing the net in later life: a review of the literature and pilot study of computer use and quality of life. J. Appl. Gerontol. **18**(3), 358–378 (1999)

Interactions with Elderly

Understanding the User's Acceptance of a Sensor-Based Ambient Assisted Living Application

Christina Jaschinski[1,2] and Somaya Ben Allouch[1(✉)]

[1] Saxion University of Applied Sciences, Enschede, Netherlands
{c.jaschinski, s.benallouch}@saxion.nl
[2] University of Twente, Enschede, Netherlands

Abstract. In this paper the acceptance of a sensor-based Ambient Assisted Living (AAL) application is investigated. To get an insight into the users' perception and needs, three fictive use scenarios were created that illustrated the potential features of the technology. Consequently, the scenarios were presented to primary (i.e., older adults) and secondary (i.e., formal and informal caregivers) user groups. Through focus groups and semi-structured interviews in France, UK and Belgium, fourteen design implications could be identified based on the preliminary analyses of the users' feedback. These implications will direct the future testing and development of the conceptual technology and can be meaningful to related AAL applications.

Keywords: Ambient Assisted Living (AAL) · Older adults · Technology acceptance behavior · User-centered design

1 Introduction

The vision of Ambient Assisted Living is to develop advanced ICT solutions that foster the autonomy, health, self-confidence, mobility and social participation of the aging community. The overall goal is to facilitate healthy and independent aging, support and unburden the care network and ultimately, control the expenses for health and social care [1, 2].

From a social and economic point of view, the development of these innovative technologies is almost inevitable, considering the demographic transition we experience. The elderly population is growing at a rapid rate and prognoses state that by 2050, one in every three persons in the more developed regions will be 60 years or older [3]. This leads to several challenges, including an aging workforce, more people with chronical conditions and in need of care, a shortage of caregivers and more responsibilities for family caregivers [2, 4]. However, more optimistic voices focus on the opportunities of this demographic shift. They consider this age group – especially the more affluent seniors – as an emerging market for innovative products and services that support healthy and active aging and help them to make the most of their third age [2, 5].

A.A. Salah et al. (Eds.): HBU 2015, LNCS 9277, pp. 13–25, 2015.
DOI: 10.1007/978-3-319-24195-1_2

1.1   Ambient Assisted Living

As stated by Van Den Broek, Cavallo and Wehrmann [2]: "There is no common view about the precise definition of AAL" (p. 15). However, after considering different attempts for describing and defining AAL [2, 4, 6] we found some common ground.

AAL builds on the principle of Ambient Intelligence [7] by developing a new generation of assistive technologies which are embedded (i.e., unobtrusively integrated into the environment); context-aware (i.e., aware of the environment); personalized (i.e., tailored to the specific needs of the individual user); adaptive (i.e., responsive to the user and the situational context); and anticipatory (i.e., anticipating the user's needs and desires without explicit request). The overall aim is to create digital environments that are empowering, supportive and safe for the elderly user.

AAL comprises various state-of-the-art technologies including smart homes, robotics and ambient, mobile and wearable sensors. Those technologies are combined with several advanced techniques, including activity recognition, context modeling, location identification, planning and anomaly detection (see [4] for a detailed review). In accordance with the variety of tools and techniques, the application domains of AAL are diverse. According to Van Den Broek, Cavallo and Wehrmann [2] AAL can be divided into three general application domains with each domain covering several sub-domains:

1. Ageing well at home
   (a) health, rehabilitation and care
   (b) coping with impairments and disabilities
   (c) activity management and monitoring
   (d) safety and security (personal and home)
   (e) activities of daily life oriented support
   (f) other common activities (i.e., shopping, eat and drink, social interaction)
2. Ageing well in the community
   (g) social inclusion
   (h) entertainment and leisure
   (i) mobility
3. Ageing well at work
   (j) access to working space
   (k) assuring environmental working conditions
   (l) support work activities
   (m) prevention of work-related diseases and injuries
   (n) safety and health regulation for employees

The current study was conducted as part of the SONOPA (SOcial Networks for Older adults to Promote an Active life) project. SONOPA focusses on the domains of aging well at home and aging well in the community. The following section describes the project and the conceptual application in more detail.

1.2 The SONOPA Project

The SONOPA project is part of the 5th AAL Joint Program Call termed 'ICT-based Solutions for (Self-)Management of Daily Life Activities of Older Adults at Home'. SONOPA aims to empower older adults to stay autonomous, active and socially connected and at the same time support and unburden their family caregivers [8]. Following this objective, SONOPA strives to provide an integrated solution, which combines smart home technology, a social network environment and activity recognition and matchmaking techniques. In essence, the conceptual SONOPA system consists of three major subcomponents.

1. A smart home environment with low-resolution visual sensors, PIR sensors and an intelligent user-interface. The intelligent user-interface is a web application that pushes information and recommendations at the appropriate time to the elderly in the home environment. The intelligent user-interface derives its input from various sources for example from the user's agenda, the social network activity, information pushed by family members and feedback from the SONOPA controller based on the sensor data. It is set up as a cloud-based solution can run on tablets or a smart TV.
2. An adapted and simplified social network that hosts all social interaction components like message system, friend management, activities and interest groups as well as real time chat and video calls.
3. The SONOPA controller that receives and processes all sensor data and data retrieved from the social network with advanced activity recognition and matchmaking algorithms.

At this stage the system is still in a prototype stage. By closely involving prospective users in the development and testing of the system, the system will be further improved and adapted to the user's feedback.

1.3 The Importance of User Involvement

AAL technologies could be the key to healthy and autonomous aging. However, while those technologies offer a promising outlook on the future of our aging society, technology adoption among older adults is typical low [9, 10]. Stereotyping, insufficient need assessment, and the cultural gap between developers and the older adult users are often reasons for non-adoption [9, 11]. Therefore, in the development and design of AAL technologies, it is crucial to closely involve older adults throughout the design and development process in order to fully understand their context, needs and desires [11, 12]. In addition, one should also pay attention to other stakeholders such as family and professional caregivers [4], as they are also facilitators of a successful adoption of AAL technologies. By closely involving the future users in this study, we aim to improve SONOPA to better correspond with their needs and hence be more likely to get accepted.

2 Method

To derive a better understanding of the users' needs and perceptions with regard to the conceptual SONOPA system, three use scenarios were developed and presented to the primary (i.e., older adults) and secondary (i.e., formal and informal caregivers) user groups. Focus groups and semi-structured interviews were conducted in the project's target countries France, United Kingdom and Belgium to collect the users' perspective.

2.1 Scenario Development

A workshop with all SONOPA consortium members was hold to create use scenarios for the SONOPA system. The consortium consists of professionals from different backgrounds including behavioral researchers, computer scientists, technical developers, marketing professionals and professionals working closely with the primary and secondary target group. The workshop started with a brainstorm session to specify the potential features of the SONOPA system. Thereby, we included the results from an initial user study that was conducted at the very beginning of the project. After grouping similar features together, the session resulted in 38 features, which after discussion, were further narrowed down to 14 features. The remaining features were then grouped into three topics:

1. **Smart Secretary:** focusing on sensor-based reminders and activity suggestions as well as fostering the connection with family members and providing some peace of mind;
2. **Matchmaking:** focusing on exchanging knowledge and services, matching users with similar interest across generations and providing opportunities for volunteering;
3. **Activity Game and Care Logbook:** focusing on gaming to monitor and encourage activity and coordinating care.

The consortium split up into 3 subgroups to compose the first version of each scenario. Subsequently, each scenario was presented to the other consortium partners and feedback was collected to finalize the scenarios (see Annex 1).

2.2 Participants

The participants from the primary and secondary user groups were recruited through the network of the end-user consortium partner in each of the target countries.

Primary User Group. In total, 17 older adults aged between 55 and 82 years (M = 73.41, SD = 6.88) participated in this study. Gender distribution in this user group was fairly equal with ten female participants and seven male participants. Only five participants lived alone, the others lived with a partner, friend or family member. The majority of the older adults was retired, one participant was self-employed and another was a voluntary worker. Concerning their ICT experience, 76 % of the older adults in this study indicated to use ICT tools (e.g., computer, smartphone or tablet) on a daily basis, mostly for purposes such as communication and mailing, writing and text editing, administration and finances, and information research. Only two participants rarely or never used ICT tools. About half of the older adults in this study used social network sites on a daily (n = 6) or weekly (n = 2) basis, the other had little experience with social network sites and rarely (n = 1) or never (n = 8) used social networks. The older adult participants in this study felt fairly healthy, active and socially connected according to their self-reported measures on a seven-point Likert scale (M^{Health} = 6.12, SD = 1.36; $M^{Physical}$ = 5.88, SD = 1.73; M^{Social} = 6.18, SD = 1.19).

Secondary User Group – Informal Caregivers. Five female informal caregivers participated in this study. They were aged between 63 and 81 years (M = 73.80, SD = 7.56) and most of them (n = 4) were retired. Two participants took full-time care of their husband, one participant took full-time care of her daughter, another was looking several times a day after her mother and the last one was the informal caregiver of a friend who she supported several times a week. They were fairly experienced with ICT tools and all but one informal caregiver used these tools on a daily basis, mostly for the purpose of mailing and communication, and information research. Moreover, three participants were experienced and frequent social network users.

Secondary User Group – Formal Caregivers. Five female formal caregivers, aged between 26 and 56 years (M = 45.8, SD = 12.38) participated in this study. Their average work experience in the field of elderly care was M = 15.00 years, SD = 8.94. They were experienced ICT users and used these tools for professional and various private purposes. All but one participant in this group used social network sites on a daily or weekly basis.

2.3 Procedure

Before starting the focus groups and semi-structured interviews, the participants were asked to fill in an informed consent form and a short questionnaire to gather some demographic data. After that, a short introduction of the SONOPA project was provided. In the first part of each session, several questions accessed the user's general experience and opinion with regard to social networks, sensors and other care-related ICTs. In the second part, each use scenario was presented to the user and evaluated with several follow-up questions. The third part concluded with a short demo and subsequent usability evaluation of the first prototype of the smart user-interface, displaying different types of information, which could be pushed to the intelligent interface in the user's home. Each session lasted about 60 to 90 min and was recorded and transcribed for subsequent analyses. The recorded material was then coded and grouped into common themes.

3 Preliminary Results

3.1 General Impression

This section describes the participants' overall impression of each use scenario.

Scenario 1. The focus of the 'smart secretary' scenario was on sensor-based reminders and activity suggestions as well as fostering the connection with family members and providing some peace of mind. The older adults regarded the features in this scenario especially useful for people who live on their own, with limited ICT skills and who start to experience some problems in their daily routine. However, the formal caregivers could also imagine these features to be helpful for clients who are still active and mobile, to get some extra incentives for activities and to prevent age-related decline. The older adults believed that the features in this scenario could stimulate the user to be more active and feel socially connected. The formal caregivers agreed that the prompts provided by the system could stimulate activity, but had their doubts that the features could improve the user's level of social connectedness. The support and peace of mind for the family, and the stimulating reminders were viewed as key benefits of this scenario. Concerns included among others, the potential intrusiveness of the system and also the burden it could put on a family member to be constantly in the loop of the whereabouts of his relative.

Scenario 2. The 'matchmaking' scenario focused on exchanging knowledge and services, matching users with similar interest across generations and providing opportunities for volunteering. Older adults, informal caregivers and formal caregivers thought that the features described in this scenario could stimulate activity and foster social connectedness. The participants thought that the key benefit of this scenario was that older adults were not just on the demand site but also contributed with their own skills and knowledge. Moreover, the features in this scenario helped the users to engage in new activities and find people with similar interests. Concerns were raised about the lack of added benefits compared to existing volunteer networks and the difficulty to find enough reliable and suitable volunteers.

Scenario 3. The 'activity game and care logbook' scenario put the focus on using gaming to monitor and encourage activity and coordinate care through an automated care logbook. Older adults, informal caregivers and formal caregivers perceived the features described in the scenario most suitable for older adults with an advanced need of care. The participants thought that the capabilities of the system to foster activity and social connectedness were limited as activity would be housebound and social interaction computer-mediated. A game that is entertaining and functional at the same time was viewed as a main advantage of this scenario. From the older adults' and the informal caregivers' perspective, another advantage was the possibility to get an objective view on the received level of care, which in turn increases the accountability of formal caregivers. However, according to the formal caregivers' feedback, the care logbook did not provide a lot of added value, as they already have systems and procedures in place for coordinating and exchanging with other caregivers.

3.2   Design Implications

After analyzing the collected data, several common themes were identified from the users' feedback and translated into specific design implications.

Specific and Flexible Value Propositions. The participants' feedback showed, that we have to rethink and specify some of SONOPA's suggested value propositions. For instance in contrast to our expectations, the formal caregivers showed little interest in using the collected sensor data in their role as professional caregiver. Moreover, gaming (scenario 3) was not perceived as suitable for all older adults. Several participants mentioned a lack of added value compared to existing solutions, e.g. with regard to the volunteer network (scenario 2) or the caregiver logbook (scenario 3). Another issue was the lack of need realization. One formal caregiver emphasized that some older adults do not realize that they need help and therefore, would not be receptive to technologies like SONOPA. Indeed, the older adults in this study found most features useful for other frail and lonely elderly, but not for themselves. To counter these issues, SONOPA should offer all services optional, so that the system appeals to the individual user's needs, wishes and abilities. These needs can change over time and SONOPA should be able to adapt to this change. For instance in scenario 1, a person with beginning cognitive decline should get more pushed information (i.e., reminders, alerts) than a person with better cognitive abilities. Flexibility is also important with regard to the context. For instance, in an emergency situation alerts should be pushed to the informal caregivers, while in a regular use mode sensor information could be pulled by the informal caregiver, whenever seen fit. Formal caregivers emphasized that SONOPA's value propositions must be clearly communicated to the older adults (e.g. by means of a short video) and that formal caregivers and informal caregivers could have a stimulating role in encouraging the older adults to try the system.

Foster Social Connectedness. The social interaction components of the SONOPA system (matchmaking, video calls, interest groups, event suggestions) were positively perceived by participants from all user groups. In general, the users believed that SONOPA could help older adults to stay in touch with family and friends, get linked to peers with the same interests, and consequently feel more connected and less lonely. In scenario 2, the informal caregivers and older adults especially liked that interaction was intergenerational. Moreover, the informal caregivers could imagine to use the social network component to connect to other informal caregivers in order to exchange personal experiences. However, participants emphasized that social interaction should not be limited to computer-mediated interaction, but that SONOPA should also foster face-to-face meetings.

Provide Leisure and Activity Features. In general, participants were positive about the suggested activity and leisure components. They liked that SONOPA could provide information and reminders about local events and stimulate activity. Participants suggested that SONOPA should be used as a channel to promote activities of local clubs and associations. A few older adults also liked the gaming aspect (scenario 3). The formal caregivers thought that the activity reminders (scenario 1) were also suitable for clients who are still active and mobile to prevent beginning functional decline.

Offer Information, Reminders and Daily Life Support. The participants in this study thought that the SONOPA reminders (scenario 1) were a good prompt to help the user to remember important things such a eating regularly or visiting the doctor, especially for people with beginning cognitive problems. The older adults also liked the social network for exchanging services (scenario 2) as it would offer them a platform to ask for help with daily life tasks. It was suggested that SONOPA should also include other informational features such as date, time, contact information of doctors and caregivers, and opening hours from local stores.

Include Health and Safety Features. Although the focus of SONOPA is not on health and safety features, informal caregivers and older adults suggested including pill reminders in the SONOPA system. One formal caregiver also suggested, that for older adults to adopt sensors in their home, more health or safety benefits have to be added to the SONOPA system. Older adults from the UK perceived the main benefits of scenario 3 to be the increased accountability and traceability of caregivers, to ensure that proper care is provided and nothing gets stolen from the house.

Empower Not Patronize. It was emphasized multiple times, that SONOPA should empower and not patronize the elderly user. Luckily, several formal caregivers perceived the reminders and event suggestions (scenario 1) as a positive stimulation. One formal caregiver even viewed SONOPA as a "buddy" who gives suggestions for activities without forcing them on the older adult. However, others feared the reminders could be perceived as annoying, intrusive and possibly infantilizing. Following this argumentation, participants liked about scenario 2, that older adults were not just on the demand site but also contributed with their own set of skills and knowledge. This in turn might increase their level of self-confidence. Moreover, the older adults liked that the users in this scenario decided on their own whether they needed help. In line with this, formal caregivers and informal caregivers alike, stressed that the clients or relatives should be in control of their life and decide if they want to use SONOPA; where sensors are placed; and which data is shared and with whom.

Provide Peace of Mind without Burdening the Informal Caregiver. Participants from each user group appreciated that SONOPA can support the informal caregivers and provide some peace of mind, by allowing them to check on the older adult from distance, alerting them in case of abnormal behavior, provide recommendations and reminders on their behalf, and logging care visits to the older adult's home. SONOPA was perceived as a useful support tool for the primary informal caregiver as well as for the supportive informal caregiver, who might live further away from the older adult. However, older adults and formal caregivers were concerned that SONOPA could put an extra burden on the informal caregivers by pushing too much information about the well-being of the older adult. This could be countered, by leaving it up to the informal caregiver, which data is consulted and when.

Clear Roles. A related requirement concerns the role allocation within the SONOPA context. The formal caregiver emphasized that is has to be clear, which caregiver is in charge of checking on the older adult to avoid conflicts with other caregivers. Another role conflict could emerge if professional caregivers become part of the SONOPA social network. They underline that there should be a clear distinction between the seniors' profiles and the professional caregivers' profiles as they just want to be contacted in their role as a professional.

Do Not Replace Human Contact. Participants from all user groups stressed that technologies like SONOPA cannot and should not replace the human caregiver and personal, face-to-face interactions. SONOPA was acknowledged as an supportive tool but not as a substitute, e.g. when coordinating care (scenario 3) or stimulating activity (scenario 1). Communication via the SONOPA system should strengthen family bonds and not replace personal visits. Ideally, computer-mediated communication via SONOPA should lead to face-to-face encounters.

Beware of Unwanted Side Effects. The participants' feedback made us alert for potential unwanted side effects of the SONOPA technology. First, SONOPA should not take over tasks, which the older adults can still perform on their own, thereby taking away their own initiative, instead of stimulating autonomy. Second, computer-mediated activities should not replace outdoor activities (scenario 3). Third, informal caregivers should not be overloaded with information, to avoid that notifications of serious events will perish in the sheer amount of data.

Increase Usability. According to the feedback of the participants, the SONOPA system needs to be user-friendly and easy-to-use. Luckily, the first impression of the intelligent user-interface was rather positive with regard to the overall usability and design. To further increase the usability, SONOPA should be able to integrate existing ICT systems and services that are already used by the prospective users. This way, they do not have to get acquainted to yet another new system.

Ensure Reliability and Data Security. It is of high importance that AAL technologies like SONOPA are reliable and work properly. The feedback of the participants made us alert for several challenges. First, it is a mistake to presume that older adults have the same routine every day and our activity recognition algorithms have to be able to cope with that. Second, for scenario 2 it could be difficult to find good matches between the older adults and the service providers. Third, in scenario 3 some caregivers doubted the quality and completeness of the collected activity data. Finally, another critical aspect is data security. Informal and formal caregivers pointed out that all sensitive and personal data collected by the system must be managed and stored securely, so the data cannot be misused.

Ensure Privacy and Unobtrusiveness. Privacy concerns and intrusiveness were prevalent concerns with regard to SONOPA, especially in scenario 1. Therefore, SONOPA reminders have to be adjusted to the individual user's needs and wishes. Moreover, the system should not be too visible or noisy, and should not tolerate intrusive advertisements in the social network environment.

Make the System Accessible and Affordable. Based on the feedback of the participants we can conclude that costs are a major decisive factor for adopting AAL technologies like SONOPA. Therefore, SONOPA should strive to be reasonably priced and accessible to all older adults, despite their potentially limited income.

4   Conclusions and Future Work

In this paper, we tested a conceptual sensor-based AAL application called SONOPA. To investigate potential acceptance issues, three fictive use scenarios were developed and presented to primary (i.e., older adults) and secondary (i.e., formal and informal caregivers) user groups. After a preliminary analyses, the collected feedback was grouped into common themes and translated into fourteen design implications that will guide the future development and testing of the SONOPA technology: (1) Specific and Flexible Value Propositions, (2) Foster Social Connectedness, (3) Provide Leisure and Activity Features, (4) Offer Information, Reminders and Daily Life Support, (5) Include Health and Safety Features, (6) Empower Not Patronize (7) Provide Peace of Mind without Burdening the Informal Caregiver (8) Clear Roles, (9) Do Not Replace Human Contact, (10) Beware of Unwanted Side Effects, (11) Increase Usability, (12) Ensure Reliability and Data Security, (13) Ensure Privacy and Unobtrusiveness, (14) Make the System Accessible and Affordable.

Although these implications derive from a small sample and data were collected in the context of a specific AAL application, these results follow up on previous work. For instance, Peek et al. [13], conducted a systematic review of factors influencing the acceptance of technologies for aging in place and identified 'high cost' and 'privacy implications' as most frequent concerns, while 'safety' was the most prevalent benefit. The 'perceived need' for a technology was also a very important acceptance factor in that study. Beer and Takayama [14] who studied the acceptance of a mobile remote presence system for older adults found 'privacy' and less 'face-to-face contact' among the major concerns while 'socialization' was perceived as a benefit. Therefore, it can be assumed that the identified design implications are not just relevant for the further development of SONOPA, but that these guidelines are also meaningful to other AAL technologies.

Future work will focus on expanding the data analyses and testing SONOPA in the field, to gather feedback in a more natural use-setting. Despite their preliminary nature, we believe that the identified implications will be valuable for the improvement of SONOPA and provide other researchers and developers of AAL technologies with valuable insights to shape their own technology according to the users' needs.

Acknowledgements. Part of this research is supported by the AAL Joint Program under contract number AAL-2012-5-187. We would like to thank our partners for their effort and support and express our appreciation to all participants for their contribution.

Appendix 1

Scenario 1. *Mary's wake-up call at 07:00 didn't happen, because Sonopa detected that she is already out of bed and in the bathroom, but Sonopa does remind her, on the tablet by her bed, that she has an appointment with the optician. Sonopa sees that Mary has not planned any activities after the optician's appointment, as a result a recommendation is proposed to her via the tablet to go to an art exhibition that takes* *place 15 min from the optician's place. She still has time to prepare and enjoy a fine breakfast. She is following some advice that she got from Sonopa about the importance of having a nutritious breakfast. The Sonopa system had noticed that Mary often skips breakfast.*

As she is preparing to leave the house, Sonopa detects her presence in the corridor near the main door, and as she picks up the keys, Sonopa registers that she is about to leave the house and reminds her to buy some groceries. Mary consults her grocery list which her son, Steve, left in Sonopa when he visited yesterday and inspected the fridge. When Mary comes back after an eventful day, Sonopa tells her via the big screen in the kitchen that today was the last day of school for her granddaughters, and maybe she can send them a message and ask about their grades? Mary sends a text message via a speech messaging tool. Fifteen minutes later, Susan (her grandchild) pushes her school report to Mary's tablet and requests a short video chat via the screen. Mary and Susan have a nice video chat and Mary tells Susan that her eyes are improving and that she enjoyed the art exhibition afterwards. Since Mary uses Sonopa she feels more in touch with her family, especially with her grandchildren. Her family also likes Sonopa because of Mary's shared sensor data that they can consult. This way, they always know how Mary is doing and have more peace of mind.

Scenario 2. *Charles is 70 years old and lives alone as his wife passed away a couple of years ago. Charles was always engaging in a lot of different activities with his wife such as cycling or hiking but since she died, he has not found the motivation to do that anymore. He feels that since he has stopped being active, his general wellbeing has decreased. Charles often feels lonely now and doesn't have the energy to do much. He also gets out of breath more easily than before. This worries him and his family. Charles' family is trying to organize activities with him but they are living three hours away from his place, which makes it hard to meet on a regular basis. That is why his daughter has suggested to him to try the Sonopa system that puts him in touch with people who carry out different activities with him in his hometown. Charles has created a Sonopa profile on which he indicates that he is looking for persons who could motivate him to go more outdoors and carry out activities with him. Via the Sonopa matchmaking platform Charles got matched up with John. John is 35 year old and lives in Charles' hometown. He is currently out of work but wants to start a career as a fitness trainer. To try out his coaching skills and get some experience in this field he applied to be a member of the Sonopa network. The Sonopa company screened John to verify that he is a trusted coach. John offers fitness coaching via telepresence and also organizes fun fitness activities such as hiking tours every Sunday. Charles immediately got interested when Sonopa suggested to him to meet with John as he loves hiking. He also likes the video-training which he can conveniently perform at home. Additionally, the Sonopa system provides Charles simple activity recommendations based on the sensed activity levels. For instance, based on the weather report, the system will recommend a walk in the afternoon, but only if Charles has not left the house before noon, and only after 14:30, because the system has discovered that Charles usually takes a nap until then. Charles and John are very happy that the Sonopa sensor data shows that Charles has been much more active since he started using Sonopa. Therefore, Charles continues to participate in John's activities every Sunday where he* *also made a couple of new friends. At least once a week Charles gets in touch with his family via the video calling tool included in Sonopa. During these calls he explains the different activities he has carried out during the week and his daughter understands that the Sonopa system has helped him to become more active and involved.*

Scenario 3. *Emma receives a notification on her screen that another elder in the Sonopa social network wants to play a game. She accepts and joins the game. Challenges are proposed to them using the screen that make them move in the whole house such as 'go in your room and look for an old object, come back and show it to the screen'. This is an opportunity for them to talk face to face and remember past events. While she goes to her room to retrieve the object, the PIR sensors follow her movements and compare her speed with the measures from previous games. Players pass levels, get rewards, and new, more complex challenges are proposed (e.g. increase the number of visits, which could be motivation to call relations, family or neighbors to participate and come). Each time one of the carers who visit Emma comes, his entrance is logged by the visual sensor placed at the entrance of the house. All carers receive periodically by email a report on earlier visits of caregivers when they came, and how intense was the visit (how long, in how many rooms). The information is also archived in a shared agenda(*). This information will aid them to coordinate their help. Also are included monitoring parameters such as long term behavior changes, and a profile of the user's activity. Without Sonopa, (1) carers such as family would have to rely on asking the elder about visitors during the week, and about their activity levels. The answers would be subjective and not very accurate. This is a well-known phenomenon even for people with top mental capabilities, let alone for possibly forgetful erders. (2) carers do not know who has visited the elder. Several professional organizations come to the elder's home, but today there is no exchange of information, and these agencies do not always know what other professional carers do. Thanks to the report, they can know each other and coordinate their activities. Sonopa provides the care givers with more in-depth, comprehensive and objective information about the elder's activities. The report is the basis for quickly focusing on what is most relevant for the specific user and for sharing information more quickly, knowing for example if a carer had any problem (such as missing money to go shopping, or lack of drug.) It also gives a measure of the elder's socialization, if the elder went outside or if the elder has moved to hospital. This also helps to reassure the family. Using the Sonopa system the help can be given to the right person at the right time.*

References

1. Ambient Assisted Living Association. http://www.aal-europe.eu/about/objectives
2. Van Den Broek, G., Cavallo, F., Wehrmann, C.: AALIANCE Ambient Assisted Living Roadmap. IOS press, Amsterdam (2010)
3. United Nations: DESA: World Population Ageing: 1950-2050. United Nations Publications, New York (2002)
4. Rashidi, P., Mihailidis, A.: A survey on ambient-assisted living tools for older adults. IEEE J. Biomed. Health Inform. **17**, 579–590 (2013)

5. Kohlbacher, F., Herstatt, C.: The Silver Market Phenomenon: Business Opportunities in an Era of Demographic Change. Springer, Heidelberg (2008)
6. Kleinberger, T., Becker, M., Ras, E., Holzinger, A., Müller, P.: Ambient intelligence in assisted living: enable elderly people to handle future interfaces. In: Stephanidis, C. (ed.) Universal Access in HCI, Part II, HCII 2007. LNCS, vol. 4555, pp. 103–112. Springer, Berlin Heidelberg (2007)
7. Aarts, E., Encarnação, J.: True Visions: The Emergence of Ambient Intelligence. Springer, Heidelberg (2006)
8. SONOPA Consortium. www.sonopa.eu
9. Lee, C., Coughlin, J.F.: Perspective: older adults' adoption of technology: an integrated approach to identifying determinants and barriers. J. Prod. Innovat. Manag 32, 747–759 (2014)
10. Heart, T., Kalderon, E.: Older adults: Are they ready to adopt health-related ICT. Int. J. Med. Informat. 82, e209–e231 (2011)
11. Eisma, R., Dickinson, A., Goodman, J., Syme, A., Tiwari, L., Newell, A.F.: Early user involvement in the development of information technology-related products for older people. Univ. Access Inf. Soc. 3, 131–140 (2004)
12. Ballegaard, S.A., Hansen, T.R., Kyng, M.: Healthcare in everyday life: designing healthcare services for daily life. In: Proceedings of the SIGCHI Conference on Human Factors in Computing Systems, pp. 1807–1816. ACM, New York (2008)
13. Peek, S.T., Wouters, E.J., van Hoof, J., Luijkx, K.G., Boeije, H.R., Vrijhoef, H.J.: Factors influencing acceptance of technology for aging in place: a systematic review. Int. J. Med. Informat 83, 235–248 (2014)
14. Beer, J.M., Takayama, L.: Mobile remote presence systems for older adults: acceptance, benefits, and concerns. In: Proceedings of the 6th International Conference on Human-Robot Interaction, HRI 2011, pp. 19–26. ACM, New York (2011)

Sleep Analysis for Elderly Care Using a Low-Resolution Visual Sensor Network

Mohamed Eldib[1]([✉]), Francis Deboeverie[1], Wilfried Philips[1],
and Hamid Aghajan[1,2]

[1] TELIN-IPI-IMINDS, Ghent University,
Sint-Pietersnieuwstraat 41, Ghent, Belgium
mohamed.eldib@telin.ugent.be
[2] Department of Electrical Engineering, Stanford University,
350 Serra Mall, Palo Alto, CA, USA

Abstract. Nearly half of the senior citizens report difficulty initiating
and maintaining sleep. Frequent visits to the bathroom in the middle of
the night is considered as one of the major reasons for sleep disorder.
This leads to serious diseases such as depression and diabetes. In this
paper, we propose to use a network of cheap low-resolution visual sensors (30 × 30 pixels) for long-term activity analysis of a senior citizen
in a service flat. The main focus of our research is on elderly behaviour
analysis to detect health deterioration. Specifically, this paper treats the
analysis of sleep patterns. Firstly, motion patterns are detected. Then,
a rule-based approach on the motion patterns is proposed to determine
the wake up time and sleep time. The nightly bathroom visit is identified using a classification-based model. In our evaluation, we performed
experiments on 10 months of real-life data. The ground truth is collected
from the diaries in which the senior citizen wrote down his sleep time
and wake up time. The results show accurate extraction of the sleep
durations with an overall Mean Absolute Error (MAE) of 22.91 min and
Spearman correlation coefficient of 0.69. Finally, the nightly bathroom
visits analysis indicate sleep disorder in several nights.

Keywords: Sleep disorder · Sleep analysis · Visual sensor networks ·
Ambient assisted living

1 Introduction

Sleeping is of the utmost importance to everyone, especially for the elderly.
According to the following study [8], the authors have found that 30 % of the
people have trouble to sleep. In another study [7] on more than 9000 elderly
subjects, more than 4500 subjects have reported difficulty falling asleep due to
frequent visits to the bathroom at night for voiding, waking up too early, or
sleeping late.

Nocturia is defined as the awakening from sleep to urinate after an individual has gone to sleep. In a recent study [20], Nocturia-related awakenings are

© Springer International Publishing Switzerland 2015
A.A. Salah et al. (Eds.): HBU 2015, LNCS 9277, pp. 26–38, 2015.
DOI: 10.1007/978-3-319-24195-1_3

reported to cause significant sleep disorder and fatigue in elderly patients. Sleep disorder increases the risk of poor physical function and decreases the cognitive function. This dangers the quality of life of the senior citizens. The diseases associated with insufficient sleep for the senior citizens have a significant impact on health care.

In the approaching decade, the institutions that take care of the senior citizens will run into operational and financial problems. Aging-in-place presents itself as a promising solution for health care systems. Recently, aging-in-place has gained a lot of attention due to the fact that many senior citizens prefer to age and maintain their independence as long as possible in their own homes [5], because of the emotional and physical associations, memories and comfort. Aging-in-place promotes well-being of older people without sacrificing the quality of life in a familiar environment and maintains valuable social networks. The success of aging-in-place depends on Ambient Assisted Living (AAL) tools, which have witnessed tremendous improvements in the last few years. AAL tools provide supervision and assistance with activities of daily living (ADL) to prevent and cure health conditions, and improve wellness of seniors.

We have been monitoring a senior citizen living in a service flat in Belgium for one year using a network of 10 low-resolution visual sensors. In this paper, we discuss our efforts to analyze sleep patterns. We are still developing approaches and algorithms to recognize more ADLs to detect increasing or decreasing health conditions. The main contributions of this paper are: (1) indirect detection of sleep durations and nightly bathroom visits. (2) The evaluation of the sleep analysis approach on a real-life dataset covering 10 months by comparing the results to ground truth, and (3) studying the relation between sleep disorder and the number of the nightly bathroom visits.

The paper is organized as follows. In Sect. 2, we present related work. Section 3 explains our approach of detecting sleep durations and nightly bathroom visits. Section 4 describes our experimental results. Finally, Sect. 5 offers some conclusions.

2   Related Work

The sensors used in AAL tools can be divided into two main categories: (1) wearable sensors, smartphone and (2) ambient sensors. In the first category [2,10], various wearable sensors, such as accelerometers, gyroscopes, proximity sensors and e-textile sensors, could be attached to the subject of interest to monitor vital signs such the heart beats, the respiration, the blood pressure and the glucose level and the muscle activity. In [16] the authors used a chest strap and a wristband wearable device to analyze the sleep patterns, and to identify the most relevant sleep parameters for stress detection. They evaluated their approach on 10 healthy pilgrims for 18 days. Zhenyu Chen et al. [4] presented an approach for measuring sleep duration based on a novel best effort sleep (BES) model. The BES model infers sleep using smartphones in a completely unobtrusive way. Their approach achieved an accuracy of 42 min on 8-persons for 7 days.

Bed occupancy sensor (BOS), tele-actimeter and sleep logs have been used in [14] to analyze total sleep time and sleep quality. However, wearable sensors and smartphones face a few disadvantages, such as battery life, high cost, being forgotten to be worn by the user, and the requirement to be worn on specific body parts to provide reliable measurements.

In the second category, ambient sensors are installed in the home environment by mounting them on the wall or the ceiling, embedded in furnitures and appliances. Passive Infrared Motion (PIR) sensors, visual sensors and Radio Frequency Identification (RFID) are the most popular among researchers. In [17], the authors used pressure sensor matrix to monitor the elders sleep behavior in bed. Enamul Hoque et al. [11] presented a sleep monitoring system based on active RFID-based sensors equipped with accelerometers. They evaluated their system for six nights on one subject. Despite the popularity of PIR sensors, they are known of having the following problems: (1) highly bursty output which limits PIR systems to single-person scenarios; (2) self-triggering due to sudden changes in environmental conditions such as heating, ventilating, and air conditioning; (3) PIR cannot sense people who are standing still [19].

There has been a few attempts to use camera for sleep analysis. In [9], the authors proposed a camera-based system combining video motion detection, motion estimation, and texture analysis with machine learning for sleep analysis. Their system should be installed in front of the bed to perform the sleep analysis. They used six video sequences with six different subjects to validate their system. A sleep monitoring system using Kinect has been proposed in [13]. The system used depth and infrared images to track the body for posture and movements analysis. The system has been evaluated on 20 simulated use-cases for 7 hours. In [15]. The authors used Kinect and contact-based pressure mattress to build a sleep monitoring system. The system combined rule-based and supervised learning methods to recognize sleep patterns of 7 different individuals simulating their sleep habits. In another study [12], the authors introduced a Kinect-base setup where a number of measures are computed to quantify the amount of relevant motion. Then, a binary classifier is used for the actual sleep detection.

Our approach of sleep analysis is different than those proposed in [9,13,15]. The authors used a high-resolution camera in front of the bed for sleep analysis which raises concerns about the privacy. In contrast, we opted to use low-resolution cameras, and not cameras with regular imaging resolutions which often raise privacy concerns and increase the cost of the sensor network. Also, no visual sensor has been installed inside the bedroom for sleep analysis. In [4,9,11,16], they performed sleep analysis on small datasets (several days) and the datasets were captured in lab environments. On the contrary, we perform long-term sleep analysis on 10 months of real-data recordings in a real service flat setup.

3   Sleep Analysis Approach

We used the low-resolution visual sensors [3] in previous studies [6,18] for person tracking in our lab, as a first step, towards building a sensor network in a

Fig. 1. The camera consists of stereo pair of image sensors controlled by a digital signal controller. Each image sensor delivers an image with a resolution of 30 × 30 pixels.

service flat for activity analysis. The sensor network deployed in the service flat is composed of 10 cameras as shown in Fig. 1. Each camera includes a stereo pair of visual sensors producing images of 30 × 30 pixels, and a digital signal controller. The visual sensor images often suffer from artifacts due to read out problems such as electrical interference, and it does not have built-in processing capabilities such as lens shading correction resulting in a reduction of the image's brightness (vignetting). This can be solved by performing devignetting on the digital signal controller.

The results in this paper are obtained from a system setup in a service flat, covering an area of 8 × 4.4 m². Figure 2 displays the living space layout with camera positions. The voluntary older person participating in the installation is 83 years old with diabetes and decreased mobility due to a partial paralysis. However, the resident has a very clear mind. No instructions were given to the senior citizen about the way and the time of performing the sleep activity. The senior citizen was hospitalized in April 2014, December 2014 and January 2015 for 18, 8 and 9 days, respectively.

One of the major challenges of the current setup is the unavailability of the visual sensors in the bedroom and the bathroom, which increase the difficulty of detecting accurate sleep durations and nightly bathroom visits.

We propose a simple approach that estimates the presence of the senior citizen in the room. Let $p_k(t)$ be the average number of foreground pixels in frames $t \ldots t + L - 1$ of camera k. Then, we output a motion feature vector $\vec{x}_t = (p_k(t) \ldots p_m(t))$ where m is the number of the visual sensors. In this paper, we opted to use the correlation method as a foreground/background subtraction algorithm for its good performance with the visual sensor of [3], as indicated in a previous study [18]. The obtained results were good enough for detecting motion patterns produced by the senior citizen as shown in Fig. 3.

We use a rule-based approach to detect the wake up time and sleep time. The inference rules have the generic form: IF A AND/OR B THEN C. The wake up time is detected when the senior citizen produces sufficient motion in the service flat in the morning. The motion should last for several minutes (e.g., more than 30 min) to indicate the senior citizen has actually woken up, and not

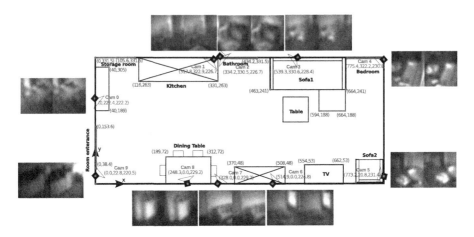

Fig. 2. Living space layout showing the configuration of ten visual sensors (each containing stereo image sensor) covering an area of 8×4.4 m^2.

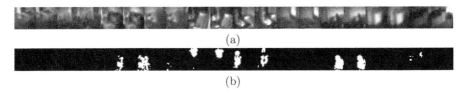

(a)

(b)

Fig. 3. (a) Original images, (b) foreground images produced by the correlation method.

to be confused with the nightly bathroom visit. Wherein, sleep time is detected by considering the last motion the senior citizen produces (e.g., turning off the TV at night). The TV status is detected by computing the intensity values of the TV's region of interest. If the intensity proceeds a threshold, then the TV status is on. Otherwise, the TV status is off.

Let w_d be the wake up time of day d and s_{d-1} be the sleep time of day $d-1$. Then, the sleep duration u_d of day d is computed as

$$u_d = w_d - s_{d-1} \tag{1}$$

For the nightly bathroom visits, we use a Support Vector Machine (SVM) classifier with RBF kernel for detecting the nightly bathroom visit. The training data of the nightly bathroom visit D are defined as:

$$D = \{\vec{x}_i, y_i | y_i \in \{0,1\}\}_{i=1}^n, \tag{2}$$

where the y_i is either 0 (not in the bathroom) or 1 (inside the bathroom), indicating the class to which the feature vector $\vec{x}_i$ belongs. In the training step, we annotate one week of data containing the nightly bathroom visits. Then, we use the annotated data to build an SVM model. After building the model, the motion feature vectors are computed for the test days and classified. Finally, the nightly bathroom visit is valid when:

1. The bathroom visit happens after 30 min from the time the senior citizen goes to sleep.
2. There is a time difference of 60 min between two consecutive bathroom visits.
3. The bathroom visits take place between the bedtime and 5 am.

4   Experiments

To validate the performance of our proposed approach, we collected 10 months of real-life recordings using a network of 10 low-resolution visual sensors producing an image of 30×30 pixels at a frame rate of 50 fps. Video capturing is time-synchronized. The data of each day correspond to a 24 hour period, starting from midnight.

In this section, we compare the estimated sleep durations against ground truth. The ground truth is collected from diaries in which the elderly wrote down his sleep time and wake up time. The ground truth obtained from the diary has been validated by a health insurance partner. Our health insurance partner is actively involved in the organization and coordination of care and accompaniment of patients in home care. Especially, the participation in the deliberations and consultations 'around the patient's bed'. The data are interpreted in real-time by visualizing the wake up time and sleep time on a smart display to the caregiver and the senior citizen.

Figure 4 shows the comparison between the estimates and the ground truth of sleep duration for two different periods. The vertical error bars in Fig. 4 shows the overestimates and the underestimates of sleep durations. About 20 % of the cases are overestimated and 6 % of the cases are underestimated by more than 30 min. There are more overestimates than underestimates of sleep durations due to standing up without putting the lights on. Figure 5 shows the estimates and the ground truth of the wake up time. The overestimates of the wake up time can be clearly seen in the winter period (Fig. 5b) than the summer period (Fig. 5b). Similarly, Fig. 6 shows the estimates and the ground truth of the sleep time.

Next, we compute the cumulative score (CS) to evaluate the sleep duration performance within error ranges. The cumulative score $CS(j)$ is defined as $\frac{N_{e \leq j}}{N} \times 100\%$ where $N_{e \leq j}$ is the number of days on which sleep duration estimates have an absolute error not higher than j minutes. Figure 7 shows the CS of the sleep duration estimates. At an absolute error range of 25 min, we achieve an accuracy of 70 %. The accuracy reaches 80 % with an absolute error range of 40 min. We use the Mean Absolute Error (MAE) to measure the performance of the senior citizen sleep duration estimates:

$$MAE = \sum_{d=1}^{N} \frac{|u_d - u'_d|}{N},\tag{3}$$

where u_d is the sleep duration estimate of day d, u'_d is the actual sleep duration of day d and N is the number of ground truth days. The MAE of the sleep duration estimates is 22.91 minutes. Then, the Relative Absolute Error (RAE) is computed to measure the error percentage:

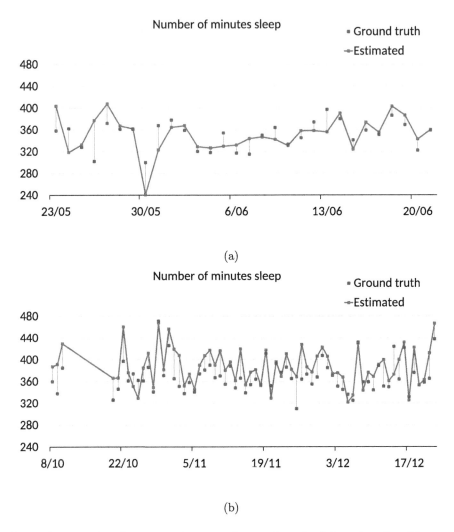

Fig. 4. A comparison between estimates and ground truth of sleep duration. The vertical error bars show the overestimates and the underestimates of sleep duration: (a) May and June, (b) October, November and December.

$$RAE = \frac{\sum_{d=1}^{N} \frac{|u_d - u'_d|}{u'_d}}{N} \times 100 \qquad (4)$$

The RAE of the sleep duration is 6.39 %. Despite waking up without putting the lights on, our approach of estimating the sleep duration provides promising results close to the ground truth. The accuracy can be increased by using other sensors inside the bed room, such as PIR sensors and thermopiles.

Finally, we measure the Spearman's rank correlation coefficient to assess how well the relationship between the sleep duration estimates and the ground truth

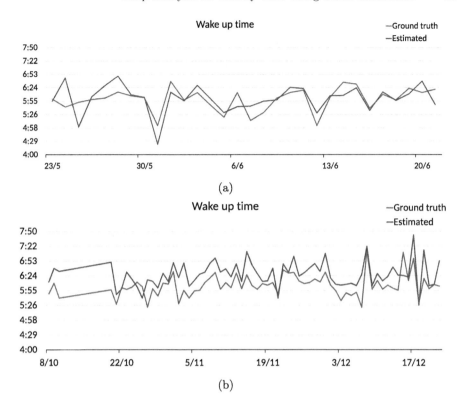

Fig. 5. A comparison between the estimates and the ground truth of wake up time: (a) May and June, (b) October, November and December.

is approximated. Let u_i be the sleep duration estimates set, and let π_{u_i} be the set of corresponding ranks. Similarly, let $\pi_{u'_i}$ be the ranks of the ground truth set $u'i$. Let d_i be the difference between the two ranks π_{u_i} and π_{u_j}. The Spearman's rank correlation coefficient r_s is defined as:

$$r_s = 1 - \frac{6d_i^2}{n(n^2 - 1)}, \tag{5}$$

where n is the number of ground truth days. The Spearman correlation coefficient r_s is 0.69. This value shows that the correlation between the sleep duration estimates and the ground truth is high. Figure 8 shows the correlation between the sleep duration estimates and the ground truth.

Next, we measure the number of the bathroom visits in the middle of the night to discover sleep disorders. We used SVM for detecting the nightly bathroom visits. 10 % of the output results (30 days) from the SVM have been visually checked. In most of the cases, the nightly bathroom visits were detected correctly. In few cases, the nightly bathroom visits were not detected due to standing up without putting the lights on. Figure 9 shows the number of the

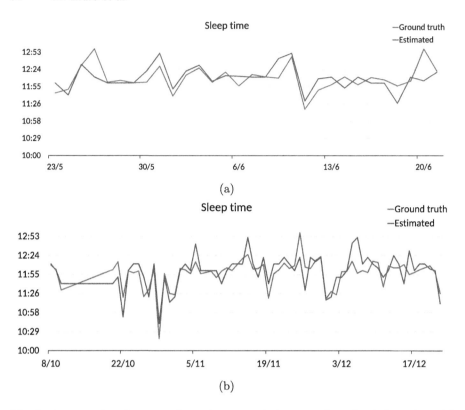

Fig. 6. A comparison between the estimates and the ground truth of sleep time: (a) May and June, (b) October, November and December.

nightly bathroom visits per day from April to December. The senior citizen goes to the bathroom on average from one to two times per day. There are few days when the senior citizen went to the bathroom for three times per day. These days are possible indications of sleep disorder [1]. Figure 10 shows the number of the nightly bathroom visits per month. There are more nightly bathroom visits in June and August (46) than in the other months. This indicates a high possibility of sleep disorder. April (16), May (31) and December (35) have the least bathroom visits, because the senior citizen was hospitalized. Finally, Fig. 11 shows the probability of sleeping and visiting the bathroom in the middle of the night according to the preference of the senior citizen. The senior citizen prefers to sleep around the midnight with a probability of 50 % and around 11 pm with a probability of 30 %. He most likely visits the bathroom between 2 am to 5 am with probabilities of 27 %, 29 % and 29 %, respectively. There is a possibility of 15 % that he goes to the bathroom around 1 am after he sleeps for one hour.

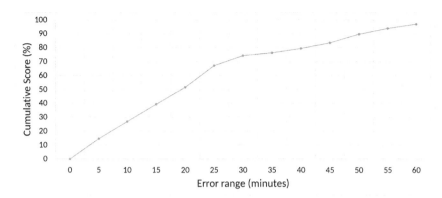

Fig. 7. The cumulative score of the sleep duration estimates at absolute error levels from 0 to 60 minutes.

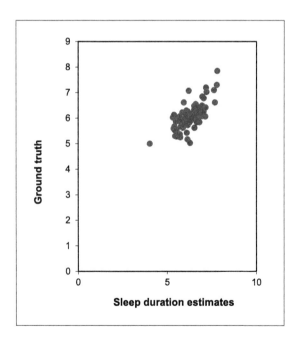

Fig. 8. The correlation coefficients between the sleep duration estimates and the ground truth.

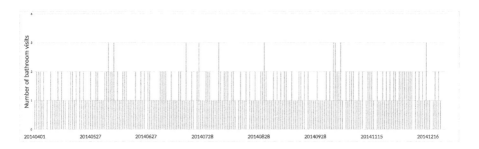

Fig. 9. The nightly bathroom visits per day from April to December.

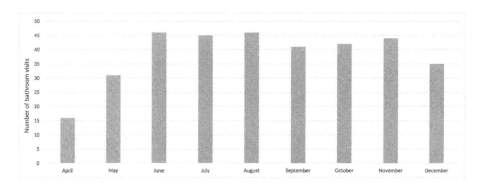

Fig. 10. The nightly bathroom visits per month from April to December.

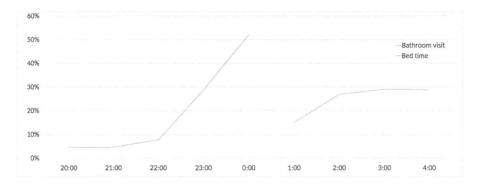

Fig. 11. The probability of sleeping and visiting the bathroom in the middle of the night.

5   Conclusions

In this paper, we presented a network of low-resolution visual sensors installed in a service flat of a senior citizen in Belgium. Our approach of detecting sleep durations is promising and does not require to install visual sensors inside the bedroom. We analyzed the sleep patterns and the nightly bathroom visits indirectly to indicate sleep disorders. The wake up time and sleep time were identified using a rule-based approach based on the motion patterns. The nightly bathroom visits were detected using SVM classifier. We collected 10 months of real-life video recordings. Our approach of estimating sleep durations against ground truth achieved MAE of 22.91 min and r_s of 0.69. Then, we studied the relation of the nightly bathroom visits and sleep disorder. The study showed several nights of sleep disorder. In the future, we aim at integrating and fusing visual information with data from other types of sensors (e.g. in the bed frame), and controllers (e.g. X10 or PIR) for detecting more activities to show health deterioration or improvement.

Acknowledgments. This research has been performed in the context of the project "LittleSister" and the European AAL project "Sonopa". This research has been financed by the agency for Innovation by Science and Technology (IWT), the Belgian National Fund for Scientific Research (FWO Flanders), and iMinds.

References

1. Ancoli-Israel, S., Bliwise, D.L., Nrgaard, J.P.: The effect of nocturia on sleep. Sleep Med. Rev. **5**(2), 91–97 (2011)
2. Anliker, U., Ward, J., Lukowicz, P., Troster, G., Dolveck, F., Baer, M., Keita, F., Schenker, E., Catarsi, F., Coluccini, L., Belardinelli, A., Shklarski, D., Alon, M., Hirt, E., Schmid, R., Vuskovic, M.: Amon: a wearable multiparameter medical monitoring and alert system. IEEE Trans. Inf. Technol. Biomed. **8**(4), 415–427 (2004)
3. Camilli, M., Kleihorst, R.: Demo: mouse sensor networks, the smart camera. In: 2011 Fifth ACM/IEEE International Conference on Distributed Smart Cameras (ICDSC), pp. 1–3, August 2011
4. Chen, Z., Lin, M., Chen, F., Lane, N., Cardone, G., Wang, R., Li, T., Chen, Y., Choudhury, T., Campbell, A.: Unobtrusive sleep monitoring using smartphones. In: 2013 7th International Conference on Pervasive Computing Technologies for Healthcare (PervasiveHealth), pp. 145–152, May 2013
5. Doblhammer, G., Ziegler, U.: Future elderly living conditions in europe: demographic insights. In: Backes, G.M., Lasch, V., Reimann, K. (eds.) Gender, Health and Ageing, pp. 267–292. VS Verlag fr Sozialwissenschaften, Wiesbaden (2006). http://dx.doi.org/10.1007/978-3-531-90355-2_13
6. Eldib, M., Bo, N.B., Deboeverie, F., Nino, J., Guan, J., Van de Velde, S., Steendam, H., Aghajan, H., Philips, W.: A low resolution multi-camera system for person tracking. In: 2014 IEEE International Conference on Image Processing (ICIP), pp. 378–382, October 2014

7. Foley, D., Ancoli-Israel, S., Britz, P., Walsh, J.: Sleep disturbances and chronic disease in older adults: results of the 2003 national sleep foundation sleep in america survey. J. Psychosom. Res. **56**(5), 497–502 (2004). http://www.sciencedirect.com/science/article/pii/S0022399904000327
8. Foley, D.J., Monjan, A.A., Brown, S.L., Simonsick, E.M., Wallace, R.B., Blazer, D.G.: Sleep complaints among elderly persons: an epidemiologic study of three communities. IEEE Pervasive Comput. **18**(6), 425–432 (1995)
9. Heinrich, A., Geng, D., Znamenskiy, D., Vink, J., de Haan, G.: Robust and sensitive video motion detection for sleep analysis. IEEE J. Biomed. Health Inf. **18**(3), 790–798 (2014)
10. Hodgins, D., Bertsch, A., Post, N., Frischholz, M., Volckaerts, B., Spensley, J., Wasikiewicz, J.M., Higgins, H., Von Stetten, F., Kenney, L.: Healthy aims: developing new medical implants and diagnostic equipment. IEEE Pervasive Comput. **7**(1), 14–21 (2008)
11. Hoque, E., Dickerson, R.F., Stankovic, J.A.: Monitoring body positions and movements during sleep using wisps. In: Wireless Health 2010 (WH 2010), pp. 44–53. ACM, New York (2010). http://doi.acm.org/10.1145/1921081.1921088
12. Krüger, B., Vögele, A., Herwartz, L., Terkatz, T., Weber, A., Garcia, C., Fietze, I., Penzel, T.: Sleep detection using a depth camera. In: Murgante, B., Misra, S., Rocha, A.M.A.C., Torre, C., Rocha, J.G., Falcão, M.I., Taniar, D., Apduhan, B.O., Gervasi, O. (eds.) ICCSA 2014, Part I. LNCS, vol. 8579, pp. 824–835. Springer, Heidelberg (2014). http://dx.doi.org/10.1007/978-3-319-09144-0_57
13. Lee, J., Hong, M., Ryu, S.: Sleep monitoring system using kinect sensor. Int. J. Distrib. Sens. Network. **501**, 875371 (2015)
14. Merilahti, J., Saarinen, A., Parkka, J., Antila, K., Mattila, E., Korhonen, I.: Long-term subjective and objective sleep analysis of total sleep time and sleep quality in real life settings. In: 29th Annual International Conference of the IEEE Engineering in Medicine and Biology Society (EMBS 2007), pp. 5202–5205, August 2007
15. Metsis, V., Kosmopoulos, D., Athitsos, V., Makedon, F.: Non-invasive analysis of sleep patterns via multimodal sensor input. Pers. Ubiquit. Comput. **18**(1), 19–26 (2014). http://dx.doi.org/10.1007/s00779-012-0623-1
16. Muaremi, A., Bexheti, A., Gravenhorst, F., Arnrich, B., Troster, G.: Monitoring the impact of stress on the sleep patterns of pilgrims using wearable sensors. In: 2014 IEEE-EMBS International Conference on Biomedical and Health Informatics (BHI), pp. 185–188, June 2014
17. Ni, H., Abdulrazak, B., Zhang, D., Wu, S., Yu, Z., Zhou, X., Wang, S.: Towards non-intrusive sleep pattern recognition in elder assistive environment. In: Yu, Z., Liscano, R., Chen, G., Zhang, D., Zhou, X. (eds.) UIC 2010. LNCS, vol. 6406, pp. 96–109. Springer, Heidelberg (2010)
18. Nyan, B.B., Deboeverie, F., Eldib, M., Guan, J., Xie, X., Niño Castañeda, J., Van Haerenborgh, D., Slembrouck, M., Steendam, H., Veelaert, P., Kleihorst, R., Aghajan, H., Philips, W., Van de Velde, S.: Human mobility monitoring in very low resolution visual sensor network. Sensors **14**(11), 20800–20824 (2014). http://dx.doi.org/10.3390/s141120800
19. Teixeira, T., Dublon, G., Savvides, A.: Physical and mental health effects of family caregiving. ENALAB Technical report (2010)
20. Umlauf, M.G., Chasens, E.R., Greevy, R.A., Arnold, J., Burgio, K.L., Pillion, D.J.: Obstructive sleep apnea, nocturia and polyuria in older adults. Sleep **27**(1), 139–144 (2004)

How Are You Doing? Enabling Older Adults to Enrich Sensor Data with Subjective Input

Marije Kanis$^{(\boxtimes)}$, Saskia Robben, and Ben Kröse

Amsterdam University of Applied Sciences, Wibautstraat 2-4,
1091 GM Amsterdam, The Netherlands
{M.Kanis, S.M.B.Robben, B.J.A.Krose}@hva.nl

Abstract. Technology designed to sense behavior, often neglects to directly incorporate subjective input from (elderly) users. This paper presents experiences in deploying technology that considers the elderly user and their subjective input as a way to enrich sensor data systems and empower the user. For this purpose, the paper draws on: (1) Observations of shortcomings in terms of capturing objective data from sensors as experienced in long-term deployments in the homes of older adults; (2) The design and evaluation of a wide range of applications especially designed to enable older adults to give subjective input on how they are doing, including an interactive television quiz, a talking picture frame and a tangible mood board, and (3) The development and field study of one application, the 'Mood button' in particular, that was tested in real-world sensing settings to work with a commercial sensing system. In doing this, this work aims to contribute towards successful sensing deployments and tools that give more control to the (elderly) end-user.

Keywords: Ubiquitous computing · Sensor monitoring · Ambient assisted living (AAL) · Real-world deployment · Autonomy and control · Invisible computing · Affective computing

1 Introduction

Recent funding initiatives, technological improvements, such as small inexpensive sensors and advances in the field of sensor-based activity recognition [1], have stimulated a renewed interest in real-world approaches (e.g. [2]) to the deployment of ubiquitous sensing applications (e.g. [3–5]) to understand, augment and infer people's activities and behavior in their everyday life. These sensing technologies are offering a new generation of applications that are enabling innovative human-machine interactions that are characterized by pervasive, unobtrusive, and anticipatory communications.

Real-world sensing deployments such as smart homes that support Ambient Assisted Living (AAL) (e.g. [6]) have received particular interest from the research community. Ambient monitoring systems (also referred as residential monitoring) typically involve monitoring the Activities of Daily Living (ADLs) and safety of residents to detect changes in their daily routines. Most often, the advantages of sensor (monitoring) technology –such as the opportunities for helping people to live longer independently in their home and more effective care– are highlighted. However, the

© Springer International Publishing Switzerland 2015
A.A. Salah et al. (Eds.): HBU 2015, LNCS 9277, pp. 39–51, 2015.
DOI: 10.1007/978-3-319-24195-1_4

ubiquitous sensing of people's activities and behavior also raises issues which merit more attention [7, 8]. Particularly important are issues regarding the (elderly) user and ways that are enabling them to truly participate, control and behave autonomously.

Since Weiser's vision of ubiquitous computing [9], many have embraced and celebrated the perceived invisibility and seamlessness of sensing devices. However, the shift to ubiquitous computing, resulting in many people dealing with many computers, together with the increasing invisibility of ubiquitous, sensing technology also poses a threat to people's autonomy and control. Some have noted that 'invisible' computing and the implicit disappearance of user interfaces [10–12] indeed come with complications that need more attention, particularly when it comes to including the elderly user. Already, studies [13, 14] have shown that existing technology often does not cater for the needs and abilities of elderly people. Invisible sensing devices with no visible clues or user interfaces for direct control make it even more difficult to engage and participate in human sensing interactions. Therefore, tools are needed that enable older adults to actively participate and contribute to sensing outcomes. Addressing these concerns, this paper presents the design of user-centered solutions for enabling older adults to complement 'invisible' data derived from sensor networks with their own affective input. This paper starts with describing our experiences with deploying residential sensing systems and difficulties in terms of obtaining, understanding and engaging with objective sensor data, as in consciously, willingly and actively contributing to the intent and output of sensor monitoring. Seeing the shortcomings of objective information captured with these sensors, a study was conducted to investigate the design and use of devices that enable the users to give *subjective* feedback with regards to their affective status. The contribution of this paper is a number of design exemplifications that particularly consider the affective input of the (elderly) end-user, of which one (the *Mood button*) was tested in commercial real-world sensing settings and described in more detail.

2 Living Labs: Experiences from the Field

In developing ubiquitous (monitoring) technology and applications, it has been recognized that a potential 'technology push' should be abandoned in favor of working from the perspective of its actual users [8, 15]. Despite major efforts in human-centered fields such as HCI, in the development and uptake of sensor (monitoring) technology, the engagement of users is still often identified as a major barrier [15]. On top of this, technological opportunities offered are frequently not taken-up in everyday practice [8]. With that in mind, the Living Lab approach was chosen, which gives great importance to users' physical and realistic surroundings and the users themselves. Through adopting the Living Lab approach, the relevant stakeholders and users could be involved in technology development at an early stage and play an active role in the research trajectory.

In 2006, our first Living Lab for sensor monitoring was set up in Naarderheem, The Netherlands. Subsequently, several care complexes and residences were equipped as Living Lab environments to support the design and development of new care solutions using sensing technology, together with its users and stakeholders. In the residential monitoring project, which experiences are the motivation for this work, 28 apartments were equipped with sensor-monitoring systems for the purpose of investigating the monitoring of daily activity patterns and detecting a decline in daily functioning. Our long-term experiences with residential sensor monitoring deployments provide real-world context in terms of obtaining, understanding and engaging with ambient sensor data.

2.1   Obtaining Sensor Data

In our Living labs, it was not always possible to obtain (sufficient and reliable) data from the installed sensor networks. Insufficient project management, local resident selection criteria and consent issues were one predominant reason. This meant that eight dwellings with sensor networks installed were not considered for subsequent data analysis. Also failing technology and sensors (e.g. false positives from sensors due to incorrect placing, sensors not transmitting data and short battery life) was problematic. Eventually, our sensor data analysis study included 20 participants (from the original $N = 28$) with monitoring systems installed for 11705 days in total. However, 5746 days needed to be removed from that data set. Thus in this instance, almost half of the data (49 %) that could have been used, was lost.

Insight: In explorative real world sensing settings, technological infrastructures are not typically robust. Consequently, the collection of satisfactory amounts of reliable data from residential sensor networks for effective usage can be a problematic process that requires lots of commitment and resources. When information about users' behavior and status is desired, other more robust, but also simpler techniques –for example, less sensors or more input from other (human) sources– might be more effective and should therefore also be considered.

2.2   Understanding Sensor Data

Once data has been collected, interpreting sensor data to acquire relevant information is not an easy and straightforward process. For measuring 'functional health', sensor patterns need to be recognized and classified, such as for emergency situations (e.g. if one has fallen), activities of daily living (e.g. cooking, sleeping), and to predict slow-moving, latent problems. A number of researchers (see [1] for an overview) have dedicated their work towards detracting such meaning from objective sensor data and identifying relevant deviations in patterns. In most cases, machine-learning techniques are used that need annotated sensor data. For example, if a sensor indicates a high frequency of a door being opened, this could be a sign of frequent social or medical visits, or simply something else. In short term lab situations, annotation is often done by a human observer (on-site) looking at the behavior of the participant. For long-term experiments, annotation of activity patterns and achieving true contextual under-standing of sensor output in general is much harder to obtain. Especially for older participants, it seemed to be difficult to continuously keep a precise diary of their status and activities. The deployment of cameras in private homes for this purpose is also not an optimal solution, for obvious privacy concerns.

Insight: For meaningful and effective usage of sensor data, annotation and additional interpretation is needed, which can be hard to obtain from older participants for the long-term. To make better sense out of data, durable solutions enabling richer data annotation would be helpful.

2.3   Engaging with Sensor Data

Engaging with sensor data in terms of having a clear understanding of how to actively and willingly control and contribute to the system's output and implications was found to be a concern. Namely, sensor technology can uncomfortably emphasize a person's limitations and so subsequently be confronting and less empowering. For example, some could perceive the technology and its data output as an indication that a person is less independent. In some cases (see also [8, 16]), potential participants did not want to adopt sensor monitoring technology because of the stigmatizing effect. Also, sensor data interpretations, such as minimal sensor activity output from a door sensor could uncomfortably or inaccurately reveal a person's lack of social contact. A way to add personal interpretations to the sensor data would help to empower the user in this process.

A disadvantage of having small, embedded, nearly invisible sensing technology without visible affordances is that it becomes more difficult to understand and actively control the system and its data implications. Consequently, some (potential) users in previous study thought that the sensor networks implied the use of cameras to observe them (in the shower) and control them [8], which can raise concern in terms of what happens to personal data.

Without highly legible systems and interfaces for managing, understanding and actively contributing to 'smart sensing' with its pervasive, unobtrusive, and anticipatory communications, it is likely that people can feel powerless, lost or frustrated. Indeed, as sensing systems record people's personal activity and data, according to Arnall [11], invisibility is exactly the wrong approach. It is important to develop visual cues and user interfaces that show the workings of technology (such as [8]) and enable the user to actively control and contribute to the system (instead of letting the system control them and disappear as user).

Insight: For true autonomy and better engagement with sensor data, the user should be provided with visible, active means to control and contribute to the sensor system.

3   Technology that Asks How You Are Doing

Sensing technology often neglects to directly incorporate input from its users, making users –to some extent– less autonomous. For example, the described sensor monitoring deployments that typically focus on the automatic detection of daily activities and status of older adults, do not directly ask how they are doing. Having observed the shortcomings of sensor monitoring systems in terms of obtaining, understanding and engaging with sensor data, indicate the potential for systems that incorporate users' input. Particularly, input of affective states might add more value to sensed behavior.

Furthermore, although social media, mobile technology (e.g. [17]) and Internet offer opportunities for distilling affective states, as well as expressing oneself, studies on the use of Internet [13] and Twitter [14] show that older adults are en masse not typically included in the process of such communication technology usage. To address this, the 'How are you doing?' project is presented, which aim was to develop elderly-centered communication technologies that directly ask the user's input on their affective status. Adding or enabling affective input from older adults could serve many goals, namely:

- Provide an additional verification when a sensor system detects that something might be wrong or when the technology is failing;
- Empower and enable users to indicate an alarming situation themselves;
- Make the user feel more democratically in control of the technology and connected with the outer world by giving the opportunity to initiate interactions themselves;
- Increase the feeling of wellbeing through expressing how you are doing. Seeing that a large body of research (e.g. [18–20]) has shown that the act of self-expression alone can be beneficial for one's physical and mental health.

Fig. 1. Prototypes of the 'How are you doing' project: Talking picture frame and mood board.

Addressing these goals, groups of Communication & Media Design students were given the assignment to design solutions for enabling elderly users (>65 years old) to communicate their affective status. This resulted in eight different applications that are all able to inquire how the user is doing and are especially designed to relate to the elderly's world of experience. Students were encouraged to involve elderly participants in the early design stages, and to frequently show them interim results for small-scale user research. For this reason, many of the solutions employ metaphors that might come more naturally to older adults. The resulting applications are described in the following sections.

TV-Friend. The TV-friend is an application that runs on a regular television. The first questions of the interactive TV-quiz are about the users' status, while the other quiz questions function as a fun reward. The front-end of the TV-friend includes a small media player and a remote. The back-end includes a Content Management System for creating new questions so that specific data on how someone is doing can be obtained from the user. Just like other interactive television applications (such as [21]), the reason for using a television in this concept is that many older adults are more familiar with this device than with computers or tablets.

Going Out. This is a social network application for arranging and making (short) walks. It aims to make older adults less isolated by encouraging them to go out together. The application enables the users to initiate walks or to arrange walking together, such as setting a specific time slot to walk to the grocery store together. Based on their walking activities and behavior, the application asks the user how they are doing.

Mood Board. The tangible mood board is a wooden frame with an embedded screen and real magnets that enable the user to communicate how one is doing (see Fig. 1). The board comes with several questions and magnets representing a certain answer, for example a positive versus negative response to questions relating to one's status. The user is asked to put the magnet into an answer area whereby the board uses RFID technology to identify the answer. This answer is registered on the screen, and the screen provides the option to share this answer with different parties (such as family and formal care givers) through simple touch actions. Inspirations for the tangible mood board were fridge magnets. These were frequently observed to hold notes and reminders in the homes of the elderly participants.

Tell me How You Are Doing. This application makes simple conversations using solely speech. From the answers, the application detects positive or negative feelings. The prototype uses the Google Speech API for determining which words were spoken and compares the first few words with an internal list of words with either positive or negative associated valence. The application comes with a CMS so that, for example, caregivers can monitor how the older adult is doing. This interface has been inspired by the premise that using speech as a way to communicate comes natural to most people.

Talking Picture Frame. This product enables the elder user to show and (digitally) exchange pictures with others via an object that is already rather familiar to them: a picture frame. Other researchers have also considered picture frames as an attractive and inspiring object for digital usage (e.g. [22, 23]). The Talking picture frame has the added ability to attach voice message recordings, so to avoid strenuous keyboard interactions. Furthermore, the system engages family and friends in monitoring the wellbeing of the elderly user.

Social Calendar. This application enables elderly to keep track of their social events. Users can make connections in the real world and catch up on how they are doing. The social calendar is a web-based application, using real-life metaphors, such as post-its for making digital notes. The application enables the planning of social events by means of inviting others to an event or responding to other events. It uses the calendar information on daily routines as contextual source to question the user about his emotional and physical state.

Mood Box. This physical box with embedded (iPad) screen is 'alive' like a Tamagotchi. The Mood box, a web-based iPad-application, asks questions about the user's state. When the user fails to respond regularly, the mood box starts to express a sad face so to call upon the user's need to care.

Mood (dial) Button. The Mood button is a tangible device for the explicit communication of how you are feeling. With the tangible, radial dial button a person can indicate how (s)he feels by turning the switch from left (not feeling well at all) to right (feeling very well), while a smiley face is changing accordingly from very happy to very sad (see Fig. 2). Just like other tools for registering sentiment –such as the AffectButton [24], Funometer and Smileyometer [21] – the Mood button enables the user to explicitly capture one's feelings in a simple and dynamic way. However, instead of being a rating tool, the Mood button is a physical, tangible device for expressive self-report that has particularly been designed with older adults in mind. The primary design phase of the button was informed by iterative design studies with elderly users ($n = 6$), which suggested that colors and smiley's (as opposed to using words and bar charts) for indicating one's mood were best understood by the participants. This is supported by other research [25] which also found that a simple, visual and language-independent tool (using smiley's) was desirable for practical usage with elderly in clinical context. Furthermore, an ordinary dialing mechanism, often used in devices such as room thermostats, inspired the Mood button, so that users can interact in a way familiar to them.

Fig. 2. Prototype of the mood dial button.

Insight: Engaging with elderly's world of experience and using metaphors from daily life can be a true source of inspiration for accessible interfaces and technology. The results show that there are many different possible ways in terms of designing enabling and inclusive technology that consider elderly's status input.

4   User Study

Besides the iterative design sessions for developing each of the systems individually, different small-scale studies were conducted to evaluate the expressive applications from the 'How are you doing?' project. This included the following studies:

- *Feedback and demo event*. All the eight applications were shown and demoed by its different makers in a social meeting hall in an elderly care home. This event was open to all people interested. Custom-made stickers with predefined space for feedback and commenters' details were provided for rating the different applications in terms of most useful, and best technical, creative and overall achievement. The goal of this event was to gauge initial understanding of how the different applications compared and were valued;
- *User group sessions (n = 4) and semi-structured interviews with elderly users* ($N = 5$, > 65 years old). These were conducted by occupational therapists to evaluate the different expressive applications all together. The aim of this study was to gain a general overview of how the applications were used and valued by *the elderly participants*;
- *Additional user group sessions (n = 4+3, > 65 years old) and structured interviews* with *elderly participants* to evaluate and inform the iterative design of the Mood button to work in combination with a commercial sensor system in more detail.

4.1   Findings from the User Studies

The different small-scale studies provided insights with regards to the design and attitudes towards the technology. The initial design sessions affirmed design lessons from other human-centered studies (e.g. [26]). For example, the study stressed that when designing for elderly users, text and buttons could never be large enough. It also stressed the importance of engaging the user from the beginning, as all the eight concepts were improved and very much influenced by the elderly target group. Technology that is based on familiar devices (such as a television or photo frames) and activities (walking or talking) was found to be a good starting point for elderly-centered design.

From the first, demo event, in which participants awarded 32 stickers in total, it was found that all the applications were positively valued for different aspects. For example, 'Tell me how you are doing' was awarded with 40 % of the 'best technical achievement' stickers, while the Mood button (21 %) and the Mood board received most sticky votes in total (27 %). Unfortunately, the raters were mostly the younger people present. One explanation was that it was difficult for some older adults (e.g. in wheelchair) to move between the displayed projects. The younger people present made insightful comments such as *"I think my father would like this"* (female, 51) and *"The physical remote and TV will appeal to the experience of elderly people"* (male, 44) when rating the TV-friend. However, a different study approach was clearly needed as to obtain views from the elderly users themselves more directly. For this reason, and to avoid a technology bias, the second study included solely the 65 + years-old target group in fixed settings, and was conducted by occupational therapists (and one HCI-expert as guide and observer), as they have typically more experience with dealing and engaging with older adults [17].

The findings of the user group studies stressed the importance of making the technology as simple, robust, mature and accessible as possible. Interacting with the lower-fidelity prototypes and the touch screens of some applications was particularly observed to be difficult for the elder participants. Tangible buttons and devices might therefore be a better option, but more extensive study is needed to further verify this. The elderly study participants found two-way interaction (as to be heard by another party) one of the key important elements. Interestingly, for the elderly participants, novelty and innovation was not considered important. Being highly aware of their old age (one participant even dramatically proclaimed: "my coffin is already waiting for me!"), important for the participants was how they could instantly use and integrate the technology in their daily lives without a steep learning curve.

5   Field Study with the Mood Button

Closely working together with a commercial sensor installation company, the ideas stemming from the 'How are you doing?' project were further explored for integration with an existing commercial sensor system. The Mood dial button was particularly positively reviewed, because of its perceived low costs, simplistic, attractive and tangible form, and so further developed (Fig. 3). Eventually, the Mood button was further iterated for integration with a commercial sensor system in the home, so that objective sensor data could be enriched with affective input from users.

In this process, it became clear that for an end product to be used in real-settings, production (e.g. screen) costs need to be limited. This meant that some good ideas had to be abandoned, and that the most fruitful ideas that will eventually make it, may not necessarily be the most innovative solutions. However, this approach is more realistic and required for faster uptake and usage of technology in real-world daily practices.

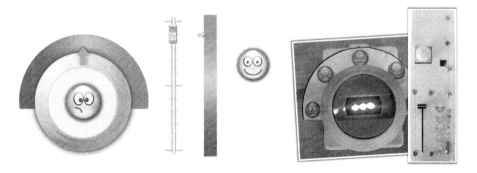

Fig. 3. Dial and slider prototype versions of the mood button.

On the basis of these findings, the mood button was further developed and evaluated in a field study ($n = 2$, > 65 years old) that focused on the use of the Mood button in real context. The Mood button was installed in the homes of two older adults (both widowers) that had already commercial sensor networks installed. Two versions (dial and slider) of the Mood button were tested each for one week in the homes of the elderly. They were requested to use the applications, but not set specific usage totals or set times. Their usage data was recorded and participants were interviewed afterwards.

Figure 4 presents the results of the actual use of the mood buttons (dial and slider) by the two participants. Participant A shared his mood once a day, not at a specific set time. During the final interview, he indicated having sometimes forgotten about the Mood button, despite of its visual presence. Reminder functionality (that could potentially be based on sensor activity) would suit him well. Participant B frequently and regularly shared his mood. He stated that he had never forgotten about the Mood button, because he had linked the action of setting his mood to post-meal time.

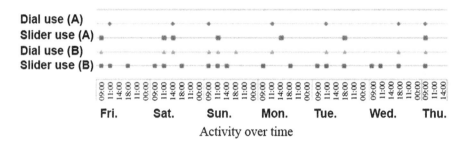

Fig. 4. The use of the Mood buttons throughout the week. The first two rows indicate the use of the prototypes by participant A, and the lower two rows indicate the use of the prototypes by participant B.

Being able to effectively combine and compare the subjective input with objective sensor data is one important aspiring goal of this work. As a proof of concept, a PIR sensor and light sensor were integrated in the mood button slider. Figure 5 displays the mood values, set with the slider throughout the week, for participant A. This figure shows that the participant was able to change and submit his mood status over time. For conducting a meaningful activity analysis that includes the personal affective state, a more advanced sensor system would be needed than now tested. As a proof of concept however, this figure shows that with the technology presented in this paper, the sensor data can be augmented with the affective state from users.

The participants used the expressive system in their daily lives and homes and found the ability to enrich their 'objective' sensor data with their own subjective data a valuable contribution.

Insight: Older adults are able to use a novel, simple tangible interface for sharing their affective state in their daily routines and can so become active participants and contributors in the sensor monitoring process.

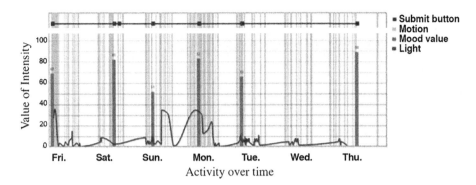

Fig. 5. Usage of the mood button slider by the first participant during the week. The neon green bars indicate the mood rating (on a scale from 0–100), in relation to the sensor output from sensors on the slider. Motion detected in front of the device is indicated by the small salmon red lines, while the blue line shows the intensity values coming from the light sensor. Finally, the dark green squares indicate the active use of the submit button, which is useful in case the mood is constant, but the user wants to set and share the same mood status.

6 Discussion and Conclusion

This paper presented a critical reflection of our experiences and challenges in terms of obtaining, understanding and engaging with objective sensor data when deploying residential sensing systems. To enhance and enrich such sensor data, this paper presented practical solutions and design exemplifications that particularly consider the active input and participation of the (elderly) end-user.

People's autonomy and engagement with technology considerably declines at older age. To respect the autonomy of the elder user, we not only need to engage elder users in the design process, we need data sensing approaches that avoid thinking with a third-person and emphasize realistic integration in daily life. Having observed the difficulties with obtaining, understanding and engaging with data derived from sensor systems, this paper presented a more elderly-focused approach in using sensor technology by presenting a wide range of different enabling applications for affective user input, that connect with the elderly's world of experience. Emphasis was placed on the Mood button as adapted to work in realistic settings in combination with a real-world sensing system. More studies still need to be done, particularly in terms of actually and effectively combining objective data derived from sensors with affective status input from users long-term. This work hopefully sets direction in inspiring the community in the design of ubiquitous technologies that engage with the elderly user and consider their autonomy, real-life practice and their 'subjective' input.

Acknowledgments. We thank our study participants, collaborators and colleagues, particularly Frank Kloos for their valuable contributions to this work. We thank the students from Communication and Media Design, particularly Mark Jongkind, Ron Geertsma & Marcel Stommel, and also acknowledge Patrick Post & Andranik Matshkalyan, and Amber Mollee & Rossy Lazarov for their involvement in the development and evaluation of the prototypes. This research was supported by the Blarickhof foundation, Agentschap NL (project Health-lab) and SIA (Smart Systems for Smart Services program). This research is also supported by ZonMW (EU-AAL project Care 4 Balance), COMMIT/ (VIEWW project) and HvA's Urban Vitality program.

References

1. Chen, L., Hoey, J., Nugent, C., Cook, D.: Sensor-based activity recognition. IEEE Trans. Syst. Man Cybern. Part C Appl. Rev. **42**, 790–808 (2012)
2. Crabtree, A.: Wild Sociology: Ethnography and Design. Sociology Department, Lancaster University (2001)
3. Storz, O., Friday, A., Davies, N., Finney, J., Sas, C., Sheridan, J.: Public ubiquitous computing systems: lessons from the e-campus display deployments. IEEE Pervasive Comput. **5**, 40–47 (2006)
4. Tilak, S.: Real-World deployments of participatory sensing applications: current trends and future directions. ISRN Sens. Netw. **2013**, 8 (2013)
5. Groen, M., Meys, W., Veenstra, M.: Creating smart information services for tourists by means of dynamic open data. In: Proceedings of Ubicomp 2013. ACM, Zurich (2013)
6. Rantz, M., Skubic, M., Miller, S.: Using sensor technology to augment traditional healthcare. In: Proceedings of Engineering in Medicine and Biology Society 2009, pp. 6159–6162. IEEE, Minneapolis (2009)
7. Froehlich, J., Kay, M., Larsen, J.E., Thomaz, E.: Workshop on Disasters in personal informatics: the unpublished stories of failure and lessons learned. In: Proceedings of Ubicomp 2014, Seattle, USA (2014)
8. Kanis, M., Robben, S., Hagen, J., Bimmerman, A., Wagelaar, N., Kröse, B.: Sensor monitoring in the home: giving voice to elderly people. In: Proceedings of Pervasive Health, pp. 97–100. IEEE, Venice (2013)
9. Weiser, M.: The computer for the 21st century. Sci. Am. **265**, 94–104 (1991)
10. Abowd, G., Mynatt, E.: Charting past, present, and future research in ubiquitous computing. ACM Trans. Comput. Hum. Interact. (TOCHI) **7**, 29–58 (2000)
11. Arnall, T.: No to NoUI (2013). http://www.elasticspace.com/writing
12. Dey, A., Ljungstrand, P., Schmidt, A.: Distributed and disappearing user interfaces in ubiquitous computing. In: CHI 2001 Extended Abstracts. ACM, Seattle, Washington (2001)
13. Consumer Panel Ofcom: Older people and communications technology: An attitudinal study into older people and their engagement with communications technology (2006)
14. Smith, A., Brenner, J.: Twitter Use 2012. Technical report. Pew Research Institute (2012)
15. Eriksson, M., Niitamo, V., Kulkki, S.: State-of-the-Art in Utilizing Living Labs Approach to User-Centric ICT Innovation – A European Approach. Lulea University of Technology, Lulea (2005)
16. Pol, M., van Nes, F., van Hartingsveldt, M., Buurman, B., de Rooij, S., Kröse, B.: Older people's perspectives regarding the use of sensor monitoring in their home. Gerontologist Gerontol. Soc. Am. **5**, 180–181 (2014)
17. Gravenhorst, F., Muaremi, A., Bardram, J., Grünerbl, A., Mayora, O., Wurzer, G., Frost, M., Osmani, V., Arnrich, B., Lukowicz, P., Tröster, G.: Mobile phones as medical devices in mental disorder treatment: an overview. Pers. Ubiquit. Comput. **19**, 335–353 (2015)
18. Kanis, M., Brinkman, W.-P., Perry, M.: Designing for positive disclosure: What do you like today? Int. J. Ind. Ergon. **39**, 564–572 (2009)
19. Smyth, J.M.: Written emotional expression: effect sizes, outcome types, and moderating variables. J. Consul. Clin. Psychol. **66**, 174–184 (1998)

20. Frisina, P., Borod, J., Lepore, S.: A meta-analysis of the effects of written emotional disclosure on the health outcomes of clinical populations. J. Nerv. Mental Dis. **192**, 629–634 (2004)
21. Stojmenova, E., Debevc, M., Zebec, L., Imper, B.: Assisted living solutions for the elderly through interactive TV. Multimedia Tools Appl. **66**, 115–129 (2013)
22. Mynatt, E.D., Rowan, J., Jacobs, A., Craighill, S.: Digital family portraits: Supporting peace of mind for extended family members. In: Proceedings of CHI 2001, pp. 333–340. ACM (2001)
23. Dibeklioğlu, H., Hortas, M.O., Kosunen, I., Zuzánek, P., Salah, A.A., Gevers, T.: Design and implementation of an affect-responsive interactive photo frame. J. Multimodal User Interfaces **4**, 81–95 (2011)
24. Broekens, J., Brinkman, W.-P.: AffectButton: towards a standard for dynamic affective user feedback. In: Affective Computing and Intelligent Interaction (ACII) (2009)
25. Lee, A.C.K., Tang, S.W., Yu, G.K.K., Cheung, R.T.F.: The smiley as a simple screening tool for depression after stroke: a preliminary study. Int. J. Nurs. Stud. **45**, 1081–1089 (2008)
26. Van der Geest, T.: Conducting usability studies with users who are elderly or have disabilities. Tech. Commun. **53**, 23–31 (2006)

Rethinking the Fusion of Technology and Clinical Practices in Functional Behavior Analysis for the Elderly

Juhi Ranjan[✉] and Kamin Whitehouse

University of Virginia, Charlottesville, USA
{juhi,whitehouse}@virginia.edu

Abstract. Functional assessment is the test of the ability of a person to perform basic self-care activities that are instrumental for living safely and independently in a home. Gerontology classifies these self-care activities as Activities of Daily Living (ADL). There exist many clinical and systems measures for performing functional assessment. This paper critically reviews the state of art in these assessments. This paper also talks about the disconnect between the clinical and the technological measures. It also discusses future directions to establish a practical and objective method of conducting functional assessments.

1 Introduction

New advances in health care, and improved quality of life have increased the average life expectancy of a person. As a result, people are aging longer, and the elderly (aged 65 and above) are becoming a major segment of the population. While the projected population of elderly is expected to double from 2000 to 2020 from about 11 % to 22 % [1], the number of health care professionals is only expected to increase by 10 % [2]. In the next five years, the gap between the population and care will increase to the extent that it will lead to a high cost of health care services. As a result, there is a high emphasis to support the concept of *aging-in-place*, where the elderly are encouraged to live in their homes for as long as it is possible. However, aging-in-place needs adequate supervision and support to ensure the safety of the elderly in their residence.

The safety of an elderly person in a home is highly correlated to their ability to perform basic functions that allow them to socialize, work, etc. These fundamental self-care activities have been labeled *Activities of Daily Living*, or ADLs. The analysis of a person's ability to perform ADLs is referred to as *functional behavior analysis* or *functional assessment*. Many elderly people experience problems in ADLs because of illnesses or health-related disabilities. For example, people suffering from heart failure or lung infections may lack the physical stamina to manage household tasks like cleaning, cooking, and laundry on their own. A functional assessment can identify if an elderly person needs outside help, such as home care, moving to an assisted living facility, etc.

© Springer International Publishing Switzerland 2015
A.A. Salah et al. (Eds.): HBU 2015, LNCS 9277, pp. 52–65, 2015.
DOI: 10.1007/978-3-319-24195-1_5

Designing a functional assessment requires making two main decisions: what activities need to be examined, and what is the scale on which each activity needs to be rated. There have been studies conducted by clinical researchers, as well as systems researchers, to develop such an assessment tool. Clinical researchers have conducted large-scale population studies and proposed multiple instruments of functional assessment. Systems researchers, working in the *Activity Recognition* community, have also proposed a technological methods to automatically sense the decline in functional abilities of the elderly. In this paper, we critically review the state of the art in ADL assessment using clinical practices as well as technological measures. We discuss a number of limitations in the these measures, to make a case for these two communities to address the challenges jointly.

A review of the various clinical instruments of functional assessment reveals the strengths and limitations of their proposed methods. These instruments are designed as self-reports or interview style questionnaires. In the US, each state has its own instrument derived from the numerous clinical scales that exist. Once an elder checks into a formal service system, such as an assisted living facility, they start undergoing a mandated semi-annual/annual functional health assessment. The clinical instruments do not focus on the dormant abilities of a person by asking questions such as 'Can you bathe?'. This is because the answer may be unrelated to the person's actual performance of the activity. Instead, they assess the ADLs that are actually performed by a person by asking questions such as, 'Do you bathe?'. Each ADL on the list is rated in different degrees of the person's ability to perform it - ranging from 'Able to perform independently', to 'Requires partial assistance', to 'Requires total assistance'. In spite of the proliferance of clinical instruments, there are many limitations in this body of methods. One such limitation is the non-uniformity of the ADLs monitored across the different instruments. The non-uniformity can result in a person being assessed differently across states within the same country. Also, the human-in-the-loop factor imposes limitations on the scalability of these methods with the increasing elderly population.

Technology is a great way to address the issues of non-uniformity and scalability present in the clinical assessment methods. This is because once setup, the cost of making additional measurements is negligible. Systems sensing methods are mainly based on the heuristic that if we can detect when a person performs a certain ADL, we can monitor the decline in the frequency of performance of the ADL and conclude that the person is losing the ability to perform that ADL. Another heuristic monitors the changes in fine-grained usage pattern of an object to determine loss of functional ability.

In either of the heuristics, systems are expected to be able to monitor the object usage in homes using sensors. Systems researchers have explored the use of various sensing modalities such as accelerometers, reed switch sensors, cameras, microphones etc., in order to sense various ADLs. Some systems use just a single wearable device, while others derive their inference from wearable devices worn at multiple locations. Some systems depend on instrumentation of all the salient objects in a home, while others focus on using single point sensing of water and electricity mains to determine the object usage based ADLs in the home. One of the limitations in the systems based methods is the lack of clinical validation of the heuristics the systems are based on. Its unclear if this type of monitoring can be used to conclusively determine any deterioration of functional abilities.

This rest of this paper is organized in the following manner: Sect. 2 describes the need to monitor functional capability at an ADL granularity. Section 3 critically reviews the clinical methods of ADL assessment. Section 4 critically reviews the technological solutions of ADL assessment. Section 5 reviews future work and directions in this domain.

2   Background

In 1984, the WHO Scientific Group on the Epidemiology of Aging reported that the ability to function independently was a good indicator of the state of health of the elderly [4]. Since then, many clinical studies have been conducted to determine how to assess functional ability. The outcomes of some of these studies have been tools or instruments of functional assessment. These instruments take into consideration the ability to perform certain tasks crucial to daily life [8, 9, 16], which are referred to as Activities of Daily Living or ADLs.

The two main subcategories of ADLs are Basic ADLs, such as 'Dressing,' which refer to the ability of a person to live within a home, and Instrumental ADLs such as 'Driving', which refer to a person's ability to live within a community. However, within these sub categories, each clinical scale has its own set of labels, some of which may specify activities very specifically such as 'brushing teeth', and others just refer to broad categories, such as 'grooming'. The instruments of functional assessment intend to track the ability to perform certain basic and instrumental ADLs.

Changes in functional abilities of an elder are usually the manifestation of the changes in the cognitive and physical abilities of the elderly, such as changes in how well elders are able to perform task such as meal preparation, grooming, ease of transferring between bed and chair etc. Since these tasks are performed in a routine manner by the individuals on a regular basis, they may not notice the changes in their own abilities. Therefore it becomes important to monitor the functional status of an individual.

This is done at an ADL level granularity for many reasons. Firstly, knowing what ADLs an elder needs help with, determines the type of assistance they require. For example, if someone needs help with bathing, they can pay for a weekly home care service. But if someone needs help with transferring from bed to chair and vice-versa, they may need someone to assist them everyday. These decisions are crucial as they determine the expenses of recruiting care. Secondly, monitoring all ADLs can show if there is a functional decline due to normal aging or a medical problem. This is because the after-effects of a major surgery or a medical condition may affect certain functional abilities only.

There are federal and state funded programs in the US that provide free care to the elderly using Medicare and Medicaid [3]. Every individual enrolled in this care service is assessed not only medically but also functionally. Functional behavior analysis is important in these programs so that the limited care resources are utilized optimally among the elderly.

3   Survey of Clinical Methods of ADL Assessment

There are broadly two types of clinical assessments that can be performed to determine an elder's ADL functions [5]. One type of assessment focusses on what ADLs an elderly person currently does and how they do it. This type of assessment is referred to as *Task Frequency*. The other type of assessment measures the degree of how well an elder can perform each ADL, which referred to as *Task Ability*.

Task frequency, is the most common type of elderly functional assessment. In this type of assessment, a scale or an instrument is used to test the person on a pre-defined set of ADLs. The scales are usually easy to administer and score, and are typically designed to be completed within an hour. Their formats may vary from a self-assessment form to an interview with an human assessor. The set of ADLs present in the scale is empirically identified by the researchers proposing the assessment. For each label of ADL, the assessor marks a score according to the scoring function specified by the scale. For example, for the ADL 'Walking', a person can be scored from 0–6, where 0 is 'no assistance required', 1 is 'uses some mechanical help', 2 is 'uses human supervision', 3 is 'uses human assistance', 4 is 'uses mechanical assistance and human supervision', 5 is 'uses human and mechanical assistance' and, 6 is 'cannot perform this ADL' [6].

There are many different indices for measuring an elder's ability to live independently. Some of them are the Katz Index of Independence in Activities of Daily Living [8], The Lawton Instrumental Activities of Daily Living [9], The Barthel Activities of Daily Living Index [10], Bristol Activities of Daily Living Scale [11], The Bayer Activities of Daily Living Scale [12], The Frenchay Activities Index [13], Nottingham Extended Activities of Daily Living [14], TMIG Index of Competence [15], Klein-Bell Activities of Daily Living Scale [16], Myasthenia Gravis Activities of Daily Living Profile [17], Guttman health scale for the aged [18] and Older Americans Resources and Services (OARS) Activities of Daily Living scale [19]. In addition to these, in the US, the state governments have their own instruments derived from existing clinical instruments. For example, the Uniform Assessment Instrument is used in Virginia [6] and the Hospital and Community-Patient Review Instrument is used in New York [7]. Once an elder checks into any formal service system, they are monitored using these state mandated instruments on a annual/bi-annual basis.

Different instruments can use different labels to refer to the same activity or finer aspects of the same activity. For example, [11] refers to the act of using the toilet as 'Elimination', whereas [6] refers to the same activity as 'Continence', and further sub-categorizes it into 'Bowel' and 'Bladder'. Some ADL labels are present in many instruments, such as 'Bathing'. While other labels such as 'Write Letters' are present in only one or two instruments [14]. Figure 1 shows a tree

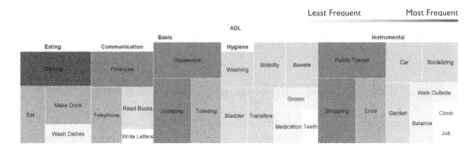

Fig. 1. A tree map of all the ADLs listed in different interments of ADL assessment reveals that there is a varied emphasis on different activities that are considered most basic for self-care. While some activities such as 'Dressing' and 'Bathing' are common to many instruments, other activities such as 'Write Letters' are more niche to a certain instruments

map of the various ADLs present in the twelve indices. We can see that some ADL labels are more niche, while others are more common across the different measures.

The task frequency type of assessments are easy to conduct. Therefore, the state can mandate it in the entire formal elder care service sector. On the other hand, task ability type of assessments are more niche and currently mandated by government in nursing facilities only. This type of assessment is not easy to conduct, and requires an occupational therapist to administer them. To conduct this assessment, the therapist may interview the person, in addition to using observation to rate the ADL abilities. Some examples of such assessments are the Melville-Nelson Evaluation System [20] and the Performance Assessment of Self-Care Skills (PASS) [21]. In this type of instrument, a compound task is broken down into atomic tasks. An elder is then asked to perform the compound task, and every atomic task is rated for independence, safety and adequacy. For example, the task of 'Telephone Use' for using a cordless phone and automated pharmacy is further sub-divided into atomic tasks such as: 'Reads handout from therapist and selects a pharmacy', 'Locates telephone', 'Dials pharmacy number', 'Positions telephone receiver for call', 'Navigates phone menu choices', 'Ends call appropriately' and 'Reports information' [5].

Critique: Despite an over abundance of scales to measure ADL function, the field of elder assessment largely remains subjective and therefore not scalable with the increasing population of elderly. Future work in developing the scales could benefit from considering the following:

– *Creating a dictionary of ADL labels*
  One of the main differences between the instruments of functional assessment is the choice of ADL labels. The ADLs are different not only in the type of activities that they represent but also the granularity of each activity type that is monitored. The inconsistency in what needs to be monitored is confusing, because there is no obvious basis on which labels should be selected for

any elder. Every state in US has its own set of ADLs, which is then applied uniformly to all elderly within the state. So while elders are monitored differently and therefore possibly treated differently in each state, individuals having different lifestyles, cultures, and socio-economical backgrounds within the same state are monitored with the same set of ADLs. A dictionary of ADLs would help create have a unique label for every activity. It can also help create labels that represent different activities performed in different lifestyles. For example, there may be a special interest in monitoring 'Making Tea' in Japan. In fact there are internet kettles sold in Japan which intend to monitor how often an elder is making tea, and send this across to their children [22]. For the children, this simple action can provide a measure of the elder's well being.

– *Elder's value of activity*
All the scales of ADL have one thing in common: they each propose a fixed set of ADLs that they deem are important for independent living. As such this poses a problem when the scales are used for the purpose of determining if an elder needs to be moved from the community to an institution and what care facilities would the elder require at the institution. However, a big factor of the decision to institutionalize, depends on the perceived value of an activity from an elder's standpoint. For example, many of the ADL indices enlist Cooking' as a primary function that the elder should be able to perform. However, a person may not like to cook, or even know how to cook. And in spite of not knowing how to cook, can lead a healthy life, because they have either someone cooking for them or order food from outside.

– *Valuing practicality with reliability*
An index may have many detailed activities in it. A detailed set of activities in an index, attempts to capture the full details of an elder's functions. However, it also increases the number of activities that need to be assessed. Fewer activities in a scale however make it more practical, since it minimizes the assessment effort. It could be helpful if we could identify a few compound activities that encapsulate a large number of motor functions to have a good marriage of practicality with reliability.

– *Measurability using technology*
When the scales were developed, they focussed on activities that could be assessed using interviews. The biggest challenge with this method, is that it requires a person to visit the elderly, and assess them. This is a fairly expensive method, especially when conducted frequently. Having activities that are measurable using technology has many advantages. The activities can be monitored more cheaply. frequently and most importantly in an objective manner.

4   Survey of Systems Methods of ADL Assessment

From a technological and automatic sensing standpoint, the field of determining the activities of daily living (ADLs) aligns strongly with the field of 'Activity Recognition'. We selected top 25 of the well cited research papers in activity recognition returned by Google Scholar [23], eliminating survey type papers [24,47].

Our survey also confirms that one of the most common motivations for research in this field is the need to detect the decline in functional and cognitive abilities in the elderly, or eldercare.

The use of a technological method to assess functional behavior can be justified by three main reasons: 1. provides an objective measure of ADLs, 2. it is scalable because of the potential of sensing being cheap in future, 3. it can be used to assess an elder more frequently mainly because there are no additional costs per measurement.

The work in this field broadly relies on two types of heuristics to perform functional assessment:

1. Task frequency heuristic - The decline in the frequency of an ADL performance is indicative of decline in functional and/or cognitive ability.
2. Task ability heuristic - Changes in the time and pattern of performing atomic tasks to complete a single compound task, is indicative of decline in functional and/or cognitive ability.

Table 1. Survey of technology used in different systems

Paper	Activities	Type of Sensors Used
[25, 27, 29, 36, 37]	Ambulation	Tri/bi-axial accelerometers on body
[28, 33]		Smartphone accelerometer
[34, 41]		Cameras in home
[26, 35]	Basic ADLs	State sensors on objects in homes
[30, 42]		State, temperature, humidity sensors on home objects
[31, 32, 39]		Cameras in Home
[38, 40, 45]		RFID gloves and tagged objects
[46]		Cameras+RFID tagged objects

The solutions proposed by the researcher can be classified into various sensing modalities, as shown in Table 1. Some sensing modalities are more typically used for ambulation related ADLs such as walking, running, climbing stairs etc., such as bi/tri-axial accelerometers worn in a device on the body. Over time, researchers have improved the number of activities that can be detected using fewer number of wearable accelerometer devices on the body with more precision. The use of other modalities such as RFID tagging is more commonly used for detecting basic ADLs such as cooking, making coffee etc.

In the current state of art, the sensor based data is expected to be useful for providing feedback to the elder for improving self-awareness on how his/her individual abilities might be changing over time. This type of data is also expected to be useful to a gerontologist to help diagnose the functional abilities of an elder, although it isn't very clear in what format would the data help them with a diagnosis [5].

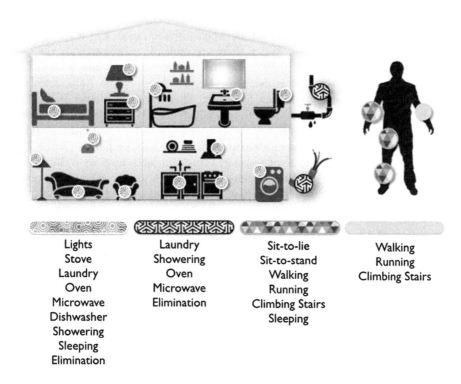

Lights	Laundry	Sit-to-lie	Walking
Stove	Showering	Sit-to-stand	Running
Laundry	Oven	Walking	Climbing Stairs
Oven	Microwave	Running	
Microwave	Elimination	Climbing Stairs	
Dishwasher		Sleeping	
Showering			
Sleeping			
Elimination			

Fig. 2. While more number of sensors can detect a richer set of ADLs, it is more practical in terms of cost and maintenance to have systems that can infer ADLs from fewer sensing points

Based on where the sensor is located, the main body of sensing modalities in this field can be classified in the following way:

1. Body Wearable Device- Single/Multiple locations [24, 25, 29]
2. Instrumented Home - Mains/Per-Fixture Monitoring [26, 42–44]
3. Combination of Body Wearable Device/Instrumented Home [45–47]

Figure 2 shows a list of ADLs that can be sensed using these sensing modalities. Since there is no single/standard instrument of ADL assessment, researchers in the field of activity recognition select and focus on ADLs labels of their own choosing. While some researchers have created sensing solutions focusing on a wide variety of ambulation related ADLs such as walking and running, others focus on the basic ADLs that require the use of appliances and water fixtures in the home, such as bathing and cooking. In general, a review of the literature suggests that instrumenting the person is the most common method of detecting ambulation, while instrumenting the home appliances, and/or the electric and water mains is the most common method of detecting basic ADLs.

Instrumenting multiple points usually gives much detailed information about the activities. For example, single point sensing of electricity of a home cannot infer the source small electrical events such as 'Switching on a light', and single wearable device cannot differentiate between different modes of a rested body such as lying down vs. sitting. When there are multiple people sharing the same space, the use of a wearable device and the fixtures in the home is one of the common ways to detect who is using the fixture. Most of the ADL detections are based on the Task Frequency heuristic. These systems detect every time that a person performs a certain ADL and construct a timeline of the frequency with which an elder performs that ADL. There is a smaller subset of researchers in this community who focus on detecting ADL with an emphasis on the Task Ability heuristic. In this type of sensing, typical objects used in ADL such as the coffee machine, are highly instrumented and each atomic step in the object usage is monitored for deviations in pattern of typical usage.

Critique: While technology is a good solution that can scale with the increasing population of the elderly, it has a few challenges that prevent it from being applied for functional assessment in the current state of the art.

– *Packaged Solution*
  The sensing solutions for detecting different ADLs are varied. Some use RFID tagged objects and wearable gloves to detect certain activities such as cooking food, while others use multiple sensors attached to the body to determine when a person is sitting vs. lying down. One of the problems with the current state of art in activity recognition is the fact that every system configuration is different. There is no principle to pack the various sensing modalities into a single solution. A principle of integrating the multiple technological needs to be identified, where all the activity recognition solutions use a unified framework.
– *End-to-end solutions*
  Until now, most of the research focussed on getting the sensing right. For example, vision based activity recognition can identify the low level behaviors of people and determine what activity they are doing. The main challenge is that this system needs to be able work out of the box in different unstructured environments, subject to different constraints. For example in a vision based system, it should have the ability to work in low light conditions, have a coverage of the living space, ensure privacy in homes, etc. While a basic installation cost may be acceptable to elders, tasks that require major configurations and precise calibration, increase the installation costs and may prove to be a deterrent in the widespread adoption by elders.
– *Empirical evaluation*
  Almost all of the activity recognition research papers cite elderly monitoring as a compelling motivation, and yet few of them actually test their system on the elderly. Understandably, the biggest challenge to elderly testing is the recruitment of elderly participants. Elderly participation is also a challenge since many times the systems are chunky prototypes, and the experiments conducted are controlled in nature. Experiments having an in-situ component with wearables that can actually be worn comfortably by the elderly are important to ensure that a solution has been validated for the correct end user.

Experimenting with the researchers can often remove the noisy signal characteristics that can be present when an elder uses the system. For example, a wearable device with accelerometer will probably register a lot of shakiness when used by a person suffering from Parkinson's.

– *Consideration of Multi-Occupants*
According to a recent statistic, almost two-thirds of the elderly population in US actually live in a multi-resident home [1]. This means that infrastructure-mediated sensing paradigms such as Non-Intrusive Load Monitoring (NILM) systems need to consider that the activities sensed based on the use of different objects in the home can be attributed to multiple individuals. Therefore, any system that purely detects activities from an object-use stand point also needs to be able to integrate a method of determining which person actually used the object.

– *Capture competence of activity*
The paradigm of activity recognition should not be restricted to sensing activities alone. An important aspect informing the state of health of the elderly is their competence in performing the activity. By simply capturing the fine-grained performance of an activity such as cooking, we cannot know of behavior such as spills during cooking, which is important in ascertaining if the elder is in danger of a potential accident while performing the activity.

5   Discussion

One of the biggest challenges in future of functional behavioral analysis of the elderly will be the ability to scale up to the population increase. By 2050, there are expected to be 2 billion adults in the world, aged 65 and above [1]. The current means of functional assessment is highly dependent on experts such as gerontologists, care givers and occupational therapists. Technology, especially cheap sensing technology, is promising in that it is widely pervading the homes and lives of people. There are various modalities of sensors that can provide rich information about the activities that people are performing. The concept of connected homes along with the advent of Bluetooth Smart, has made the appliance usage information more accessible. More homes are getting smart electric meters, making the mains information easily available as well. As appliances get old and are replaced with the appliances supporting these new sensing technology, the cost of instrumenting the fixtures in homes becomes negligible. Wearable gadgets are already available commercially. These gadgets have a wide variety of sensors on board, such as Inertial Measurement Unit, Wi-fi, GPS, microphone etc., which are used the activity recognition community.

While there is sufficient evidence that supports the idea that eventually in future, obtaining sensing information for elderly monitoring will be available very cheaply and widely, there are other things that we need to consider to make sure we are going on the right track as a community. This is because the two main heuristics used in this community aren't validated in clinical studies. The disconnect between the clinical research community and the technological research

Table 2. Limitations in the state of the art in functional behavior assessment methods

Clinical Methods	Technological Methods
Dictionary of ADL labels	Packaged Solution
Elders value of activity	End-to-end solutions
Valuing practicality with reliability	Empirical evaluation
Measurability using technology	Consideration of Multi-Occupants
	Capture competence of activity

community, and the limitations in the current state of art (Table 2) need to be addressed before we can claim that technology can detect changes in the functional behavior in the elderly. Interviews with gerontologists and occupational therapists [5] have revealed that they do not understand how to interpret the quantitative nature of the data yet. One of the main reasons for this is that it is not clear when to treat changes in pattern as an anomaly, that indicates functional decline, or a conscious change in person's lifestyle. A system that generates a large number of false alarms is unlikely to be adopted by the masses.

While the aim of this paper is not to undermine the contributions of activity recognition in elder monitoring, it seems important that there be an explicit declaration in the community that, at this point, claiming that a system can detect functional decline in the elderly using the existing heuristics, is likely to be over ambitious. There is danger of a *snowball effect*: a large number of papers claiming to perform the functional analysis by simply detecting ADLs, might influence other researchers into believing that this is a clinically validated fact.

One of the main reasons why this major disconnect exists, is because the methods used by the clinicians to determine functional abilities were not designed to be objectively measured by sensing technology. It seems like its time for both these communities construct a dialogue around these issues and develop some guidelines, so that together they can design methods can meet the needs of the future more efficiently. New alternative solutions can be designed. For example, the use of systems like Apple's ResearchKit [48] can be used to determine the efficacy of a sensing solution over a wide range of population.

Acknowledgement. We would like to thank our reviewers for providing many helpful critiques and suggestions. This work is supported by the National Science Foundation under Grants 1038271 and 0845761, and the NSF Graduate Research Fellowship Program under Grant 0809128.

References

1. World Health Organization. http://www.who.int/ageing/en/
2. US Labor Employment Projections. http://www.bls.gov/news.release/pdf/ecopro.pdf

3. Program of All-inclusive Care for the Elderly. http://www.medicare.gov/your-medicare-costs/help-paying-costs/pace/pace.html
4. World Health Organization. The uses of epidemiology in the study of the elderly: report of a WHO Scientific Group on the Epidemiology of Aging [meeting held in Geneva from 11 to 17 January 1983] (1984)
5. Lee, M.L.: Task-based embedded assessment of functional abilities for aging in place. Diss, Georgia Institute of Technology (2012)
6. Uniform Assessment Instrument. http://www.vda.virginia.gov/pdfdocs/uai.pdf
7. Hospital and Community- Patient Review Instrument. https://www.health.ny.gov/forms/doh-694.pdf
8. Brorsson, B.E.N.G.T., Asberg, K.H.: Katz index of independence in ADL. Reliability and validity in short-term care. Scand. J. Rehabil. Med. **16**(3), 125–132 (1983)
9. Graf, C.: The Lawton instrumental activities of daily living scale. AJN Am. J. Nurs. **108**(4), 52–62 (2008)
10. Collin, C., Wade, D.T., Davies, S., Horne, V.: The barthel ADL index: a reliability study. Disabil. Rehabil. **10**(2), 61–63 (1988)
11. Fish, J.: Bristol activities of daily living scale. Encycl. Clin. Neuropsychol. **452–453**, 13 (2011)
12. Hindmarch, I., Lehfeld, H., de Jongh, P., Erzigkeit, H.: The bayer activities of daily living scale (B-ADL). Dement. Geriatr. Cogn. Disord. **9**(Suppl. 2), 20–26 (1998)
13. Schuling, J., De Haan, R., Limburg, M.T., Groenier, K.H.: The frenchay activities index. assessment of functional status in stroke patients. Stroke **24**(8), 1173–1177 (1993)
14. Harwood, R.H., Ebrahim, S.: A comparison of the responsiveness of the Nottingham extended activities of daily living scale, london handicap scale and SF-36. Disabil. Rehabil. **22**(17), 786–793 (2000)
15. Koyano, W., Shibata, H., Nakazato, K., Haga, H., Suyama, Y.: Measurement of competence: reliability and validity of the TMIG index of competence. Arch. Gerontol. Geriatr. **13**(2), 103–116 (1991)
16. Klein, R.M., Bell, B.: Self-care skills: behavioral measurement with Klein-Bell ADL scale. Arch. Phys. Med. Rehabil. **63**(7), 335–338 (1982)
17. Wolfe, G.I., Herbelin, L., Nations, S.P., Foster, B., Bryan, W.W., Barohn, R.J.: Myasthenia gravis activities of daily living profile. Neurology **52**(7), 1487–1487 (1999)
18. Rosow, I., Breslau, N.: A Guttman health scale for the aged. J. Gerontol. **21**, 556–559 (1966)
19. Doble, S.E., Fisher, A.G.: The dimensionality and validity of the older americans resources and services (OARS) activities of daily living (ADL) scale. J. Outcome Meas. **2**(1), 4–24 (1997)
20. Melville, L.L.: The Melville-Nelson Occupational Therapy Evaluation System for Skilled Nursing Facilities and Subacute Rehabilitation, Toledo. University of Toledo, Toledo (2001)
21. Holm, M.B., Rogers, J.C., Hemphill-Pearson, B.: The performance assessment of self-care skills (PASS). In: Hemphill-Pearson, B., et al. (eds.) Assessments in Occupational Therapy Mental Health, 2nd edn, pp. 101–110. SLACK, NJ (2008)
22. Internet-Connected Tea Kettle. http://www.mimamori.net/index.html
23. Google Scholar. http://scholar.google.com
24. Lester, J., Choudhury, T., Borriello, G.: A practical approach to recognizing physical activities. In: Fishkin, K.P., Schiele, B., Nixon, P., Quigley, A. (eds.) PERVASIVE 2006. LNCS, vol. 3968, pp. 1–16. Springer, Heidelberg (2006)

25. Bao, L., Intille, S.S.: Activity recognition from user-annotated acceleration data. In: Ferscha, A., Mattern, F. (eds.) PERVASIVE 2004. LNCS, vol. 3001, pp. 1–17. Springer, Heidelberg (2004)
26. Tapia, E.M., Intille, S.S., Larson, K.: Activity Recognition in the Home using Simple and Ubiquitous Sensors. Springer, Berlin Heidelberg (2004)
27. Ravi, N., Dandekar, N., Mysore, P., Littman, M.L.: Activity recognition from accelerometer data. Proc. AAAI **5**, 1541–1546 (2005)
28. Kwapisz, J.R., Weiss, G.M., Moore, S.A.: Activity recognition using cell phone accelerometers. ACM SigKDD Explor. Newsl. **12**(2), 74–82 (2011)
29. Maurer, U., Smailagic, A., Siewiorek, D.P., Deisher, M.: Activity recognition and monitoring using multiple sensors on different body positions. In: International Workshop on Wearable and Implantable Body Sensor Networks (2006)
30. Van Kasteren, T., Noulas, A., Englebienne, G., Kröse, B.: Accurate activity recognition in a home setting. In: Proceedings of the 10th International Conference on Ubiquitous computing, pp. 1–9. ACM (2008)
31. Duong, T.V., Bui, H., Phung, D.Q., Venkatesh, S.: Activity recognition and abnormality detection with the switching hidden semi-markov model. In: IEEE Computer Society Conference on Computer Vision and Pattern Recognition, **1**, pp. 838–845. IEEE (2005)
32. Messing, R., Pal, C., Kautz, H.: Activity recognition using the velocity histories of tracked keypoints. In: IEEE 12th International Conference on Computer Vision, pp. 104–111. IEEE (2009)
33. Huynh, T., Schiele, B.: Analyzing features for activity recognition. In: Proceedings of the 2005 Joint Conference on Smart Objects and Ambient Intelligence: Innovative Context-aware Services: Usages and Technologies, pp. 159–163, ACM (2005)
34. Ben-Arie, J., Wang, Z., Pandit, P., Rajaram, S.: Human activity recognition using multidimensional indexing. IEEE Trans. Pattern Anal. Mach. Intell. **24**(8), 1091–1104 (2002)
35. Wilson, D.H., Atkeson, C.G.: Simultaneous tracking and activity recognition (STAR) using many anonymous, binary sensors. In: Gellersen, H.-W., Want, R., Schmidt, A. (eds.) PERVASIVE 2005. LNCS, vol. 3468, pp. 62–79. Springer, Heidelberg (2005)
36. Khan, A.M., Lee, Y.-K., Lee, S.Y., Kim, T.-S.: A triaxial accelerometer-based physical-activity recognition via augmented-signal features and a hierarchical recognizer. IEEE Trans. Inf Technol. Biomed. **14**(5), 1166–1172 (2010)
37. Yang, J.-Y., Wang, J.-S., Chen, Y.-P.: Using acceleration measurements for activity recognition: an effective learning algorithm for constructing neural classifiers. Pattern Recogn. Lett. **29**(16), 2213–2220 (2008)
38. Wyatt, D., Philipose, D., Choudhury, T.: Unsupervised activity recognition using automatically mined common sense. Proc. AAAI **5**, 21–27 (2005)
39. Bodor, R., Jackson, B., Papanikolopoulos, N.: Vision-based human tracking and activity recognition. In: Proceedings of the 11th Mediterranean Conference on Control and Automation, **1**(2003)
40. Gu, T., Wu, Z., Tao, X., Pung, H.K., Lu, J.: Epsicar: An emerging patterns based approach to sequential, interleaved and concurrent activity recognition. In: IEEE International Conference on Pervasive Computing and Communications, pp. 1–9. IEEE (2009)
41. Ribeiro, P.C., Santos-Victor, J.: Human activity recognition from video: modeling, feature selection and classification architecture. In: Proceedings of International Workshop on Human Activity Recognition and Modelling (2005)

42. Hong, X., Nugent, C., Mulvenna, M., McClean, S., Scotney, B., Devlin, S.: Evidential fusion of sensor data for activity recognition in smart homes. Pervasive Mobile Comput. **5**(3), 236–252 (2009)

43. Fleury, A., Vacher, M., Noury, N.: SVM-based multimodal classification of activities of daily living in health smart homes: sensors, algorithms, and first experimental results. IEEE Trans. Inf Technol. Biomed. **14**(2), 274–283 (2010)

44. Patel, S.N., Robertson, T., Kientz, J.A., Reynolds, M.S., Abowd, G.D.: At the flick of a switch: detecting and classifying unique electrical events on the residential power line. Lect. Notes Comput. Sci. **4717**, 271–288 (2007)

45. Patterson, D. J., Fox, D., Kautz, H., Philipose, M.: Fine-grained activity recognition by aggregating abstract object usage. In: Proceedings Ninth IEEE International Symposium on Wearable Computers, pp. 44–51. IEEE, October 2005

46. Wu, J., Osuntogun, A., Choudhury, T., Philipose, M., Rehg, J.M.: A scalable approach to activity recognition based on object use. In: IEEE 11th International Conference on Computer Vision, IEEE, October 2007

47. Hong, Y. J., Kim, I.J., Ahn, S.C., Kim, H.G.: Activity recognition using wearable sensors for elder care. In: Proceedings of the Second International Conference on Future Generation Communication and Networking, **2**, pp. 302–305. IEEE (2008)

48. Apple Research Kit. https://www.apple.com/researchkit/

Mobile Solutions

Push or Delay? Decomposing Smartphone Notification Response Behaviour

Liam D. Turner$^{(\boxtimes)}$, Stuart M. Allen, and Roger M. Whitaker

Cardiff School of Computer Science and Informatics, Cardiff University, Cardiff, UK
{TurnerL9,AllenSM,WhitakerRM}@cardiff.ac.uk

Abstract. Smartphone notifications are often delivered without considering user interruptibility, potentially causing frustration for the recipient. Therefore research in this area has concerned finding contexts where interruptions are better received. The typical convention for monitoring interruption behaviour assumes binary actions, where a response is either completed or not at all. However, in reality a user may partially respond to an interruption, such as reacting to an audible alert or exploring which application caused it. Consequently we present a multi-step model of interruptibility that allows assessment of both partial and complete notification responses. Through a 6-month in-the-wild case study of 11,346 to-do list reminders from 93 users, we find support for reducing false-negative classification of interruptibility. Additionally, we find that different response behaviour is correlated with different contexts and that these behaviours are predictable with similar accuracy to complete responses.

Keywords: Interruptibility · Smartphone notifications · Interruptions · Context awareness · Implicit sampling · Mobile

1 Introduction

Over the last decade the rise of the smartphone has had a profound effect on society, providing an ever-present opportunity for information retrieval and delivery. The *app* culture has extended the diversity of interruptions from phone calls and SMS messages to include *notifications* - snippets of information from diverse services, intended to inform or prompt reaction. Inappropriately timed interruptions are a fundamental issue, being at best an annoyance and at worst a dangerous distraction. Techniques are needed to enable services to determine and exploit interruptible moments, in order to deliver the right information at the right time.

Intelligent systems capable of predicting the success of individual notifications are highly desirable, yet this is dependent on the nature of the service [14]. For example, an appropriate time to prompt the user for a health related intervention is unlikely to be the same as one to notify them of a social network update. Similarly, the former may require them to undertake a specific and

© Springer International Publishing Switzerland 2015
A.A. Salah et al. (Eds.): HBU 2015, LNCS 9277, pp. 69–83, 2015.
DOI: 10.1007/978-3-319-24195-1_6

timely action (e.g. report their progress *in situ*), while the later is simply delivering information, and could safely be ignored. Currently, the delivery of notifications is largely at the interrupter's discretion, leaving the interruptee to reactively assess the appropriateness, or manually manage blanket-rules. The smartphone's ubiquity brings further opportunities, particularly with the evolving habitual role interruptions are having in our daily lives.

A fundamental issue in building intelligent interruption systems is to identify contexts where the benefit of interrupting outweighs the perceived cost on the user. Previous work has typically involved relying on the user to explicitly provide feedback after each interruption (e.g., [15, 18]), thereby classifying their interruptibility at that time. However, this creates a rigid *black-box* between delivery and feedback, leaving an outstanding issue of what to do when complete responses are not made. In these cases important information is being lost, for example, it may be that the user wasn't interrupted, or that they weren't physically interruptible to the extent that they changed focus, or that they were but didn't want to provide feedback. Identifying the attentiveness of users [15] through partial responses forms the focus of this study.

Previous interruptibility studies have identified that the abstract convention of an interruption and a response is a staged process of decision making and information exchange [12]. However, developing this in the context of smartphones has received little attention. Additionally, previous work has shown that smartphone interactions vary based on the level of focus available [17]. Therefore we hypothesise that, in comparison to a black-box approach, decomposing response behaviour to notifications will enable more cases of interruptibility to be observed and ultimately avoid misclassification. We present a model that decomposes response behaviour from notification delivery through to notification consumption. By developing and deploying a bespoke to-do list reminder app on Android smartphones, we find empirical evidence supporting this approach. In particular we are able to reduce misclassifications by separating out truly unsuccessful interruptions from partial responses where some degree of interruptibility was shown.

2   Current Conventions

The general convention for studying interruptibility is to issue interruptions under different contexts and see if a response is given (Fig. 1). For smartphone notifications, this has the benefit of issuing interruptions through mechanisms that the user already adopts. This has typically involved explicitly interrupting the user to ask how interruptible they are, an arguably redundant practice if the user responds. Other studies attempt to implicitly operate through useful applications such as a reminder function in a Mood Diary [18]. However across these studies, each interruption attempt is typically represented in a similar way - as a feature representation of the current context and a label of the user's interruptibility given that context.

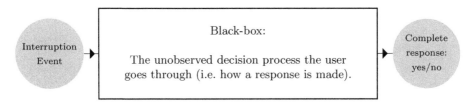

Fig. 1. The current underlying convention for determining interruptibility.

2.1 Representing the Current Context

The influential factors of interruptibility have been widely debated, particularly between: user characteristics (e.g., cognitive load), interruption properties (e.g., notification content) and the local environment (e.g., location or activity) [4, 11]. Additionally, the definition of what it means to be interruptible is also fragmented, with some studies focusing on: the physiological ability to switch focus (e.g., [2,10]); the affect the interruption would have on the current task (e.g., [6,7,14]) or the user's sentiment towards the interruption (e.g., [15]).

The data sources sampled from also vary greatly in the literature, with peripheral hardware (e.g., wearable accelerometers [5]) historically used. The introduction of the smartphone has enabled many of these sensors to be contained within a single device that isn't alien to the user. Although smartphone sensors have some issues with accuracy and consistency [8], similar issues affect user annotation and bespoke equipment is impractical for large-scale, "in-the-wild", and longitudinal studies. Software APIs such as those tracking UI events [1,14] have also been used, however these are often platform dependent or limited to moments when the user is performing a task on the device.

2.2 Labelling Response Behaviour

After initiating an interruption, studies across the literature typically judge success by either observing whether a response is made (e.g., [16]) or by requesting a self-assessment of its appropriateness (e.g., [3,15,19]). In either case, this resembles a *black-box* system that either succeeds or fails. However in reality, a user can exhibit a degree of interruptibility without completing the response. For example, if a response is started but abandoned, it may be the case that all notifications are unsuitable at this time, or only those from that application (e.g., all emails) or just the particular content in question (e.g., emails from the particular sender). If the user doesn't provide feedback or provides incomplete feedback, the *black-box* approach can't distinguish between these cases. For intelligent systems, this could lead to misclassifications of partial responses as null-responses, where no observable attempt to respond is made.

Retrieving a Label. Determining a quantified and unbiased measure of interruptibility remains an ongoing challenge. A common method for capturing this

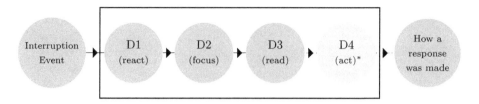

Fig. 2. Decomposing the decision process for Android notifications. *D4 may not apply to all notifications.

has been through self-reports, also known as Experience Sampling Methods (ESM) (e.g., [15,22]). On the positive side, due to the smartphone's ubiquity, this enables the collection of user opinion in situ, however it has several drawbacks for interruptibility studies. Firstly, it introduces an additional task that the user has to be sufficiently interruptible for and willing to complete. Secondly, it assumes that a user can accurately and consistently quantify their interruptibility, making it prone to errors across users and contexts [13]. Thirdly, it is also subject to potential behavioural bias from the consistent reminder that behaviour is being monitored [13].

An alternative is to use software events to implicitly capture indicators of interruptibility. For example, Smith et al. [21] infer interruptibility by noting whether incoming phone calls are answered. This measures what the user does rather than what the user thinks, providing consistency over subjective self-reporting, but it is limited to externally observed behaviour.

3   Modelling a Response as a Decision Process

To observe within the *black-box*, we decompose notification response behaviour into a sequence of atomic (possibly subconscious) decisions that a user makes. This enables us to examine the extent to which the response is pursued and avoid assumptions about the information the user knew. It is important to note that we are not aiming to extend or change the existing response process - we are trying to observe a process that already occurs. While this concept has previously been explored for other systems [12], we are unaware of its application explicitly to smartphone notifications. Additionally the variability of notifications [14] and operating system conventions presents a non-trivial task of creating a model robust to these inconsistencies. Within the scope of this study we focus on Android, due to it's market share and open APIs to observe decision behaviour.

From a prediction standpoint, being able to predict at least a partial response is useful for some applications. An example would be an application that delivers repetitive identical reminders. The user may not want to complete the process each time as the staged information delivery wouldn't change. Instead, just knowing that they acknowledged the interruption may be suitable.

3.1   Decomposing Android Notifications

For Android notifications, user interface conventions and available APIs dictate a sequence of up to 4 atomic decisions (visualised in Fig. 2) to be observed. A decision occurs at each point new information about the notification is provided to the user. After being presented with this information (e.g., the application icon), the user makes the decision to either continue (and be presented with the next piece of information) or terminate the response at that point (e.g., turn the screen back off and resume their previous activity). Inactivity with the device represents a failed attempt to interrupt the user, i.e. null-responses. The steps in our model are listed below, with the included examples assuming that the device is not-in-use when the notification is delivered:

D1 The process begins as the device attempts to gain the user's attention through sound, vibration or visual cues. Depending on the state of the device, this may go unnoticed (e.g. if the device is in a bag). However if the user is interrupted, they decide to either *react* and switch focus towards responding to the notification or ignore it.

D2 After choosing to react (e.g. turning the screen on), an icon graphic can be seen which indicates the notifying application (e.g. an email has arrived). Given this information, the user then decides to either *focus* their attention towards a content summary (e.g. the email subject) by accessing a notification drawer, or exit and return to their previous activity.

D3 On seeing the content summary, the user makes the decision whether or not to *read* a fuller message by consuming the notification and entering the relevant application (e.g. accessing the email client).

D4 Finally, if relevant to the notification, the user decides whether or not to *act* on the content, (e.g. send documents in reply to the email).

3.2   Model Generality

The stages visualised in Fig. 2 represent the maximum observable decisions that a user goes through, however, this could vary due to notification inconsistency. Some decision steps can be obscured by properties such as a recognisable tone, such as the distinction between D1 and D2. Similarly, this may occur if the notification summary contains the complete content (e.g., a repetitive reminder) rather than dynamic meta-data (e.g., email sender). Additionally, when the device is not-in-use, the unlock process provides distinct points to observe decisions being made (Table 1). However, if the device is already unlocked (i.e., in-use), D1 and D2 cannot be easily distinguished due to limitations in observable UI events (e.g. accessing the notification drawer). However, the ability to observe some degree of partial response behaviour still offers improvement over relying on completed responses.

4   Case Study: Timely Android Notifications

To determine the extent our decision model captures complete and partial responses to notifications, we collected data "in-the-wild", using a bespoke Android application. From this we explore how many additional cases of interruptibility are captured in comparison to a *black-box* approach and identify correlations between the context before an interruption and response behaviour. Finally we assess the extent individual response behaviour can be predicted through machine learning algorithms.

For this case study we focus on notifications that require timely delivery to be effective and provide the user with information in stages, consistent with the model in Fig. 2. Whilst this doesn't represent all possible variations of notifications, it is representative of a subset where interruptibility is critical for success and is in-line with similar work [18]. We also used Android's default parameters where possible, including using the default tone, vibration pattern and LED pattern.

4.1   Data Collection: Interruption Experiment

We developed an Android smartphone application, called ImprompDo, designed to deliver notifications, collect detailed context data and record response behaviour. So that a participation incentive naturally exists beyond our research purpose [18], this took place implicitly behind the functionality of a to-do list productivity tool.

Application Setup. After installation the user is guided through a short setup process of consenting to participate in the study and authorising access to their existing to-do lists (Todoist or Google Tasks). The user is then presented with optional preferences (Fig. 3), modifiable at any time. Notifications could begin from the start of the next hour.

Notification Delivery and Response. Notifications were delivered within a user defined hour range (9 am to 9 pm by default) and maximum frequency (from once an hour up to once a day). If an interruption occurs, a response follows the

Fig. 3. The preferences screen.

same process as any other notification (shown in Figs. 4, 5 and 6). Although it would be possible to check whether the user did complete the to-do item (D4), these decisions are largely dependent on individual to-do list usage behaviour, hence to maintain generality, we chose not to consider this step.

Fig. 4. The application icon shown for an example ImprompDo notification.

Fig. 5. The notification drawer with a ImprompDo notification summary.

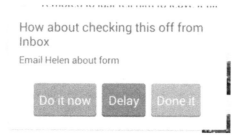

Fig. 6. The application content shown if the ImprompDo notification is consumed.

At the beginning of each period, a random trigger was chosen that dictates if and when the notification would occur. Inspired from related works, these triggers were: at a random time, at the end of a period of acceleration, a temporal online learning model (using hours) and a multi-modal online learning model using logistic regression with features extracted from captured context. This follows a 1×4 repeated measures within-subjects design implemented as a *N of 1 randomized trial* [15,20]. This intended to prevent skewness by not splitting users into groups for each trigger, and because user participation time "in-the-wild" cannot be guaranteed.

Each notification prompts the user once and remains active for 30 s, or until the user either selects a to-do list item action (Fig. 6) or dismisses it. After 30 s, the interruption is deemed unsuccessful in producing a response and is removed. We assume that this window provides sufficient opportunity for the user to respond if they were physically interrupted and could respond immediately. This design choice intended to keep the local context at the time the interruption consistent with the context if the user were to respond.

4.2   Data Collection: Implicit Sensing

To capture context before interruption and during response we chose data sources
that would be readily available for a real-world smartphone application - without adding any extra permissions or user tasks. With little co-agreement across
the literature [5], we adopted a bottom-up approach of collecting from a variety of local hardware sensors and software APIs. The data sources chosen to
extract feature variables from were: linear acceleration (pseudo-sensor), gravity (pseudo-sensor), light sensor, proximity sensor, charging state, screen on/off
state, lock/unlock state, volume state and the current timestamp. Whilst these
are a subset of what the smartphone is capable of, these represent what is typically available on an Android smartphone, across manufacturers and models.

Additional context about what the user is doing could be provided by calendar data or activity recognition. However, calendar data has high granularity and
is often incomplete, especially beyond working hours. Detailed activity recognition is restricted by the inability for current smartphones to do this accurately
and efficiently. Other environmental data such as location and ambient noise
(microphone) were omitted due to the additional permissions required. This
also has a tenuous link to the to-do list application and may deter users from
participating and could introduce a behavioural bias [13].

Data was collected implicitly as notifications were delivered and remained
active. Sampling begins from 5 s before the interruption until the notification is
consumed/dismissed by the user (D3) or otherwise it expires 30 s after interruption (Fig. 7). Sampling consists of taking sets of raw data vectors containing a
reading from each data source. As readings are delivered by Android asynchro-
nously, a short window is opened to listen for readings. It is closed when either:
at least 1 reading is collected from all data sources or 2 s has elapsed. When
closed, the most recent readings are taken to minimise variance between reading
times. If no readings were available after 2 s, the reading for that data source is
set to null in the vector. An attempt is made to open a new sampling window
immediately, however this is subject to device speed and system stability. The
collection of raw data vectors is then examined to extract decision behaviour,
using the criteria detailed in Table 1.

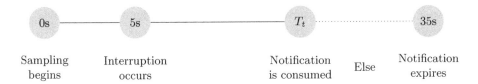

Fig. 7. Visualisation of the implicit data collection. Sampling occurs from 5 s before
delivery up until the notification is consumed at time T_t ($5s < T_t < 35s$) or it expires.

Table 1. Decision outcomes observed through progressive smartphone events. *Only observable if an Android device is not-in-use.

Decision	Continue on event	Exit early event
D1*	Screen is switched on	Screen stays off until timeout
D2*	Device is unlocked	Screen is switched back off
D3	Notification is tapped on	Notification is dismissed or timeout
D4	Application dependent	Application dependent

5   Case Study Results

After a period of 6 months, we analysed the aggregated data of all users to determine whether: capturing detailed response behaviour is beneficial; different contexts before an interruption are correlated with different behaviour; and whether partial and complete responses could be predicted. A summarised breakdown of the dataset is shown in Table 2. It should be noted that user participation was voluntary and could have occurred any time within the 6 months for any duration. Missing data prevented the extraction of whether the device was in-use or not at the time of the interruption or the decision behaviour afterwards, in 1287 of 11,346 cases (11.343 %). Of the remaining 10,059 cases, the majority of notifications were not completed, with only 1056 of 10,059 (10.498 %) consuming the notification - consistent with other studies (e.g., [15]).

5.1   Capturing Partial Response Behaviour

Identifying partial responses, and therefore preventing them from being misinterpreted as null-responses, is possible under our approach. When the device was not-in-use at the time of interruption, partial responses occurred in 1126/7737 cases (14.553 %). Whilst this may appear small, this increases the total distribution of cases where some degree of interruptibility was shown from 1056 cases (across in-use and not) to 2182 in 10,059, representing a substantial 106.629 % increase. Including notification dismissals when the device was in-use would increase this further. Overall, this suggests that whilst users aren't interruptible most of the time, decomposing interruptibility through our model reveals additional cases to potentially consider. If further APIs are made available (e.g. notification drawer UI events), then further cases could be captured when the device is in-use.

By assessing the exact decision stage the user discontinued responding, we can also infer why they may have exited. For example, if the user turns the screen on to show the application icon, but goes no further, they don't know what the exact to-do list item was, so their reason for stopping cannot be due to undesirable content.

Table 2. A summary breakdown of the ImprompDo dataset.

Metric	Value
Total number of users with >1 notification	93
Total number of notifications	11,346
Total number of days	178
Average number of notifications	122
Average number of days	26.457
Interruptions when the device was not-in-use	7737
- Null responses	5939
- Partial responses	1126
- Complete responses	672
Interruptions when the device was in-use	2322
- Null responses	1747
- Partial responses	191
- Complete responses	384
Interruption cases with missing data	1287
- Unknown if in-use or not-in-use	1267
- Unknown response behaviour	20

5.2 Correlating Context to Decision Behaviour

Before conducting our analysis we performed Kolmogorov-Smirnov tests, which determined the presence of non-normal variable distributions. Therefore, non-parametric equivalents to t-tests were used. For variables with 2 possible values, Mann-Whitney U tests were used. Kruskal-Wallis 1-way ANOVAs were used for those with more than 2 values, to reduce the likelihood of Type I statistical errors. We began with analysing whether a particular trigger was significantly better at producing at least partial responses. From pairwise post-hoc tests from a Kruskal-Wallis test we found that no trigger was significantly better than all others. As a result we chose to analyse the significance of each variable individually, towards building other multi-modal prediction models.

To evaluate the prospects for prediction, we analysed whether the context sampled in the 5 s before an interruption was correlated to the outcomes of each decision (continue or exit). Raw sensor readings on Android devices have previously been shown to be inconsistent [8] and require filtering [9]. Therefore to stabilise the readings over the 5-second period, we took the mean value of each data source and categorised the result (shown in Table 3). For the "Accelerating" variable, a high-pass noise filter was also applied (threshold $= 0.1m/s^2$) to ensure that acceleration was substantial.

Each variable was then tested for statistical significance by analysing the distribution of its values across each decision outcome (continue or exit). Table 3 provides an overview of the p-values from the analysis. Overall, the results reveal

Table 3. P-values indicating significance of each feature on each decision. Bold values show significance using $p < 0.05$. * Mann-Whitney U Test ** Kruskal-Wallis 1-way ANOVA

	Not-in-use			In-use
Feature Variables	D1	D2	D3	D3
Accelerating*	.186	.458	.072	**.000**
True, False				
Ambient Light**	**.000**	**.039**	**.000**	**.000**
Dark, Dim, Light, Bright				
Screen Covered*	**.000**	.187	**.000**	**.005**
True, False				
Volume State**	**.000**	**.009**	**.011**	**.000**
Silent, Vibrate, Audible				
Orientation**	**.000**	.098	**.000**	**.000**
Flat, Upright, Other				
Charging State*	**.000**	**.001**	.145	.177
True, False				
Time of Day**	**.002**	.125	.936	**.000**
Morn, Aftrn, Eve, Nght				
Day of the Week**	.509	.794	.100	**.000**
Number of cases (n)	7737	1798	1469	2322

differences in the significant variables between different decisions, as well as when the device is in-use and not, showing potential for predicting response behaviour at a finer granularity than a *black-box* model.

5.3 Response Prediction

To investigate the extent in which response behaviour can be predicted, we built predictive models from the same dataset using the machine learning tool-kit WEKA. We experimented with whether having a different model for each decision (with {continue, exit} classes) would perform better than a multi-class model predicting the exact decision the user exited the response. An exit at D3 is synonymous with a complete (consumed) response.

From frequency distributions we found that the distribution of class labels in the dataset was imbalanced. Therefore we used random-under-sampling (RUS) to prevent skewing classifier performance. We chose 7 classifiers used in related works and performed 10-fold cross validation on each model using 100 randomly under-sampled balanced datasets. The mean performance of each classifier is shown in Table 4.

The results show poor performance for the multi-label model in comparison to individual models dedicated to predicting continue or exit for eachdecision. For the

Table 4. Classifier performance using models at varying granularities. Bold values indicate the highest value across classifiers.

Classifier	Metric	not-in-use				in-use
		D1	D2	D3	MC	D3
AdaBoostM1	Precision	0.6045	**0.6064**	**0.6375**	0.2522	0.5927
	Recall	**0.6026**	**0.6045**	**0.6369**	0.2976	0.5923
BayesNet	Precision	0.5936	0.5873	0.5955	0.2532	0.4997
	Recall	0.5889	0.5831	0.5917	0.2870	0.4996
J48	Precision	**0.6065**	0.5986	0.6316	0.3376	**0.6010**
	Recall	0.6023	0.5957	0.6294	**0.3393**	**0.6002**
Logistic	Precision	0.5719	0.5791	0.6118	0.3217	0.5881
	Recall	0.5718	0.5790	0.6117	0.3272	0.5879
NaiveBayes	Precision	0.5715	0.5816	0.6195	**0.3408**	0.5889
	Recall	0.5702	0.5801	0.6174	0.3372	0.5872
RandomForest	Precision	0.5788	0.5769	0.6250	0.3277	0.5939
	Recall	0.5787	0.5768	0.6246	0.3283	0.5938
SMO	Precision	0.5664	0.5779	0.6036	0.3233	0.5941
	Recall	0.5659	0.5761	0.6017	0.3248	0.5928

individual models, the performance is in-line with similar studies (e.g., [15]), with D3 the equivalent to a black-box model. Given that this is an aggregated dataset and that humans can have varying smartphone and interruption habits this performance (of around 60 %) is neither unexpected nor unreasonable. Interestingly, the variance in classifier performance for each decision and between decisions is small for both metrics and not statistically significant. Crucially, this shows that partial response behaviour can be predicted as well as complete responses. This is also beneficial for real-world implementation as the same classifier can be used for all decisions without a detrimental affect on performance.

Additionally, although having separate models increases complexity, a single computationally cheap classifier can be used without significant performance loss - improving viability as the smartphone has limited resources. Going forward, this shows that predicting response behaviour at decision-level granularity is possible. These results provide a baseline for further work on whether performance can be improved with personalisation and online learning.

6   Limitations and Future Work

Notifications vary in content and purpose [14], so to assess the suitability of our model we've used a notification that is representative of those where untimely delivery would be useless for both the interrupter and the interruptee. However, other types of notifications, particularly less timely notifications (e.g., digest type notifications such as Twitter's notifications) and rapport-driven notifications (e.g., instant messaging) should also be explored.

We have focused on Android smartphones running version 4.0 – 4.4, which represented between 85 %-90 % of the market distribution within Android versions at the time of the study. However, the delivery and response conventions to notifications can vary across operating systems, inhibiting a *one-size-fits-all* case study. Theoretically, the premise of the model remains, the exact decisions and indicators of decisions being made may need to be adapted from *a priori* knowledge of these systems.

Going forward, several steps to potentially improve prediction performance can be taken. Firstly, the performance of alternative training methods, such as online or evolutionary learning, could be explored. Secondly, further work could explore whether personalised training data could improve performance or a mix with aggregated data. Thirdly, we've intentionally used typical data sources available for Android devices. If technical constraints and behavioural bias risks can be mitigated, the predictive power of other data sources should be explored. Finally, if additional measures to implicitly observe decision behaviour become available, this should be explored, particularly for when the device is in-use.

For the model itself, an ongoing research question remains in distinguishing between cases where the user wasn't physically interrupted (e.g. the smartphone wasn't near them) and those where they were but they didn't perform any observable actions on the device, i.e. null-responses.

7   Conclusion

Smartphone notifications have extended the diversity and frequency of interruptions we receive throughout our daily lives. Intelligent systems for inferring interruptibility and likely success of a timely response are highly desirable to the remove the reactive burden placed on users. The current conventions for modelling the response behaviour to notifications heavily rely on complete responses and the user to provide labelling. However in reality notifications have high variability [14], a user might be interruptible but not for all notifications [12].

For intelligent systems which seek to decide whether to push or delay a notification in situ, we explore whether the natural decision process that the user goes through when being interrupted [12] can be observed for smartphone notifications. We present a model of up to 4 sequential decisions a user faces when receiving and responding to notifications and find support for our hypothesis that decomposing how a response is made is worthwhile. Through an "in-the-wild" case study, we observe that including partial responses when the device is not-in-use increased the number of cases where some degree of interruptibility was shown by 106.629 % - reducing false-negative misclassifications.

Additionally, we find that this is achievable without explicit user annotations through implicitly observing how the user interacts with the device. From this we identify that different features in the context before an interruption are significantly correlated to different partial and complete response behaviour. Finally, we attempt to predict the extent in which a user pursues a response, with accuracy in-line with related work in the area, but with the benefit of also predicting partial responses.

References

1. Adamczyk, P., Bailey, B.: If not now, when?: the effects of interruption at different moments within task execution. In: Proceedings of the (CHI 2004), pp. 271–278. ACM (2004)
2. Bailey, B., Iqbal, S.: Understanding changes in mental workload during execution of goal-directed tasks and its application for interruption management. ACM Trans. Comput. Hum. Interact. (TOCHI) 14(4), 21 (2008)
3. Fogarty, J., Hudson, S., Atkeson, C.G., Avrahami, D., Forlizzi, J., Kiesler, S., Lee, J., Yang, J.: Predicting human interruptibility with sensors. ACM Trans. Comput. Hum. Interact. (TOCHI) 12(1), 119–146 (2005)
4. Grandhi, S., Jones, Q.: Technology-mediated interruption management. Int. J. Hum Comput Stud. 68(5), 288–306 (2010)
5. Ho, J., Intille, S.: Using context-aware computing to reduce the perceived burden of interruptions from mobile devices. In: Proceedings of the (CHI 2005), pp. 909–918. ACM (2005)
6. Horvitz, E., Apacible, J.: Learning and reasoning about interruption. In: Proceedings of the (ICIMI 2003), pp. 20–27. ACM (2003)
7. Iqbal, S., Bailey, B.: Effects of intelligent notification management on users and their tasks. In: Proceedings of the (CHI 2008), pp. 93–102. ACM (2008)
8. Lathia, N., Rachuri, K., Mascolo, C., Rentfrow, P.: Contextual dissonance: design bias in sensor-based experience sampling methods. In: Proceedings of the (UbiComp 2013), pp. 183–192. ACM (2013)
9. Liu, G., Hossain, K.M.A., Iwai, M., Ito, M., Tobe, Y., Sezaki, K., Matekenya, D.: Beyond horizontal location context: measuring elevation using smartphone's barometer. In: Adjunct Proceedings of the (UbiComp 2014), pp. 459–468. ACM (2014)
10. Mathan, S., Whitlow, S., Dorneich, M., Ververs, P., Davis, G.: Neurophysiological estimation of interruptibility: demonstrating feasibility in a field context. In: Proceedings of the 4th International Conference of the Augmented Cognition Society (2007)
11. McFarlane, D.: Interruption of people in human-computer interaction: A general unifying definition of human interruption and taxonomy. Technical report DTIC Document (1997)
12. McFarlane, D., Latorella, K.: The scope and importance of human interruption in human-computer interaction design. Hum. Comput. Interact. 17(1), 1–61 (2002)
13. Miller, G.: The smartphone psychology manifesto. Perspect. Psychol. Sci. 7(3), 221–237 (2012)
14. Okoshi, T., Ramos, J., Nozaki, H., Nakazawa, J., Dey, A., Tokuda, H.: Attelia: Reducing users cognitive load due to interruptive notifications on smart phones. In: Proceedings of the (PerCom 2015), IEEE (2015)
15. Pejovic, V., Musolesi, M.: Interruptme: designing intelligent prompting mechanisms for pervasive applications. In: Proceedings of the (UbiComp 2014), pp. 897–908. ACM (2014)

16. Pielot, M., de Oliveira, R., Kwak, H., Oliver, N.: Didn't you see my message?: predicting attentiveness to mobile instant messages. In: Proceedings of the (CHI 2014), pp. 3319–3328. ACM (2014)
17. Pohl, H., Murray-Smith, R.: Focused and casual interactions: allowing users to vary their level of engagement. In: Proceedings of the (CHI 2013), pp. 2223–2232. ACM (2013)
18. Poppinga, B., Heuten, W., Boll, S.: Sensor-based identification of opportune moments for triggering notifications. IEEE Pervasive Comput. **13**(1), 22–29 (2014)
19. Rosenthal, S., Dey, A.K., Veloso, M.: Using decision-theoretic experience sampling to build personalized mobile phone interruption models. In: Lyons, K., Hightower, J., Huang, E.M. (eds.) Pervasive 2011. LNCS, vol. 6696, pp. 170–187. Springer, Heidelberg (2011)
20. Sidman, M.: Tactics of Scientific Research: Evaluating Experimental Data in Psychology. Basic Books, New York (1960)
21. Smith, J., Lavygina, A., Ma, J., Russo, A., Dulay, N.: Learning to recognise disruptive smartphone notifications. In: Proceedings of the (MobileHCI 2014), pp. 121–124. ACM (2014)
22. Ter Hofte, H.: Xensible interruptions from your mobile phone. In: Proceedings of the (MobileHCI 2007), pp. 178–181. ACM (2007)

Estimating the Perception of Physical Fatigue Among Older Adults Using Mobile Phones

Netzahualcóyotl Hernández[✉] and Jesús Favela

Computer Science Department, CICESE, Ensenada, Mexico
netzahdzc@gmail.com, favela@cicese.mx

Abstract. Fatigue is one of the symptoms associated with frailty among older adults, a syndrome that signals a progressive deterioration of physical and mental capacity. It is commonly measured by clinical studies, physical tests, or questionnaires, involving effort some people can't attain. We describe a method to assess the fatigue a person experiences while walking by measuring their demand for oxygen and heart rate. The approach makes use of the accelerometer in the mobile phone, thus allowing for continuous fatigue assessment under naturalistic conditions. Results show a margin of error of less than 5 heart beats per minute and no significant difference between heart rate's base-line fatigue classification and predicted fatigue classification; which compares favourably with current approaches. The method can be used to monitor health conditions among the frail.

Keywords: Heart rate · Fatigue · Opportunistic mobile sensing

1 Introduction

Aging is an intrinsic process of demographic transition and indicator of the need of additional medical services and health. This population is characterized by losing the ability to live independently due to their limited mobility, weakness, or other physical or mental problems. According to [18] aging population will rise 16.6 % by 2030 and 21.4 % by 2050, suggesting that while in 2000 one in ten people in the world was an older adult elderly, by 2050 this figure will increase to one in five.

This increased longevity has several implications, for instance, it implies important contributions to society through active participation of the aging population within their families, carrying out voluntary activities, transmitting their knowledge and experience to new generations, participating along compensable workplace, among other activities. On the other hand, those benefits might be accompanied by health and social challenges as the aging population changes biologically; such as the decrease in vision and driving speed, loss of muscle mass, reduced lung and cardiovascular capacity, and partial hearing loss. Addressing these issues associated to frailty, such as physical fatigue, required medication consumption, counseling to improve lifestyle, specialized assistance, and care for the elderly.

© Springer International Publishing Switzerland 2015
A.A. Salah et al. (Eds.): HBU 2015, LNCS 9277, pp. 84–96, 2015.
DOI: 10.1007/978-3-319-24195-1_7

In this context, [12] predicts a massive increase in chronic diseases and age-related diseases, illustrating the important of raising awareness about the biological and psychological changes involved in aging. This requires society to change from a culture that solves health problems toward one that prevents it; involving a breach of opportunity to provide computational tools in the context of pervasive technology [8].

1.1   Perception of Physical Fatigue

Physical fatigue can be appreciated as a subjective feeling of tiredness, it is an adaptive and regulatory symptom that indicates when people need to rest [22], is a process that gets manifested progressively as muscle tension, which implies an association to blood irrigation and muscle oxygen supply [20]. It evolves progressively according to three phases: (1) incubation, characterized by one of either two conditions: the person becomes either nervous, irritating, impatient, or depressed and passive, (2) febrility, where previous symptoms get worse, and other are manifested, (3) apathy, in which a state of physical or/and psychological problems come up; requiring a medical solution. When physical demand repetitively reaches any of these phases, the muscles and nervous system get deteriorated, leading to health problems such as chronic fatigue, and as a symptom of frailty; a syndrome that reflects a progressive decline in physical and cognitive abilities that increase vulnerability to deleterious effects such as the risk of falling, fractures, and death [2].

2   Perception of Physical Fatigue Assessment

There are three main methods to diagnose the perception of physical fatigue, through a clinical test, questionnaires, or physical tests that use instruments such as the Borg scale [5] and the Workout zone [9]. These methods might be inconvenient requiring the subject to attend a lab or somewhat unreliable (e.g. based on self-report), which makes attractive the development of non-intrusive methods to detect the perception of physical fatigue while the subject performs daily activities, such as walking.

However, the problem with diagnosing physical fatigue is that it is often considered a biological reaction between stress and physical exhaustion is stereotyped with aging, which causes physical fatigue to be ignored by both patients and physicians; depriving them of diagnoses and treatments in a timely manner. Therefore, in this work we propose a methodology to unobtrusively monitor perception of physical fatigue base on technology people are already familiar with, such as mobile phones, thus patients could provide objective data regarding physical fatigue episodes, without investing on new technology [27].

Related work conducted in this context include identifying signs of sleepiness by yawning and blinking [16], and changes in the grasping force of a flywheel [3]. Mobile phones may estimate physical fatigue by using different approaches such as heart rate, which could be gathered by optical sensor ([21], CardioBuddy[1]). While others consist of a set of distributed sensors along a patient body [1,17], which in all cases, implies an economic investment some people prefer to avoid.

3 Perception of Physical Fatigue Estimation Method

As argued in the previous section, physical fatigue is commonly associated with increased heart rate. Thus, our approach considers the fact that as the body demands more oxygen, heart rate increases [7], and an increased heart rate is perceived by the individual as a symptom of physical fatigue [5]. The approach is based on estimating oxygen consumption from the amount of motion recorded by a wearable sensor while the subject walks [4]. Subsequently the approach calculates the heart rate from previous oxygen consumption, to finally estimate physical fatigue perception; opportunistically and with technology most people already have adopted (Fig. 1). To estimate motion, we use accelerometer and GPS data gathered from a mobile phone, as proposed in [24].

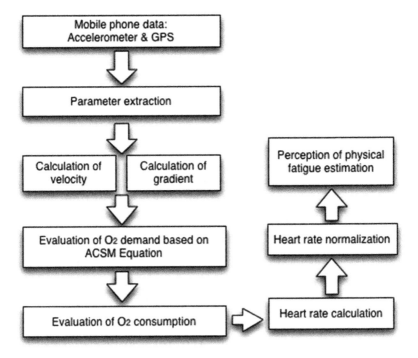

Fig. 1. Methodology flow to calculate perception of physical fatigue, according to the approach proposed.

---

[1] http://www.azumio.com/apps/cardio-buddy-2/.

3.1 Parameter Extraction

The method starts by extracting the gravity component from the accelerometer measures[2].

Afterwards, we extract the DC component (Component Direct) in regular window segments ($W = 24$ s). Subsequently, windows are analysed to infer the parameters required by the predictor method, *i.e.*, walking speed, and oxygen demand, as described next.

3.2 Velocity

We count user steps to measure walking speed based on the number of steps and stride size, as shown in Eq. 1.

$$S_k = D_k/W \quad D_k = ST_k \times SL \quad SL = D_{total}/ST_{total} \tag{1}$$

Where S is the speed (m/s), D represents the distance traveled (m), W the window size (s), ST the steps total, and SL represents the stride size.

3.3 Gradient

We determine inclination surface to the horizontal by calculating user's elevation from GPS of mobile-phones and walking distance.

3.4 Oxygen Demand

We use a formula proposed by the American College of Sports Medicine (ACSM) to calculate O_2 demand [23], and adjusted for each user as shown in Eq. 2.

$$K = R + H + V$$
$$R = 3.6145 - (0.0367 \times BMI) - (0.0038 \times age) + (0.1790 \times gender)$$
$$H = 0.1 \times speed$$
$$V = 1.8 \times speed \times gradient \tag{2}$$

Where R represents the user-customized consumption of O_2 ($ml \times kg^{-1} \times min^{-1}$) [4], H represents the horizontal component of the displacement speed (m/min), and V represents the vertical component relative to the speed (m/min) and gradient displacement (%).

3.5 Calculating Oxygen Consumption

Assuming we estimate oxygen demand periodically when the user walks (Eq. 1), we calculate oxygen consumption from its variation at each interval i.

Subsequently, a predictive model is constructed based on the parameters described earlier using a Support Vector Machine (SVM).

---

[2] http://developer.android.com/reference/android/hardware/SensorEvent.html.

3.6   Predictive Model to Calculate Heart Rate

We use WEKA to construct the predictive model using the SVM classifier [11] with a non-linear kernel, our input data consisted on mobile phone's accelerometer and GPS data. Ground truth was taken from an electrical pulse reader Zephy[3] to monitor heart rate (as described in Sect. 4.2).

3.7   Normalization

During the analysis of preliminary results, it was possible to observe a similar behaviour between the prediction model and the ground-truth, but with a shift in their amplitude. Therefore, to stabilize prediction data, we have corrected for the offset.

The normalization process begins by identifying a stabilization point set to 3 min [13] (Fig. 2-a), then the heart rate prediction converges to heart rate ground-truth to reduce the gap between them (Fig. 2-b), and finally we exclude the segment of data identified between the first reading window and the point of convergence (Figs. 2-c and d).

3.8   Perception of Physical Fatigue Inference

To calculate the perception of physical fatigue, we initially calculate the maximum heart rate [25], and subsequently classify the calculated heart rate (post-

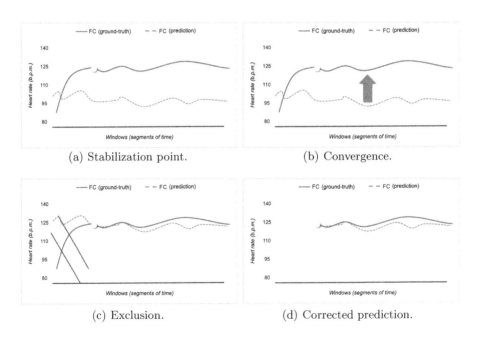

(a) Stabilization point.   (b) Convergence.

(c) Exclusion.   (d) Corrected prediction.

Fig. 2. Normalization process.

---

[3] http://www.zephyranywhere.com.

normalization) according to the five Workout zones [9], where the distance between each zone represents a margin of 10 % of the intensity of exercise supported by the human body (Table 1).

Table 1. Rating based on the perception of physical fatigue classification Workout zones.

ZONE – DESCRIPTION	% HRmax
Verylight – For a healthy person, it's equivalent to a slow walk at his own pace for a few minutes.	50 % – 60 %
Light – People with average physical condition are comfortable working at this level and can remain in this zone for long periods of time.	60 % – 70 %
Moderate – The person is aware of the difficulty in breathing; it becomes more difficult to maintain a conversation.	70 % – 80 %
High – The person is walking at a fast pace, presenting deep and forceful breathing. Cannot conduct a conversation while walking.	80 % – 90 %
Extreme – The body feels very heavy, and the person is very tired. It is a very strenuous exercise level.	90 % – 100 %

Notice that, so far, our normalization approach requires knowing the initial heart rate. In the discussion section we propose how to deal with this.

4   Evaluation

We next present the results of the evaluation of the model proposed in this work. Although we use two cell phones as part of our setup, we will only show the results from the one positioned on the right hip, since data analysis shows a high correlation between the two data sets (i.e. 0.92).

4.1   Subjects

Participants consisted of 3 elderly (2 males and 1 female) with a mean age of 68 years ($\sigma = 6.1$ years). These subjects answered a brief questionnaire with demographic and health information, which was used to determine whether they could perform maximal aerobic exercise testing. Subject were excluded if they presented an impairment to conduct exercise, were taking medication altering metabolic rate or if their physician identified cardiovascular abnormalities.

Inclusion criteria consisted of participants completing the Readiness Questionnaire Physical Activity (PAR-Q) [26], a freely mobile rating from Timed Get Up and Go Test [19], as well as fulfilling the 6MWT recommendation (i.e., resting heart rate of less than 120 b.p.m., a systolic blood pressure of less than 180 mm Hg, and a diastolic blood pressure of less than 100 mm Hg.) [10].

The participants provided a written informed consent on the use of their data for research purposes.

4.2   Procedure

Individual anthropometry data (i.e., weight and height) was measured [14] in order to calculate body mass index (BMI). Subjects were asked to attend test day under criteria for preventing cardiovascular atypical behaviour, i.e., the subjects have not eaten anything or consumed coffee or alcohol after 4 hours before testing, and they did not conduct any intense exercises during at least 20 min before testing [6].

Before beginning the test, we equipped participants with an electrical pulse reader Zephy[4] to monitor heart rate with readings at 1 Hz (ground-truth), and two Samsung Google Nexus S GT-I9020T[5] cellphones with 3 axes accelerometer KR3DM at 50 Hz. Each subject used the electrical pulse reader on the chest and cell phone on the hips as shown in Fig. 3. We used 24-seconds windows and 50 % overlapping as in [24].

4.3   Data Gathering

To collect data, subjects were asked to walk along a free of obstacles aisle under controlled criteria [10]. As a health control, we monitored the heart rate of subjects (by an electrical pulse reader Zephy) while walking.

Participants performed 2 tests each in a period of two weeks (June, 2014). They walked for approximately the same amount of time on both tests, approximately 17.33 min. The test finished either when the subjects achieved 85 % of heart rate maximum capacity, we identify any physical discomfort, or by request.

4.4   Results

Results were normalized according to previous procedure. Figure 4 shows the longest case predicted from one of the participants (i.e., 21 min walk), which achieved an 38.96 % improvement when normalized.

Analysed data by using previous described methodology shows an average error of 4.78 b.p.m. by using round-robin distribution as presented in Table 2.

4.5   Perception of Physical Fatigue Inference

The final step consists of using the percentage of maximum effort of each participant to determine the corresponding Workout classification zone. Results show high classification accuracy (97.93 %) when comparing fatigue-based reading (ground-truth) to post-normalized prediction.

---

[4] http://www.zephyranywhere.com.
[5] http://www.samsung.com.

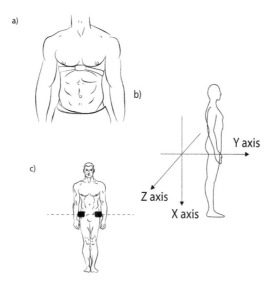

Fig. 3. (a) Position of chest band. (b) Mobile phone orientation. (c) Mobile phone positioning (i.e., hips).

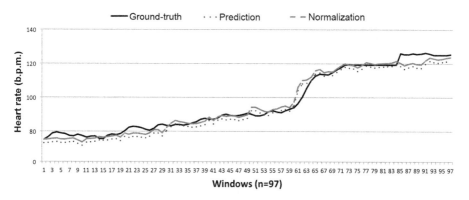

Fig. 4. Comparison between ground-truth reading and normalization prediction for Subject 3 (21 min walk performance; training with test 1 to predict test 2).

Table 2. Mean of round-robin distribution of the three subjects (A, B, C), respectively.

S-A	S-B	S-C	**AVG. ERROR (b.p.m)**	
12.67	5.44	2.77	6.14	**4.78**

5   Application

To show the applicability of the method proposed, we conducted a study in naturalistic conditions. We developed a mobile application that allows the user to report their perception of physical fatigue (Fig. 5). We asked participants to carry the mobile phone while walking as usual. Participants consisted of 4 young adults; subjects with mean age of 28.66 years ($\sigma = 2.35$ years). The data collection period was approximately one month; starting on July 7th to August 11th, 2014. 143 walking segments were collected in total, and 26 were eliminated, as they did not met the inclusion criteria *a priori* (*i.e.*, more than 7 min long, complete accelerometer, and GPS data).

(a) Fatigue report   (b) Finish walk   (c) Fatigue perception

Fig. 5. Application to gather data in naturalistic conditions.

The data collected allowed us to analyse walking context by data such as: displacement segment (Fig. 6 -top), displacement gradient (Fig. 6 -middle), and perception of physical fatigue levels associated with the movement of travel of the user (Fig. 6 -below). Naturalistic condition results show that our approach could be integrated into mobile devices applications to allow users to track their progress when conducting activities such as: performing physical exercise, experiment a recovery intervention, or simply to monitor physical deterioration of aging.

To illustrate how this method could be used, we present a scenario of monitoring physical decline in older adults.

–Sara is 67 years, she started a new medication as part of her recovery treatment derived from a surgery she had a few weeks ago. When prescribed, the physician asked her relatives to monitor Sara's progress; since secondary effects included apathy and fatigue. Sara lives with her daughter Mary; who months ago installed in her mother's cellphone an application to monitor fatigue. After breakfast, Sara usually takes a walk in the park carrying her mobile phone. One day, while Mary is in her office, she reviews her mother's physical progress (through an on-line system) to visualises her mother's health record, and observes multiple

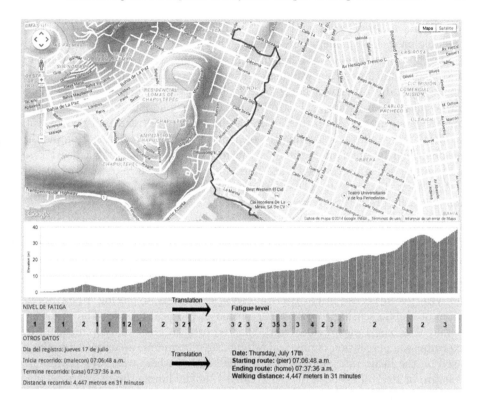

Fig. 6. Interface of a website displaying a segment of walking (top image), gradient elevation (meters) corresponding to the geographic location of an user, and his perception of physical fatigue calculation. Fatigue zones are marked by a number over each corresponding segment on the displayed bar. Zone 1= from 50 % to 60 %, Zone 2 = from 60 % to 70 %, Zone 3 = from 70 % to 80 %, Zone 4 = from 80 % to 90 %, Zone 5 = from 90 % to 100 %.

episodes of apparent fatigue since she started taking the new medication. Thus, she decides to ask for an immediate appointment with her personal physician. After performing clinical tests, the physician found that Sara is experiencing secondary effects reported to be present in 10 % of those taking the medication, and decides to change her medication.

As appreciated from the scenario, the method could be used to monitor the behavior of the older adult, possibly combined with additional parameters such as food intake or quality of sleep.

6 Discussion

The results of the experiments conducted show that by providing a personalized oxygen demand equation [23] according to each participant, using 1 walking tests as a trainer for the classifier, eliminating the first 3 min period (as stabilization samples) for normalization, and using SVM as classifier was sufficient to obtain a reliable prediction mode; as describer in this paper.

On the other hand, even though our study shows a positive result under controlled conditions when walking, it should be clear that the conditions are not always stable (*e.g.*, weather, mood, food/ingested medicine) and variations can be manifested as atypical cardiovascular behaviour [6]; even mental stress could have an impact of up to 15 % in the physical performance of people [15]. Another open challenge regarding the design of a naturalistic application (as the one described in previous section) is the requirement of a starting heart rate point, so we could process with the normalization procedure, described in our methodology. Thus, we face the challenge of integrating these parameters in a more versatile prediction model.

7   Conclusions

This paper proposes a method to identify perception of physical fatigue by measuring cardiovascular frequency through mobile phone sensing; opportunistically and with potential use in naturalistic conditions. Thus, exploring a new application of mobile sensing to detect perception of physical fatigue. The proposed technique is based on previous work that reports an error of 7 b.p.m. [24]. To determine the perception of physical fatigue, the maximum capacity (determined based on the heart rate) and Workout scale is used; where each area represents a margin of 10 % of exercise intensity carried by the human body.

The method proposed in this paper uses Support Vector Machine as classifier, and it was tested with data gathered from 3 subjects; 2 tests run each (mean: 65.50 years, $\sigma = 5.80$ years) to obtain a margin of error for predicting heart rate of 4.78 b.p.m. and 97.93 % accuracy in the classification of fatigue by comparing the base-line against post-normalized prediction.

Even though physical fatigue refers to a normal, everyday experience that most individuals report after physical exertion or inadequate rest, studies have shown that physical fatigue often precedes the manifestation of diseases, as for example: cancer, multiple sclerosis, arthritis, renal disease, and HIV infection, among other diseases. Thus, the approach presented here could be used as an auxiliary tool for medical diagnostic procedures, for early detection of diseases, monitoring post-treatment evolution, and to help assess the risk of certain medications on patients. Thus, without interrupting patient's daily life activities, who would only have to use his mobile phone as usual.

Thus, the approach presented here could be potentially used for early detection of diseases, monitoring post-treatment evolution, and to help assess the risk of certain medications on patients.

References

1. Altini, M., Penders, J., Vullers, R., Amft, O.: Estimating energy expenditure using body-worn accelerometers: a comparison of methods, sensors number and positioning. IEEE J. Biomed. Health Inform. **19**(1), 219–226 (2015)

2. Alvarado, B.E., Zunzunegui, M.V., Beland, F., Bamvita, J.M.: Life course social and health conditions linked to frailty in Latin American older men and women. J. Gerontol. A Biol. Sci. Med. Sci. **63**(12), 1399–1406 (2008)

3. Baronti, F., Lenzi, F., Roncella, R., Saletti, R.: Distributed sensor for steering wheel rip force measurement in driver fatigue detection. In: Design, Automation Test in Europe Conference Exhibition, DATE 2009, pp. 894–897, April 2009

4. Barstow, T.J., Mole, P.A.: Linear and nonlinear characteristics of oxygen uptake kinetics during heavy exercise. J. Appl. Physiol. **71**(6), 2099–2106 (1991)

5. Borg, G.: Psychophysical scaling with applications in physical work and the perception of exertion. Scand. J. Work Environ. Health **16**(Suppl 1), 55–58 (1990)

6. Compher, C., Frankenfield, D., Keim, N., Roth-Yousey, L.: Best practice methods to apply to measurement of resting metabolic rate in adults: a systematic review. J. Am. Diet Assoc. **106**(6), 881–903 (2006)

7. Corbin, C.: Concepts of Fitness. McGraw, New York (2011)

8. Dishman, E.: Inventing wellness systems for aging in place. Computer **37**(5), 34–41 (2004)

9. Edwards, S., Snell, M., Sampson, E.: Sally Edwards' Heart Zone Training: Exercise Smart, Stay Fit, and Live Longer. Adams Media Corporation, Holbrook (1996)

10. Enright, P.L.: The six-minute walk test. Respir Care **48**(8), 783–785 (2003)

11. Hall, M., Frank, E., Holmes, G., Pfahringer, B., Reutemann, P., Witten, I.H.: The weka data mining software: an update. SIGKDD Explor. Newsl. **11**(1), 10–18 (2009)

12. Kaye J, Z.T.: Overview of healthcare, disease, and disability. In: Bardram, J.E., Mihailidis, A., Dadong, W. (eds.) Pervasive Computing in Healthcare, pp. 3–20 (2006)

13. Krogh, A., Lindhard, J.: The changes in respiration at the transition from work to rest. J. Physiol. (Lond.) **53**(6), 431–439 (1920)

14. Lohman, T.G., Roche, A.F.: Anthropometric Standardization Reference Manual. Human Kinetics Pub, Champaign (1988)

15. Marcora, S.M., Staiano, W., Manning, V.: Mental fatigue impairs physical performance in humans. J. Appl. Physiol. **106**(3), 857–864 (2009)

16. Mohd Noor, H.A., Ibrahim, R.: Fatigue detector using eyelid blinking and mouth yawning. In: Bolc, L., Tadeusiewicz, R., Chmielewski, L.J., Wojciechowski, K. (eds.) ICCVG 2010, Part II. LNCS, vol. 6375, pp. 134–141. Springer, Heidelberg (2010)

17. Mokaya, F., Nguyen, B., Kuo, C., Jacobson, Q., Zhang, P.: [mars] a real time motion capture and muscle fatigue monitoring tool. In: Proceedings of the 10th ACM Conference on Embedded Network Sensor Systems, SenSys 2012, pp. 385–386. ACM, New York (2012). http://doi.acm.org/10.1145/2426656.2426721

18. Organization, W.H.: Aging (2011). www.who.int

19. Podsiadlo, D., Richardson, S.: The timed up and go: a test of basic functional mobility for frail elderly persons. J. Am. Geriatr Soc. **39**(2), 142–148 (1991)

20. Rodriguez, D.R., Fajardo, J.T.: Prevencion de lesiones en el deporte / Prevention of sports injuries: Claves Para Un Rendimiento Deportivo Optimo / Keys to Optimal Athletic Performance (Spanish Edition). Editorial Medica Panamericana (2014)

21. Scully, C., Lee, J., Meyer, J., Gorbach, A., Granquist-Fraser, D., Mendelson, Y., Chon, K.: Physiological parameter monitoring from optical recordings with a mobile phone. IEEE Trans. Biomed. Eng. **59**(2), 303–306 (2012)

22. Singleton, W.: Deterioration of performance on a short-term perceptual-motor task. In: Symposium on Fatigue, vol. 8, pp. 163–172 (1953)

23. American College of Sports Medicine: ACSM's Metabolic Calculations Handbook. LWW, Baltimore (2006)

24. Sumida, M., Mizumoto, T., Yasumoto, K.: Estimating heart rate variation during walking with smartphone. In: Proceedings of the 2013 ACM International Joint Conference on Pervasive and Ubiquitous Computing, UbiComp 2013 pp. 245–254. ACM, New York (2013)

25. Tanaka, H., Monahan, K.D., Seals, D.R.: Age-predicted maximal heart rate revisited. J. Am. Coll. Cardiol. **37**(1), 153–156 (2001)

26. Thomas, S., Reading, J., Shephard, R.J.: Revision of the physical activity readiness questionnaire (PAR-Q). Can J. Sport Sci. **17**(4), 338–345 (1992)

27. Vathsangam, H., Schroeder, E., Sukhatme, G.: Hierarchical approaches to estimate energy expenditure using phone-based accelerometers. IEEE J. Biomed. Health Inform. **18**(4), 1242–1252 (2014)

Online Prediction of People's Next Point-of-Interest: Concept Drift Support

Mehdi Boukhechba[1]([✉]), Abdenour Bouzouane[1], Bruno Bouchard[1],
Charles Gouin-Vallerand[2], and Sylvain Giroux[3]

[1] LIARA Laboratory, University of Quebec at
Chicoutimi (UQAC), Chicoutimi G7H 2B1, Canada
{Mahdi.Boukhechba, Abdenour_Bouzouane,
Bruno_Bouchard}@uqac.ca
[2] Tele-Universite of Quebec (TELUQ), Quebec, Canada
charles.gouin-vallerand@teluq.ca
[3] University of Sherbrooke, Sherbrooke, Canada
sylvain.giroux@usherbrooke.ca

Abstract. Current advances in location tracking technology provide exceptional amount of data about the users' movements. The volume of geospatial data collected from moving users' challenges human ability to analyze the stream of input data. Therefore, new methods for online mining of moving object data are required. One of the popular approaches available for moving objects is the prediction of the unknown future location of an object. In this paper we present a new method for online prediction of users' next important locations to be visited that not only learns incrementally the users' habits, but also detects and supports the drifts in their patterns. Our original contribution includes a new algorithm of online mining association rules that support the concept drift.

Keywords: Mobile environment · Human activities · Activity prediction · Online association rules · Spatio-temporal data mining · Concept drift

1 Introduction

The last decade has been the mobile device technologies era, where the capture of the evolving position of moving objects has become ubiquitous. Mobile wearable tracking devices, e.g., phones and navigation systems collect the movements of all kind of moving objects, generating huge volumes of mobility data. Despite the fact that data collected from mobile devices is more accurate, there are still scientific challenges regarding the use of this data. One of these important research topics is the prediction of user's next location [5, 7, 16], where results of such research are used in a wide range of fields like traffic management, public transportation, assistance of people with special needs, commercials and advertising.

Our previous work [2] proposed an online activity recognition system that offers the possibility to understand what people are doing at a specific moment by inferring incrementally people's interesting places from raw GPS data. In this paper, we are

© Springer International Publishing Switzerland 2015
A.A. Salah et al. (Eds.): HBU 2015, LNCS 9277, pp. 97–116, 2015.
DOI: 10.1007/978-3-319-24195-1_8

proposing an evolution of our previous system that estimates the users' actions in the future by predicting their next visited point of interest. We are planning to use such a system to assist people with special needs (e.g. persons suffering from the Alzheimer's disease) during their daily outdoor activities by proposing specific assistance based on their recognized activities and context. Assuming that we have some beforehand knowledge about people's destinations, our previous work was able to detect anomaly in the users' behaviors (comparing the planned and the real destination). The predictive model that we are proposing in this paper aims to launch assistance processes when users are lost, suggesting a new safe destination.

In this paper, we are addressing the issue of predicting the next location of an individual based on the observations of his mobility habits. One of the major problems met when trying to incrementally learn users' routine is the concept drift [19–21]. The concept drift means that the statistical properties of the target variable (in our case, the users' habits), which the model is trying to predict, change over time in unexpected ways. For instance, assuming that we learn a user's habits using a traditional algorithm, a user lives in "@1" for one year, after that he moves to "@2", this shifting will lead to not only shift the address but probably the habits too. Existing algorithms will take few months to detect that a user is having a new set of frequent habits (if we take a support of 60 % using the Apriori[1] algorithm [15] for example, it will take 7 months to detect the new habits), in the meantime, all what is proposed by these algorithms is probably false, since they are based on the old routines, and not the new ones.

Current work [1, 7, 8, 11, 16] that seeks to learn users' routines and to predict their future routines fail in their ability to deal with the changes in users' behaviors during the learning process, and there are only few works that attempt to incrementally predict the users' next location.

We bring a novelty to the manner of resolving this problem via a novel online algorithm that extracts association rules carrying the data drift during the learning process. Hence, the main idea is to help new habits detected to become quickly frequent, by introducing a new criterion of support calculation based on a weight distribution of data collected and not the classic number of occurrences.

The following sections detail our contribution: Sect. 2 briefly reviews related work; Sect. 3 presents our approach; Sect. 4 describes the experimentation. Finally, conclusion and future works, as well as the expected contributions, are summarized in Sect. 5.

2 Related Work

Significant research effort has been undertaken in both mobile computing and spatial data mining domains [17, 18]. Many advances in tracking users' movements have emerged resulting in several proposals for predicting future users' locations. The main

---

[1] Apriori is an algorithm for frequent item set mining and association rule learning over transactional databases. It proceeds by identifying the frequent individual items in the database and extending them to larger and larger item sets as long as those item sets appear sufficiently often in the database.

approach proposed is to learn the user's patterns from his historical locations and try to predict the next location via different techniques.

In [8] Morzy introduces a new method for predicting the location of a moving object where he extracts the association rules from the moving object database using a modified version of Apriori and uses the rules extracted when a trajectory is given via matching functions, he selects the best association rule that matches this trajectory, and then uses it for the prediction. Unfortunately, these works do not permit incremental training of the models, since it is based on a posteriori learning, secondly, the fact that authors propose matching functions in form of strategies (simple, polynomial, logarithmic and aggregation strategies) can create a computational complexities; difficulties to choose and set the rights parameters for the right strategy.

Sébastien et al. extended a previously proposed mobility model called the Mobility Markov Chain (n-MMC)[2], in order to keep track of the n previous locations visited [7]. This proposal essentially corresponds to a higher order Markov model. Authors show that while the accuracy of the prediction grows with n, choosing $n > 2$ does not seem to bring an important improvement to the cost of a significant overhead in terms of computation and space for the learning and storing of the mobility model. However, like the previous works, this one has a lack with the computational complexity and the incremental support. In addition, the three datasets used in authors' experiments were collected in a controlled environment where data was gathered from specific participants who were aware of the experiments.

Asahara et al. proposed in [1] a method for predicting pedestrian movement on the basis of a mixed Markov- chain model (MMM)[3], taking into account some complex parameters like pedestrian's personality merged to his previous status. The authors experiment their solution in a major shopping mall and report an accuracy of 74.4 % for the MMM method and, in a comparison over the same dataset, they reported that methods based on Markov-chain models, or based on Hidden Markov Models, achieve lower prediction rates of about 45 % and 2 %, respectively.

Authors in [3] present two new algorithms that use the frequent patterns tree (FP-tree) structure to reduce the required number of database scans. One of the proposed algorithms is the DB-tree algorithm, which stores all the database information in an FP-tree structure and requires no re-scan of the original database for all update cases, the algorithm stores in descending order of support all items, as well as counts all items

---

[2] MMC is a probabilistic automaton in which states represent points of interest (POIs) of an individual and transitions between states corresponds to a movement from one POI to another one, a transition between POIs is non deterministic but rather that there is a probability distribution over the transitions that corresponds to the probability of moving from one POI to another.

[3] MMM is an intermediate model between individual and generic models. The prediction of the next location is based on a Markov model belonging to a group of individuals with similar mobility behavior. This approach clusters individuals into groups based on their mobility traces and then generates a specific Markov model for each group. The prediction of the next location works by first identifying the group a particular individual belongs to and then inferring the next location based on this group model.

in all transactions in the database in its branches. The DB-Tree is constructed the same way as done in FP-Tree except that it includes all the items instead of only the frequent 1-items. The second algorithm is the PotFp-tree (Potential frequent pattern) algorithm, which uses a prediction of future possible frequent itemsets to reduce the number of times the original database needs to be scanned when previous small itemsets become large after database update. The first disadvantage of the three algorithms, with all respect to the authors, is the non-support of the concept drift, since none of them support the changes in the sequences behavior. The second problem is the restructuring of the tree to store the node in descending order of support. This technique not only increases the computational complexity, but represents likewise an invalid solution to fields where the order of items is important, like peoples' habits.

In [10], a method called dynamic clustering based prediction (DCP) of mobile user movements is presented to discover user mobility patterns from collections of recorded mobile trajectories and used for the prediction of movements and dynamic allocation of resources. Collected user trajectories are clustered according to their in-between similarity, using a weighted edit distance measure [11]. In the prediction phase, the representatives of the clusters are used. Using a simulation, the authors showed that for a variety of trajectory lengths, noise and outlier conditions, the DCP method achieves a very good tradeoff between prediction recall and precision.

While developing a rich body of work for mining moving object data, the research community has shown very little interest for the online mining of these objects, since the mainstream of related works lies on a post hoc analysis of a massive set of data to learn and to predict locations.

Moreover, one of the big issues that can easily shatter the most robust next location predictive model is the habits' drift, since from the time when the data begin to behave in a non-regular manner; the predictive models will face difficulties to do their work. Finally, to our knowledge, we are the first to support incrementally the users' habits changes, since there is no approach that handles the habits' drift during the learning and the prediction of next location process.

3   Overview of the Approach

Assuming that we track a user outdoor activities using an incremental solution such as that one presented in [2], every activity (location) detected is called a Place of Interest (POI). A POI is an urban geo-referenced object where a person may carry out a specific activity. Our approach begins by constructing a sequence of POI_j that represent the tracking of users' daily habits, every sequence is stored incrementally in a tree structure called Habits' Tree 'HT'. For every new sequence, our algorithm checks for a drift in the distribution of sequences and allocates a new weight to the sequence concerned. Finally, the algorithm predicts the next POI using the association rules drawn from HT.

3.1 Sequence Construction

This step aims to represent users' habits via monitoring of routines called sequence S_i, every sequence contains a set of disjoint singletons POI_j (c-e we can't find the same POI many times in the same sequence) and terminates with the end of the day (daily habits). For example, assuming that the user achieved the following activities during a day: home, work, restaurant, work, gym, home; the algorithm will construct incrementally two sequences from these habits:

S_1: Home, work, restaurant.
S_2: Restaurant, work, gym, home.

In fact, when Algorithm 1 detects a new POI that already exists in the sequence, like "work" in the example above, it stops constructing S1 and creates a new sequence S2, for optimizing the storage of the sequences.

Algorithm 1: Sequence construction

```
Input:
A POIⱼ;
Output:
Sequence Sᵢ;
Sᵢ = null ;
For each new POIⱼ
    If (! Sᵢ.contains(POIⱼ) and  StillTheSameDay) then
    Sᵢ = Sᵢ + POIⱼ
    Else //new sequence
        Return Sᵢ;
        If (StillTheSameDay) Sᵢ = Last POIⱼ
        Else Sᵢ = null ;
End for each
```

Algorithm 1 is executed on every POI_j arrival, when S_i is finally constructed we move to the next step: the habits' tree update. Note that an improvement can be made at this step to respect the definition of streaming learning, this improvement is based on the treatment and the storage of each POI_j in HT when it arrives without waiting for the construction of S_i.

3.2 Habits' Tree Update

Habits' tree HT is a data structure that takes form of a special tree, every node represents a POI and is characterized by a weight w_j that represents the weight of

POI_j's occurrence and an identifier ID_j that aims to identify the sequences by an integer (see 4.3.1 Sequence identification).

The work of [3] inspired us to plan this part, authors in that work proposed a new algorithm for mining incrementally association rules called DB-Tree. DB-Tree is a generalized form of FP-Tree (FP-Growth [22]), which stores in descending order of support all items in the database, as well as counts all items in all transactions in the database in its branches. The DB-Tree is constructed the same way as done in FP-Tree, except that it includes all the items instead of only the frequent 1-items.

In our habits' tree, tree data structure wasn't chosen arbitrarily; using this structure and storing all the sequences (frequents and not frequents) eliminate the need of rescanning the entire database to update the structure like it is done in Apriori and FP-tree (when previously not frequent POI_j become frequent in the new update). Indeed, the algorithm scans only the branches concerned by the new sequence, which optimizes the computational complexity. Additionally, storage optimizations are achieved using this structure, sharing paths between items in tree structure leads to much smaller size than that in a traditional database (see Fig. 2).

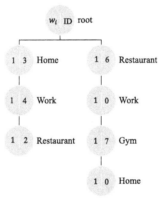

Fig. 1. HT Structure construction.

To give a brief idea on the way the data are structured in HT, we illustrated in Fig. 1 how our algorithm stored the two sequences S_1 and S_2 from the example above in a form of a succession of nodes characterized by $< name, w, ID >$.

We added two new sequences S_3 = Home, Work, Gym, Cinema and S_4 = Home, Gym, from the updated HT presented in Fig. 2, we can observe how the notion of sharing paths (in the nodes home and work) leads to a compression of the database dimension. Additionally, we can notice that the algorithm added these sequences with different weight than the previous because it detects new behaviors, more details are provided below.

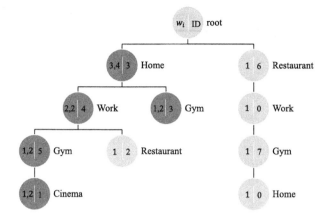

Fig. 2. Sharing paths in HT structure.

On the arrival of a new sequence S_i, the Algorithm 2 recursively processes each POI_j in S_i. If the POI_j exists in HT, the concerned node's weight is updated, otherwise, the algorithm adds a new node with a new random POI_j. ID, and a new weight POI_j. w where the details of calculation is given in the next section. For example, supposing that after a certain time of learning, user's HT is structured like on Fig. 2, the next day, the user did the following sequence: home, work, gym, @1. Figure 3 shows how our algorithm updates the nodes: home, work, gym; and adds a new POI: @1. Note that @1 was added to HT with an unknown weight because it will be calculated in the next section.

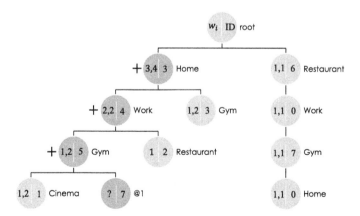

Fig. 3. Example of HT updated.

Algorithm 2: Habits' tree update

```
Input:
A sequence S_i;
Output:
HT;
ArrayListPOI = S_i.ToList() ;
For (int i=0 ; i< ArrayListPOI.Lenght; i++)
New Node = ArrayListPOI [i] ;
If (HT.contains (NewNode))
HT.UpdateNode (NewNode)   ;
HT.GoDown;
Else
// Add the remaining POI_j in S_i and leave the loop
Ht.AddAllNodes  (from  ArrayListPOI  [i]  to  ArrayListPOI
[last]);
Break;
And if
End for
```

Algorithm 2 shows how to maintain the HT on every new S_i arrival, but we haven't yet responded to our problem requirements. The next section presents how we proceed to distribute the weight in every node updated in HT. Our contribution aims to track the drift in users' habits, and to distribute the weights basing on these behavior changes.

3.3   Drift Detection

This part aims to track the changes in users' habits. Our technique is divided into two steps: firstly we formulate mathematically each new sequence and secondly we use this number to test if it is a concept drift.

Sequence Identification. In order to be able to use a concept drift test, it is crucial to parse the information contained in S_i into a quantifiable entity. The introduction of ID_j in each node was in this perspective, in fact, every new sequence will be represented by a variable called x_j where x_j is obtained from the concatenation of each POI_j. ID present in S_i. For instance, in the example cited earlier, the new arrived sequence is: Home, work, gym, @1; using each node's ID that corresponds to each POI_j (see Fig. 3), the variable x_j will take a value of 3457. Once the sequence is identified by an integer, we use this number in the next step, the concept drift test.

Concept Drift Test. We use the Page Hinkley Test (PHT) [12] to detect the changes in users' habits, PHT is a sequential analysis technique typically used for monitoring change detection. It allows efficient detection of changes in the normal behavior of a process, which is established by a model. The PHT was designed to detect a change in the average of a Gaussian signal [19]. This test considers a cumulative variable U_T defined as the cumulated difference between the observed values (in our case the sequences' identifier x_j) and their mean till the current moment.

The procedure consists in carrying out two tests in parallel. The first makes it possible to detect an increase in the average. We calculate then:

$$\begin{cases} U_t = \sum_{j=1}^t (x_j - \overline{x_t} + \delta), \ U_0 = 0 \\ m_t = \min(U_t), t \geq 1 \\ PHT = U_t - m_t \end{cases}$$

The second allows detecting a decrease in the average as follows:

$$\begin{cases} U_t = \sum_{j=1}^t (x_j - \overline{x_t} + \delta), \ U_0 = 0 \\ M_t = \max(U_t), t \geq 1 \\ PHT = U_t - m_t \end{cases}$$

where $\overline{x_t} = \dfrac{\left(\sum_{j=1}^t \overline{x_j}\right)}{t}$ and δ corresponds to the magnitude of changes that are allowed. When the difference PHT is greater than a given threshold (λ) a change in the distribution is assigned. The threshold λ depends on the admissible false alarm rate. Increasing λ will entail fewer false alarms, but might miss or delay some changes. Controlling this detection threshold parameter makes it possible to establish a trade-off between the false alarms and the miss detections. In order to avoid issues linked to the parameterization of λ, we were inspired by the work in [14], where authors propose a self-adaptive method of change detection by proving that λ_t can be self-adapted using this equation: $\lambda_t = f * \overline{x_t}$ where f is a constant called the λ factor, which is the number of required witnesses seeing the changes. In our case, habits' drift that we are tracking are brutal, in the sense that the user usually doesn't change his habits gradually, so, we don't need a big number of witnesses to detect the changes, that's why we put $f = 2$.

After having a value (PHT) that represents the stability of our users' habits, we are going to use this variable to distribute the weight in every new POI's node in HT.

3.4   Weight Distribution

On every S_i arrival, we calculate the weight w_j that will be added to every node concerned by the new sequence in HT, the distribution is realized using a variable called drift's weight (wd_j) calculated using an exponential function like follows: $wd_j = 1 - e^{-\frac{1}{2}\frac{PHT}{\lambda_t}}$, where $p_t = \frac{PHT}{\lambda_t}$ represents an indicator of the user's state, the greater is PHT than λ_t, more we are sure that the user is doing something new, and vice versa. For example, from Fig. 4, when $p_t = 0$ because PHT = 0, we are sure that the user is doing the same habits, by against, each time p_t approaches the value 1, or exceeds it, we conclude that the user has a drift in his habits.

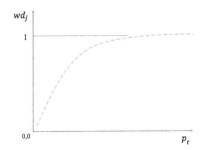

Fig. 4. Mathematical representation of wd_j.

Consequently, the weight added to HT's concerned nodes is like follows:

$$\begin{cases} w_j = 1 + wd_j, \text{ if } S_i \text{ is not frequent} \\ w_j = 1, \text{ if } S_i \text{ is frequent} \end{cases}$$

As we see, our distribution behaves in two ways (see Algorithm 3): a traditional way when the sequence S_i is frequent (adding only 1 in every node), and a special way when S_i is not frequent (adding $1 + wd_j$), the reason why we proceed this way is that we are trying to help only the new habits that aren't frequents to become frequents, once arrived, we stop our help to not promote a sequence (habit) relative to another.

Algorithm 3: Weight distribution

```
Input:
A sequence Sᵢ;
Output:
Weight wⱼ ;
xⱼ = HT.GetSequenceId(Sᵢ);
If (Sᵢ.isfrequent())wⱼ = 1 ;
Else
        Calculate λₜ,Uₜ,mₜ,Mₜ;
        Calculate PHT;
        Calculate wdⱼ;
        wⱼ = 1 +wdⱼ ;
End if
Return wⱼ
```

After calculating the weight that will be added on S_i arrival, the next step is to get the association rules from HT to predict the next activity.

3.5   Activity Prediction

Association Rules Mining. Our technique is inspired from FP-growth algorithm and one of its incremental versions called DB-Tree [3], the main difference between our work and theirs is that we introduced a weight distribution function that tracks the habits drift, secondly, our structure doesn't order the tree's items in descending order of support like done in DB-tree, in fact, DB-tree and FP-growth don't make a difference between "home, work, restaurant" and "restaurant, work, home", clearly, we can't use such technique when analyzing users' habits, otherwise, it will lead to gross errors.

Suppose we have a database with a set of items like illustrated in Fig. 2, I = {Home, gym, work, @1, restaurant, cinema} and MinSupport = 60 % of database transactions. To compute the frequent POI_j after constructing the habits tree HT, the algorithm mines the frequent POI_j that satisfy the minimum support represented by the Min-Support percentage of the maximum item's weight in HT. From Fig. 2, we have the weight of every items like follows (note that for every item we add up the corresponding weights found in all the tree, for example Home's weight = 3.4 + 1.0): I = {(Home: 4.4), (gym: 3.4), (work: 3.2), (restaurant: 2), (Cinema: 1.2)}, the minimum support will be: $MinSup = \frac{60}{100}(4.4) = 2.64$, thus, the frequent POI_j are all items greater or equal to 2.64 as {(Home: 4.4), (gym: 3.4), (work: 3.2)}.

The next steps is mining the frequent patterns from HT and association rules that are quite similar to those in FP-growth [3], thus we see no need to repeat the same process explanation.

Next Activity. After mining the association rules from HT, we get from the same example (Fig. 2) these rules: {work, gym -> home// work -> gym// home -> gym// home -> work// Home, work -> gym}, predicting the next activity lies on choosing the most appropriate association rules that represent user's situation, and using the resulting clause as predicted next activity. For example, if we know that the user is gone from home to work, using the last association rules we can predict that he will go next to the gym. Unfortunately, it's not always so simple to choose the right association rules. For instance, if we noticed that the user starts from his home and we try to predict the next activity, we will find that there are two rules that start from home, one predicts gym as next localization, and the other predicts work, and both are rights because the user has the habit of going sometimes to the gym and sometimes to work from home. This kind of conflict is managed by our algorithm (see Algorithm 4) by choosing the rule with the greater weight. Clearly, this technique doesn't rule out the risk of errors (this is what explain the error percentage presented in the experimental evaluation section) but minimizes it since we choose the most recurrent rule.

Finally, we present in Algorithm 5 the whole process that predicts the next activity from users' current location and some of their past locations if exist. First we construct a sequence of POI from the current location (or we wait until the sequence is constructed), then we calculate the weight that will be added to HT and we update the tree using this weight, we search for the association rules and we predict the next location based on the user's past activities (if exist).

Algorithm 4: Activity prediction

```
Input:
Habits tree HT;
Users past activities UPA;
Output:
Next activity;
TheRule = null;
ListRules = HT.GetAssociationRules();
ListAppropriateRules=listRules.GetAllThatContains(UPA);
If (ListAppropriateRules.size >1)
TheRule = ListAppropriateRules.GetRuleWithMaxWeight();
Else
TheRule = ListAppropriateRules.get(0);
End if
Return TheRule.getResultingClause();
```

Note that the sequence of these steps is not essentially like mentioned in Algorithm 5, we present in this algorithm the whole process to explain how to start from a simple localization to predict the next user's activity. In real life, these processes can be used differently, for example, there is no need to search for the association rules on every sequence arrival, the most correct way is to update HT on every S_i (because the update does need a whole scan of the tree, so it's not expensive in term of time calculation), and to search for the association rules in an appropriate time depending on the application requirements. For example, supposing that we try to assist a patient of Alzheimer's disease, the user tends to forget his next activities, the appropriate time that we are talking about is when the proposed system detects an anomaly in the user's behaviors (user make mistakes because he doesn't know what to do next), at this time the system searches for the association rules and predict the next activity.

4   Experimental Evaluation

In the experimentations, we address the following questions: (1) How does our algorithm compare with other states of the art? (2) How does the disparity of habits affect the algorithm results? (3) How does our algorithm behave in a mobile environment?

4.1   Datasets

We evaluate our approach using two types of data: synthetic data and real data.

Synthetic Data. We asked to three users with different profiles to note their daily habits for three months, the choosing of users wasn't arbitrary, we chose them with

---

Algorithm 5: final algorithm

```
Input:
A POIⱼ;
Users past activities UPA
Output:
Next activity;
Sᵢ = Sequence construction (POIⱼ);
wⱼ = Weight distribution (Sᵢ) ;
HT = Habits 'tree update(Sᵢ);
Next location = Activity prediction (HT,UPA)
Return Next location ;
```

---

different habits disparity level: "user 1" with very recurrent habits, "user 2" with moderately recurrent habits and user 3 with very low recurrence level.

Real Data. To push even further the level of our experiment, we used a renowned dataset from the Microsoft research project GeoLife [4]. The GPS trajectory dataset was collected in (Microsoft Research Asia) Geolife project by 182 users in a period of over three years (from April 2007 to August 2012). A GPS trajectory of this dataset is represented by a sequence of time-stamped points, each of which contains the information of latitude, longitude and altitude. This dataset contains 17,621 trajectories with a total distance of about 1.2 million kilometers and a total duration of 48,000 + hours. These trajectories were recorded by different GPS loggers and GPS-phones, and have a variety of sampling rates. 91 percent of the trajectories are logged in a dense representation, e.g. every $1 \sim 5$ s or every $5 \sim 10$ meters per point. This dataset recorded a broad range of users' outdoor movements, including not only life routines like go home and go to work but also some entertainments and sports activities, such as shopping, sightseeing, dining, hiking, and cycling.

We treated the dataset to add some information to the database like user's speed and orientation to be used in our previous work [2] to detect users' activities from their GPS traces, every POI recognized was identified by its unique combination (longitude latitude), the result was organized in dataset (see Table 1) as user's daily routines.

Table 1. Example of the inferred POIs dataset from GeoLife

ID	Longitude	Latitude	Name	Type	Date
1	116.3216	39.99190	Building 13	House	2008-10-23-02-53-30
2	116.3214	40.01119	Swissotel Beijing	hotel	2008-10-23-04-15-52
...	...	...	...	...	...

4.2   Testing Process

Test processes in association rules represent a delicate step, since how to test is related to the field of study. We created a testing process specific to us to represent as much as possible the activity prediction situation. The concept is based on the introduction of a second virtual user that will follow the real user's movements but in every sequence of POI, the virtual user will forget his next destination, in this case our algorithm will predict a next localization that will be compared with the real next activity (see Fig. 5).

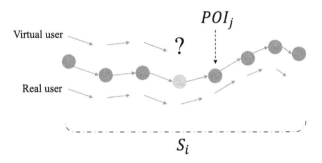

Fig. 5. Testing process with real and virtual user.

The position of the virtual user's moment of forgetting is random, in fact, on every S_i arrival, our algorithm generates a random position between 1 and S_i's length, this position represents the POI's position where the virtual user will forget his next destination.

The precision represents the number of sequences where activities were well predicted on the total number of sequences, by against, the global error GE, which is calculated using the number of sequences where the activities' predictions were mistaken on the total number of sequences.

The global error contains two types of error: learning error LE and habit error HE. LE represents an error in the prediction of the next activity when referring to the past activities. For example, the user has the habit of going sometimes from home to work and other times to drive his child to school, if we do a test starting from the POI "Home", our algorithm will predict for example work as next destination because it's the most recurrent activity after home. All the times when the user will go to drive his child to school and when we predict work as next activity, the algorithm will record a LE (this mismatching problem will be handled in our next work, please see future work section).

HE represents the disability to predict a next activity because the user's precedent POI are not frequent, this error can be seen as a similarity index, the greater is HE, the more data is scattered (there is less recurrence in the user's habits). We evaluated our approach by highlighting three dimensions: first we tested our algorithm with a standard dataset, secondly with a dataset that contained a concept drift, and finally we tested the performance of our work on the mobile environment.

4.3   Standard Incremental Activity Prediction Experiment

In this step we used four users' data, the three from the synthetic dataset and one user from Geolife dataset. Results presented in Table 2 represent the precision, GE, LE and HE of our algorithm on every user data.

Table 2. Standard incremental activity prediction results

	Simulated data			Geolife
	User 1	User 2	User 3	User 4
Precision	83 %	71 %	61 %	68 %
GE	17 %	29 %	39 %	32 %
LE	11 %	14 %	13 %	9 %
HE	6 %	15 %	26 %	23 %

From Table 2, our algorithm predicts the next activities of user 1 (with very recurrent habits) with a precision of 83 % and a global error GE of 17 % divided into 11 % of learning error LE and 6 % of habit error. User 2 and user 3 show less precision rate with respectively 71 % and 61 % of precision. User 4 data that contains 726 sequences and a total of 2831 POI shows a precision of 68 % and a global error of 32 %.

Discussion. First, it is clear that our approach shows an interesting result with an average precision of 70.75 %, moreover, analyzing the distribution of errors in every user's data, we notice a strong correlation between the global error GE and the habits error HE, indeed, the variation of learning error LE is so small that we preclude the possibility of linking between GE and LE.

We conclude that the error in our approach is sensitive to the users' habits similarity, which is somewhat logical because the definition word "Habit" is a routine of behavior that is repeated regularly, so, regularity in users' movements is important to succeed in predicting his next location.

Figure 6 tracks the evolution of HE in every user's data, results presented show globally two kinds of graphics: stepped graphic concerning user 1 and user 2 owning to the fact that those two users have some new behaviors, when arrived, the algorithm makes a mistake in that moment because the new sequence is unknown, but it catches up quickly in the next moments to recognize the sequence as frequent and predict the right activity. The second type of graphic concerning user 3 and user 4 is a moderately smoothed graphic which approaches a straight function, the user 3 and user 4 have dispersed habits which explain the continuous increase of HE over time.

4.4   Incremental Activity Prediction with Concept Drift Experiment

We compare in this section our approach with an incremental version of FP-growth called DB-Tree [3], the ideal dataset to experiment the two algorithms is a dataset where the user has made a relocation (change of address and probably of habits) using a dataset that contains a concept drift, for that, we paired two users' dataset from Geolife

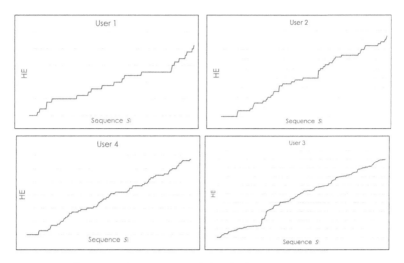

Fig. 6. Habit error HE evolution in the four users' data.

users' datasets into one dataset to say that the first user changes his address and his habits to the second user's address and habits.

Table 3 presents the results of our experiment; we divided it into three indicators, precision before and after the relocation, and the global precision.

Table 3. Comparison between our algorithm and DB-tree algorithm

	Our algorithm	DB-tree algorithm
Precision before the relocation	72 %	63 %
Precision after the relocation	69 %	51 %
Global precision	70.5 %	57 %

Discussion. Globally, our algorithm shows an interesting precision result with 70.5 % of precision contrary to DB-tree, which shows a low rate with only 57 % of precision.

First, the reason why our algorithm shows better results (72 % against 63 % for DB-tree) in normal dataset (before the relocation) is that FP-tree doesn't handle the order of POIs in sequences since it reorders the POIs to store them in descending order of support in the tree, therefore, for example, the habits of going from home to work and from work to home are the same for FP-tree, which is quite wrong.

To analyze the after location step, we tracked the error evolution of both algorithms (see Figs. 7 and 8) to justify the results shown in Table 2.

After the relocation, our algorithm shows a strength to these shifts (precision decreases only from 72 % to 69 %) and support time for habits change is small because the algorithm detects a change in the user's habits and starts to add a supplement weight (drift's weight wd_j) until that the new sequences become frequents.

Contrariwise, DB-tree encounters difficulties to revive its model after the relocation to detect the new behaviors (drop of the precision from 63 % to 51 %). Indeed, as

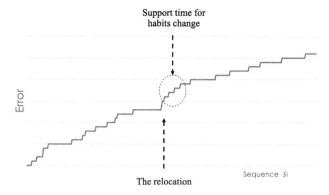

Fig. 7. Error evolution in our algorithm.

DB-tree traits all the sequences with the same manner (adds 1 to the concerned nods in the tree), it will take much time to the new habits to become frequents (the minimum support will be increased by the old habits), what explains the important support time for habits change in Fig. 8.

After the experimentation of our approach in term of precision and support of concept drift, we are going to test in the next section the computational impact of algorithm on the mobile resources.

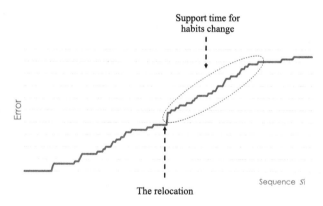

Fig. 8. Error evolution in DB-tree algorithm.

4.5   Experimentation of Mobile Resources Use

This work can be used in any environment (mobile, desktop or web applications) and using any architecture (local or distributed design), in spite of that, we are going to test our solution in a mobile environment, principally for these reasons: (1) Users movements are usually collected incrementally using a mobile device, it is more consistent to continue predicting incrementally the users' movements on the same device. (2) Mobile environment requires careful handling of the reduced storage and computing capacities, if we prove that our solution is optimal for the mobile environment, it is clear that it will be useful for the other environments that have less requirements.

We tested our algorithm using an Android smartphone from Sony (Sony Xperia S) with 1 GB of Ram and 1.5 GHz dual core processor.

The first test concerns the RAM usage, we added our solution to our precedent work [2] where we recognized incrementally users' activities, then we compared the set with a well-known GIS solutions "Waze Social GPS Maps & Traffic", one of the best free navigation applications that won the best overall mobile app award at the 2013 Mobile World Congress, the reason of such selection is that Waze has a lot in common with our approach. In fact it gathers complementary map data and traffic information from its users like police traps (can be seen as a POI in our case), and learns from users' driving times to provide routing and real-time traffic updates.

Results in Table 4 that represent the average consumption of mobile's memory of every application during 12 h show that our solution is not greedy regarding memory usage with 40 Mo of RAM usage (note that the activity recognition system alone uses 34 Mo [2]) comparing to Waze with 67 Mo.

Table 4. Comparing our solution to Waze application in term of memory usage

	Our solution	Waze
Memory usage	40 Mo	67 Mo

The second test concerns the storage capacity usage; we had to compare our solution with an algorithm that uses a traditional database structure to observe the impact of using a tree structure. We compared our approach with the Apriori algorithm, a widely used algorithm for association rule learning using a standard database design. We tracked the variation of the database size in every solution in function of the number of sequences arrived (from 1 to 1 million sequences), in order to get a such important number of sequences, we created an algorithm that generated random sequences containing between 2 to 20 POI, using 500 different POIs. Results exposed in Fig. 9 show how much the use of tree structure is benefic to the size of the database, thanks to sharing paths between items in tree structure, which leads to much smaller size than in a traditional database.

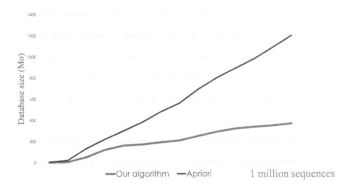

Fig. 9. Database size comparison between our solution and Apriori algorithm.

On the other hand, the maximum size of our tree (467 Mo) that is reached using one million sequences (if we take an average of 2 sequences per day, it represents more than 1388 years) represents a size widely acceptable by the requirements of mobile environment storage.

5 Conclusions and Future Work

In this paper, we proposed a new algorithm based on the online learning of users' habits to predict users' next locations taking into account the changes that can occur in their routines, our original contribution includes a new algorithm of online mining association rules that support the concept drift.

Our approach has been experimented in a real case study using Geolife project to test the accuracy of our predicting technique by comparing it to Apriori algorithm and DB-tree algorithm via several indicators like supporting users' habits changes and mobile resources usage. Results show that our proposal is well positioned compared to its similar, and represents an interesting solution to predict users' next activities without depleting the resources of users' mobile devices.

Several promising directions for future works exist. First, if this work is used in a big data context, some efforts shall be done to optimize the construction and the research process in the tree structure to minimize the response time of our algorithm. Secondly, the clustering of users' profiles represents an interesting research field, in that direction, the habits' tree represents a good structure that summarizes users' routines, clustering users' profiles basing on their habits will be reduced to the comparison of two trees (habits' trees). Thirdly, this work has to be improved by introducing a temporal dimension to the habits' tree in order to improve our algorithm precision (for example, routines made in weekends are different of those made in working days).

References

1. Asahara, A., Maruyama, K., Sato, A., Seto, K.: Pedestrian-movement prediction based on mixed markov-chain model. In: Proceedings of the 19th ACM SIGSPATIAL International Conference on Advances in Geographic Information Systems, pp. 25–33. ACM (2011)
2. Boukhechba, M., Bouzouane, A., Bouchard, B., Gouin-Vallerand, C., Giroux, S.: Online recognition of people's activities from raw GPS data: semantic trajectory data analysis. In: Proceedings of the 8th ACM International Conference on Pervasive Technologies Related to Assistive Environments, July 2015
3. Ezeife, C.I., Su, Y.: Mining incremental association rules with generalized FP-tree. In: Proceedings of the 15th Canadian Conference on Artificial Intelligence, May 2002
4. Zheng, Y., Xie, X., Ma, W.: GeoLife: a collaborative social networking service among user, location and trajectory. IEEE Data Eng. Bull. **33**(2), 32–40 (2010)
5. Zheng, Y., Zhang, L., Xie, X., Ma, W.: Mining interesting locations and travel sequences from GPS trajectories. In: Proceedings of International Conference on World Wild Web, pp. 791–800. ACM Press, Madrid (2009)

6. Zheng, Y., Li, Q., Chen, Y., Xie, X., Ma, W.: Understanding mobility based on GPS data. In: Proceedings of ACM Conference on Ubiquitous Computing (UbiComp 2008), pp. 312–321. ACM Press, Seoul (2008)

7. Gambs, S., Killijian, M., Cortez, D.P., Miguel, N.: Next place prediction using mobility Markov chains. In: Proceedings of the 1st Workshop on Measurement, Privacy, and Mobility, pp. 1–6. ACM (2012)

8. Morzy, M.: Prediction of moving object location based on frequent trajectories. In: Levi, A., Savaş, E., Yenigün, H., Balcısoy, S., Saygın, Y. (eds.) ISCIS 2006. LNCS, vol. 4263, pp. 583–592. Springer, Heidelberg (2006)

9. Morzy, M.: Mining frequent trajectories of moving objects for location prediction. In: Perner, P. (ed.) MLDM 2007. LNCS (LNAI), vol. 4571, pp. 667–680. Springer, Heidelberg (2007)

10. Katsaros, D., Nanopoulos, A., Karakaya, M., Yavas, G., Ulusoy, Ö., Manolopoulos, Y.: Clustering mobile trajectories for resource allocation in mobile environments. In: Berthold, M., Lenz, H.-J., Bradley, E., Kruse, R., Borgelt, C. (eds.) IDA 2003. LNCS, vol. 2810, pp. 319–329. Springer, Heidelberg (2003)

11. Liu, T., Bahl, P., Chlamtac, I.: Mobility modeling, location tracking, and trajectory prediction in wireless ATM networks. IEEE J. Sel. Area Commun. **16**(6), 922–936 (1998)

12. Page, E.S.: Continuous inspection schemes. Biometrika **41**, 100–115 (1954)

13. Mouss, H., Mouss, D., Mouss, N., Sefouhi, L.: Test of page-hinkley, an approach for fault detection in an agro-alimentary production system. In: Proceedings of the 5th Asian Control Conference 2, pp. 815–818 (2004)

14. Zhang, X., Germain-Renaud, C., Sebag, M.: Adaptively detecting changes in autonomic grid computing. In: Proceedings of the 11th ACM/IEEE International Conference on Grid Computing (Grid 2010) (Autonomic Computational Science Workshop), pp. 387–392 (2010)

15. Agrawal, R., Srikant, R.: Fast algorithms for mining association rules in large databases. In: Proceedings of the 20th International Conference on Very Large Data Bases, VLDB, pp. 487–499, Santiago, Chile, September 1994

16. Cheng, C., Yang, H., Lyu, M. R., King, I.: Where you like to go next: successive point-of-interest recommendation. In: Proceedings of the 23rd International Joint Conference on Artificial Intelligence, Beijing, China, pp. 2605–2611, 3 August 2013

17. Spaccapietra, S., Parent, C., Damiani, M.L., Macêdo, J., Porto, F., Vangenot, C.: A conceptual view on trajectories. Data Knowl. Eng. **65**(1), 126–146 (2008)

18. Zheng, Y., et al.: GeoLife: managing and understanding your past life over maps. In: Proceedings of the MDM 2009, pp. 211–212. IEEE Press, Beijing China, April 2008

19. Gama, J., Sebastião, R., Rodrigues, P.P.: Issues in evaluation of stream learning algorithms. In: Proceedings of the 15th ACM SIGKDD International Conference on Knowledge Discovery and Data Mining (KDD 2009), pp. 329–337. ACM Press, Paris (2009)

20. Gama, J., Medas, P., Castillo, G., Rodrigues, P.: Learning with drift detection. In: Bazzan, A.L., Labidi, S. (eds.) SBIA 2004. LNCS (LNAI), vol. 3171, pp. 286–295. Springer, Heidelberg (2004)

21. Kuncheva, L.I.: Classifier ensembles for detecting concept change in streaming data: overview and perspectives. In: Proceedings of the 2nd Workshop SUEMA 2008 (ECAI 2008), Patras, Greece (2008)

22. Hipp, J., Güntzer, U., Nakhaeizadeh, G.: Algorithms for association rule mining: a general survey and comparison. ACM SIGKDD Explor. Newsl. **2**(58), 58–64 (2000)

In the context of defining a friendship metric, decision makers are users of a given social networking. It is very subjective in a social network to define why individuals use some features or have some behavior, so we decided to have the users' perspectives as criteria and the social network variables as alternatives. A decision matrix of variables is created for each interviewed user and later normalized. Since we consider the judgment of each interviewed user equally important, the matrix of relative ranking of the criteria is filled with ones.

The comparison of alternatives in pairs is made based on a scale. So we elaborate a questionnaire to ask how important a variable is compared to others. As we have 5 variables, the questionnaire was composed by 10 questions in the form of "How important is v_i compared to v_j". We use the directive of Saaty scale to define answers' options. The answer could assume the following values: extreme importance (9), very strong importance (7), strong importance (5), moderate importance (3), equal importance (1), moderately less importance (1/3), strongly less important (1/5), very strongly less important (1/7), and extremely less important (1/9).

Each questionnaire is used to build a decision matrix of variables. The main diagonal is filled with one, meaning that one variable has the same importance when compared to itself. The questionnaire answers are the entries above the main diagonal, while their reciprocals are the entries below the main diagonal. As an example, a decision matrix of some existing questionnaire is shown in Table 1. The same procedure of building matrix is repeated to each questionnaire. Later we need to analyze the consistence of all matrixes, normalized them, and calculated the related priority vector. We then use these vectors to calculate the weights.

Table 1. Example of decision matrix of variables.

	v_1	v_2	v_3	v_4	v_5
v_1	1	1	1/7	1	1
v_2	1	1	1	1	1
v_3	7	1	1	1/3	3
v_4	1	1	3	1	1
v_5	1	1	1/3	1	1

3 The Friendship Strength Metric in Facebook

The usage of friendship maintenance strategies can vary according to individuals, for instance, in terms of age as young adults, middle age adults, and older adults [13]. Our work focuses on a specific public: the young adulthood. So, when there was a need to involve real users, we always selected different young adults, students of a college, with age varying from 18 to 26.

In the first brainstorming, we found 27 variables in Facebook, as follows: number of mutual friends (v_1), number of messages exchanged (v_2), number of pages in common that the friends liked (v_3), number of photos that the friends were tagged together (v_4), number of likes made in comments of a friend (v_5), if a friend is following the other, time online in common, number of apps in common, number of check-ins in common, age difference, number of events in common, number of groups in common, interests in common, family relationship, number of links liked in common, number of blocked pages in common, number of videos in common, work history in common, religion difference, politics difference, chat duration, chat frequency, event frequency, number of posts together, number of comments in common friend's posts, number of comments in common friend's photos, and number of comments in common friend's videos.

We submitted the list of variables, in a random order, to the appreciation of ten active Facebook users. One important decision was to determine a period of time as one month to consider time dependent variables. We then selected the following variables: number of mutual friends (v_1); number of messages exchanged in the last month (v_2); number of pages in common that the friends liked in the last month (v_3); number of photos that the friends were tagged together in the last month (v_4); and number of likes made in comments of a friend in the last month (v_5).

We invited ten Facebook users and, using an application, we collected v_i data of all their connections with friends. The quantity of connections assessed was 3855. From these relationships, we were able to collect 7244 nonzero data points that were used to plot the histograms. The histograms are shown in Figs. 1, 3, 5, 7, and 9. We also provide the CDF plots and *CDF* trendlines (*CDFT*) of all variables (Figs. 2, 4, 6, 8, and 10). The *CDF* trendlines (*CDFT*) are shown in Table 2. We checked if the polynomial approximation of each trendline was satisfactory by calculating the R-squared value. We found the following R-squared values from v_1 to v_5: 0.9909, 0.9505, 0.9947, 0.9961, and 0.9622. Our objective was to achieve R-squared value of at least 0.95 to each trendline, since a trendline is most reliable when its R-squared value is at or near 1.

Table 2. CDF trendlines of Facebook variables.

CDF trendline
$CDFT\left(v_1\right) = 4\mathrm{E} - 08v_1^3 - 3\mathrm{E} - 05v_1^2 + 0.0078v_1 + 0.1229$
$CDFT\left(v_2\right) = -0.0011v_2^4 + 0.0242v_2^3 - 0.1584v_2^2 + 0.3975v_2 - 0.213$
$CDFT\left(v_3\right) = 2\mathrm{E} - 07v_3^5 - 2\mathrm{E} - 05v_3^4 + 0.0008v_3^3 - 0.0182v_3^2 + 0.1915v_3 + 0.1632$
$CDFT\left(v_4\right) = -4\mathrm{E} - 05v_4^4 + 0.0019v_4^3 - 0.0312v_4^2 + 0.226v_4 + 0.3581$
$CDFT\left(v_5\right) = 0.0001v_5^3 - 0.0057v_5^2 + 0.0916v_5 + 0.4847$

Learning Behavior Patterns

Abnormal Behavioral Patterns Detection from Activity Records of Institutionalized Older Adults

Valeria Soto-Mendoza[1](✉), Jessica Beltrán[1], Edgar Chávez[1], Jehú Hernández[2], and J. Antonio García-Macías[1]

[1] CICESE Research Center, Ensenada, Baja California, Mexico
{vsoto,jbeltran}@cicese.edu.mx, {elchavez,jagm}@cicese.mx
[2] Softtek, Ensenada, Baja California, Mexico
jehu.hdez@gmail.com

Abstract. The automatic detection of behavioral changes in older adults living in geriatric centers is relevant for physicians and caregivers. These changes could indicate an incipient symptom of a disease or a steep decline in the health of the person. Abnormal pattern discovery has been studied in the context of an array of (wearable) sensors (i.e. accelerometers, infrared, cameras, etc.) dedicated to monitor the older adult. In this work we explore the use of manually annotated records, the type of records maintained by caregivers in a daily log. These annotations have low semantic value, and consist in a sequence of keywords about the activity being carried out by the older adult. This information is often overseen because it could be noisy, incomplete and redundant. We tested a data-driven approach to identify patterns from daily activity records, which were collected over six months from a group of older adults in a geriatric center. The results show that through simple data processing techniques it is possible to identify abnormal patterns in daily activities associated with behavioral changes over time.

Keywords: Low quality annotations · Behaviour-aware · Abnormal patterns · Older adults

1 Introduction

It has been demonstrated that daily activities of older adults are indicators of their well-being [1]. In geriatric centers, all the staff (specially the caregivers) keep an activity log [2] of every resident. Usually, caregivers are not aware of the full history of every individual resident, due to the change of personnel during shifts and other factors. In the activity log only local changes are recorded (in other words, only things happening within a shift are recorded) and the caregiver of the next shift will not review previous annotations.

This type or records may have an arbitrary level of detail; they have predefined fields with keywords as well as a free text section for comments.

© Springer International Publishing Switzerland 2015
A.A. Salah et al. (Eds.): HBU 2015, LNCS 9277, pp. 119–131, 2015.
DOI: 10.1007/978-3-319-24195-1_9

The predefined keys are not very informative. It is clear that records from a dedicated array of sensors will have more predictive power but also they can be noisy, incomplete and of of low semantic quality. However, manually annotated records have more coverage. Manually annotated activity logs are used by caring institutions in case of a lawsuit or to satisfy a request from the family of the elder. A larger number of institutions will have at least this [3].

We explore a couple of data-driven techniques which will classify the days as normal, or abnormal (three levels of abnormality). This will help caregivers to be aware of the needs of the residents (for example if one resident had a severe abnormal day; she could exert a greater degree of detail in attending the resident the current day). We acknowledge that the needs of older adults change over time and depend on the conditions they suffer. The data used is anonymized (although grouped by person) and does not compromise the privacy of the resident due to the low semantic value of the data recorded.

2   Related Work

Nowadays context-aware computing is evolving towards behavior-aware computing [4]. Even in the field there is not a precise and unique definition for behavior, the research is oriented towards estimating and anticipating people's behavior using an adhoc definition. Older adults are not the exception. In the literature, several authors have investigated how to identify patterns among elders' activities [5]. In [6] behaviors, actions and manners of patients with cognitive impairment can be amended when persuasive and pervasive technologies are designed based on identified patterns. Promising results were obtained with the combination of sensor and medical data using several techniques to determine the level of well-being in older adults while performing their daily activities [7]. In all the works above, the focus is on the use of sensors and leave out human observations, for instance, those made by caregivers or physicians. In this work, we propose to incorporate these observations to explain the context around detected abnormalities.

The elder's daily activities are a good tool to monitor the elder's decline [8]. In [9], a Markov Chains Model (MCM) was used to classify abnormal sequences of activity data. Video [10] and audio [11] data sources, as well as sensors [12], have been studied to detect abnormal behaviors using different machine learning techniques. The objective of these approaches is the integration into any assistive technology for elders [13]. Our contribution is a data driven technique able to include warnings inferred from manual annotated logs as part of the care system of a geriatric residence.

3   Searching for Behavioral Patterns

In geriatric centers, the caregivers, physicians, nurses, and managers keep manual logs with general information related to older adults. Records of their daily activities are included in these logs. Another usual approach is the installation of

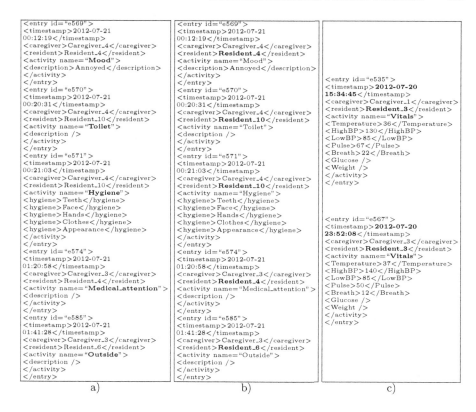

Fig. 1. Electronic records of activities for older adults.

environmental sensors coupled to information systems to track resident's activities and keep digital records of the data. With these settings, members of the staff feed the system every day with new information of the wellbeing of older adults.

The logs manually annotated by caregivers offer a rich source of information, unparalleled with an array of sensors. One person can quickly judge the wellbeing of another person. One problem with these annotations is that they are made in natural language, are prone to errors and could be incomplete and contradictory at times (think for example in the judgment of two persons about the same fact). Natural language processing techniques are not at the point of producing high level reports from noisy, incomplete logs. Hence one alternative is to simplify the logs to the point of considering just keywords, one for each activity being carried out. Each individual annotation will have a low semantic value, because it consist of a simple keyword; however, we want to prove that the accumulated data over a long period of time can be used to classify a given day as normal or abnormal. We are not aiming at eliciting the causes of the abnormality, the objective is more modest; we aim at raising a flag that would be verifiable by the caring personnel. The staff can quickly check if there is something wrong with the older adult [14].

We analyzed the skimmed manually anotated data of one geriatric center (see Fig. 1) searching for patterns in the activities. The electronic record analysis poses several challenges for automatic learning methods, they are described below.

Activity Granularity and Heterogeneity. During the day, every older adult performs different activities (see Fig. 1b) which are recorded in the system (i.e. Mood, Hygiene, etc.) Also, each activity can be integrated with various additional descriptions (for instance, Hygiene with Teeth, Hands, Clothes, etc.) (see Fig. 1a). All this variability among the data makes it hard to find a unique representation [15].

Temporal Gaps. Timestamps seem like a natural way to establish a chronological order in the activities (see Fig. 1b). However, in practice, this is far from true. In some days the activities are scheduled at different hours of the day, or the same activity is performed and registered more than once (see Fig. 1c), therefore there could be a gap in the activities sequence of the residents [16].

Missing Data. Manually annotated logs are prone to missing data, because caregivers are frequently overwhelmed with work, and the information will not be complete [17]. For sensors, this could be also the case due to power, battery or communication failures. We cannot assume the records are complete [18].

Determine a Metric or Comparison Measure. The obtained data is essentially incomplete, inconsistent and noisy. There is a challenge in designing a method to establish a measure to identify similarities and deviations in the records [19].

In general these challenges are given by: (1) the collection mechanisms of the data, and (2) the semantic of the activities. There are also dependencies between activities (i.e. *Medication* after *Lunch*). The objective is to exploit these dependencies found to be included in information systems to enrich the care process but how can these dependencies and relationships be automatically detected? With these activities' dependencies is it possible to determine which relationships are normal or abnormal during a certain period of time?, how can we detect them?; and in case of being abnormal, why those deviations occurred? To answer the above questions we start by establishing a representation of data to analyze all of them.

3.1   Representing Activities Sequences

Given D(i,j) the sequence of sorted activities of the day j performed by the resident i, where the activities' log corresponds to the set of m days

$$
\begin{aligned}
D(1,1) &= A_{1,1}, A_{1,2}, A_{1,3}, \ldots, A_{1,n_1} \\
D(1,2) &= A_{2,1}, A_{2,2}, A_{2,3}, \ldots, A_{2,n_2} \\
&\ \ \vdots \\
D(1,m) &= A_{m,1}, A_{m,2}, A_{m,3}, \ldots, A_{m,n_m}
\end{aligned}
$$

$n_1, n_2, \ldots, n_m$ are the number of activities of the day (the size can be different), and $A = (T_s, r)$, where:

T_s = start time of activity A, and $r \in R$ = {set of activities in the log}.

With this representation we incorporate the temporal factor sorting the daily sequence according to the occurrence of each activity. Moreover, the observation that every day might contain a different number of recorded activities was considered too.

3.2 Data-Driven Approach

Data-driven approaches [20] encourage the use of machine learning techniques and algorithms to analyze a dataset [21,22]. These approaches need a significant amount of data [23]. We used a dataset of activities collected during six months inside a geriatric center under natural conditions. In Table 1 we show the characteristics of our dataset.

Table 1. Characteristics of the dataset.

Number of activity records	19182
Number of residents	15
Average of days per resident	91
Average maximum number of activities per day	25
Average minimum number of activities per day	1.26
Average number of activities per day	8.63

The set of activities (see Table 2) in the logs is an adaptation of the activities of daily living (ADL) and the instrumented activities of daily living (IADL) [24] modified for the care process followed in the geriatric center.

We will use the above representation for the data to analyze the activity records based on data-driven techniques. We apply clustering and mining sequential patterns for the analysis. We discuss the use of these two techniques in the next subsections.

Clustering. This is an unsupervised machine learning technique aming at creating groups of data, which are similar inside the group, and dissimilar if they belong to different groups [25]. In particular, it is possible to find a representative sample of each group using k-means [26].

We used clustering to find when each activity is performed by an older adult during the day, since we encountered the time variable is relevant for this study. In particular, the k-means algorithm is not equivalent to the statistical mean, even if the data are one dimensional. It is known that in one dimensional data, an optimal algorithm for clustering exists [27,28].

To exemplify this, we have the timestamps of 125 days from the activities of *feeding* from subject 1, which we know is distributed as *feeding breakfast, feeding*

Table 2. Set of activities.

Activity	Sub-activity	Tag	Activity	Sub-activity	Tag
Anomaly	-	Anomaly	Medical attention	-	Medical_attention
Check over	-	Check_over	Medication	-	Medication
Check over	Asleep	Asleep	Hygiene	-	Hygiene
Check over	Awake	Awake	Hygiene	Shower	Shower
Check over	Get up	Get_up	Hygiene	Teeth	Teeth
Check over	Lay down	Lay_down	Mood	{Sad, Cheerful, Ill, Quiet}	Mood
Toilet	-	Toilet	Recreation	{Read, TV}	Recreation
Toilet	Evacuation	Evac	Social interactions	Talking	Talking
Toilet	Micturition	Mict	Feeding	{Breakfast, Lunch, Dinner}	Feeding
Inside	-	Inside	Visits	-	Visits
Outside	-	Outside	Vitals	-	Vitals

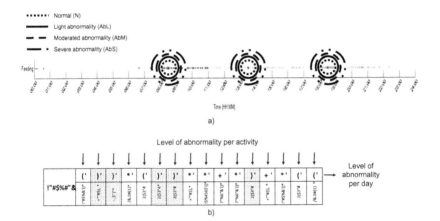

Fig. 2. Clustering settings: in (a) the centroids established for Feeding activity, and (b) the classification of the day using hours and activities.

lunch, feeding dinner. Figure 2a shows red points (at left) when *feeding breakfast* occured during the 125 days, yellow points (at center) when *lunch* and green points (at right) when *dinner.* We use the k-means algorithm, using Euclidean distance on the timestamps, to find the centroids for each activity (see Fig. 2a). For *feeding* can be typical the creation of three groups, but for other types of activities like *using the toilet* or *medical attention* the identification of centroids is helpful for discovering the behavior of each subject.

Once we have identified the centroids for each activity, we set these centroids as the normal or typical behavior (see the circles in Fig. 2a.) Then we establish a scale of abnormality (see Table 3) based on the distance of an upcoming datum of a given activity compared against the centroid of that activity.

Each day is classified as normal or abnormal depending on the deviations from the activities performed. As depicted in Fig. 2b, we classify each activity

Table 3. Levels of abnormality based on time.

Level		Distance from the centroid
Normal (N)		within 15 min
Abnormal	Light (L)	within 30 min
	Medium (M)	whitin 60 min
	Severe (S)	more than 60 min

within its corresponding level of abnormality. At the end, the day is classified as normal or abnormal, depending on the number of abnormal activities detected.

As mentioned, the clustering only considers the time of occurrence of the activities. However, this approach has some limitations. For instance, if a gap occurred because the resident overslept as a consequence of late TV watching the previous night, the clustering will tag the majority of the activities as abnormal, therefore the day will be classified as abnormal too. We tackled this limitation by analyzing the daily sequence of activities; we present this analysis in the next section. Another limitation is related with the prioritization of the activities according to their importance (for instance, deviations in medications are more relevant than recreational activities). As a consequence, the level of importance of an activity should influence the determination of the abnormality of one specific day.

Mining Sequential Patterns. Mining sequential patterns is a technique used to analyze databases of customer transactions [29] to discover purchasing patterns in the commercial context. This technique has also been used in [30] to discover the most frequent sequences of activities in older adults for activity recognition purposes.

We used the ideas of this technique to analyze the sequences of daily activities to discover the most frequent sequences in the activity records of older adults. The difference here, is that in our approach the order of the activities is crucial to identify changes of the behavior of older adults over time.

With the mining sequential patterns technique, it is possible to find patterns with different sizes. Therefore we need to define a proper sequence size. We explored with different sizes to ensure the larger coverage and at the same time a good diversity. Figure 3 shows the number of different sequences found when using a given sequence size. The maximum number of different sequences (800) is achieved with a length of 7. The computational complexity of processing increases with larger sequences. We consider that sequences of size 3 or 4 offer a good trade-off between the sequence's length and the number of patterns found.

We identified the most frequent sequences of activities of size 4 within a time window (every 15 days). Later, we analyzed those sequences within the window to discover changes in behavior from the comparison of the sequences of activities performed during that time frame.

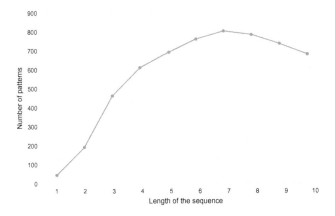

Fig. 3. Number of patterns vs. sequence size.

4   Results

We present the results obtained after applying each technique mentioned in the previous section. We only considered residents with more than 60 days of collected data and show days with at least 4 activities each.

In Fig. 4 we present the results from Resident 1 with 125 days of collected data using the clustering technique. Figure 4 illustrate some events in the logs. For instance, October 10th, 2012, was classified as *severe abnormal*. After reviewing the complete log, the expert found inconsistencies based on time of ocurrence of the activities of *Lay down*. At 12:58 the resident was in bed instead of having

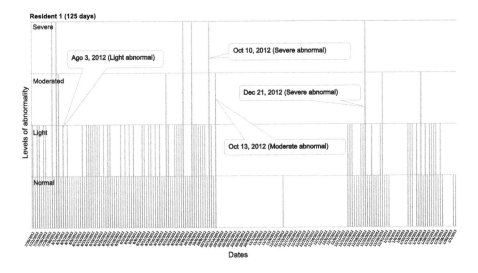

Fig. 4. Clustering results.

Table 4. Activity records of October 10, 2012 from Resident 1.

Id	Hour	Activity	Description	Comments	Caregiver
14829	00:26	Medication	Tamsulosin		C_01
14834	08:20	Hygiene	Teeth		C_02
14835	08:21	Feed	Breakfast		C_02
14836	08:22	Toilet	Evac Mict		C_02
14837	08:23	Medication	Lasilacton		C_02
14838	08:24	Medication	Ferranina		C_02
14839	08:27	Medical_attention	Consultation	Nurse took him out	C_02
14904	12:56	Inside	Back	He returned from consultation	C_02
14905	12:57	Toilet	Mict		C_02
14906	12:58	Check_over	Lay_down		C_02
14907	12:59	Hygiene	Hands		C_02
14908	13:05	Medical_attention	Special_treatment	He must rest due to his eyes surgery	C_02
14915	14:18	Feed	Lunch		C_02
14922	14:20	Check_over	Lay_down		C_02
14925	15:49	Medication	Aspirine, Protect		C_02
14926	15:50	Medication	Prednefrin		C_02
14928	16:37	Medication	Gatifloxacino		C_02
14930	17:48	Medication	Gatifloxacino		C_02
14931	17:49	Medication	Prednefrin		C_02
14940	18:27	Feed	Dinner		C_02
14941	18:28	Toilet	Mict		C_02
14944	18:32	Toilet	Mict		C_02
14957	20:46	Medication	Gatifloxacino		C_01
14960	20:47	Medication	Dutasterida		C_01
14961	20:48	Medication	Prednefrin		C_01
14995	23:15	Toilet	Mict		C_01

lunch, similarly for the same activity at 14:20. Moreover, the resident had two *Medical attention* records, which is strange because the physician consultations are once every two weeks, and having two records is atypical. Also, new records of *Medication* activities appeared. After reviewing the additional comments from the caregivers, we discovered that the resident had an eyes surgery. This explains the medical visits and the frequent intake of medications (prednefrin and gatifloxacino) for ophthalmic treatment (see Table 4). Before October 10, the resident was not receiving those drugs.

Please notice that our method does not make use of the natural language description, or the name of the medicine. Our method only triggers a flag, and

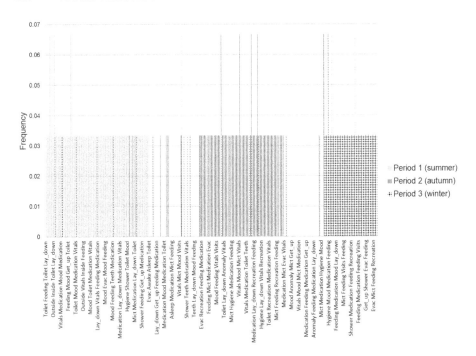

Fig. 5. Sequential patterns mining results.

the caring personnel can check the cause by manually inspecting the logs of one patient, the day before.

For testing the classification, we have used sampling. We selected 48 days, and an expert from the staff in the geriatric center manually verified the predictions and decided if the prediction was correct or incorrect. This sampling technique was used, because manually verifying events is a time consuming task. Each day of data may have up to 30 keywords and manual annotations for each patient. Each day can be reviewed by an expert in about 40 min. The entire set of 48 samples was cross-checked in four days.

From the 48 samples, the expert tagged 21 days as *Abnormal*. From the 21 *Normal* days, the clustering classified 14 as normal, six as lightly abnormal and one as medium abnormal. For the *Abnormal* days, seven were classified as normal, 13 as lightly abnormal, one as medium abnormal and six as severe abnormal. Depending on where we put the threshold for a trigger, the hit ratio can lean towards abnormality or normality. For example, if the threshold is relaxed, we can count lightly abnormal as normal, obtaining less warnings; or we can set it more strict and obtain more warnings.

With the sequential pattern mining analysis we also identify changes between different periods of time. Figure 5 shows the patterns of size 4 from Resident 6 in three different periods of time. These three different periods represent three different seasons: summer (period 1), autumn (period 2) and winter (period 3).

The differences between the periods are due to the decrease in breaks (leave times) from the residence and the number of social interactions, the number of visitors increased in the last period because of the holidays. Besides, we observe that many patterns emerged, some of them are present in all the periods; while some new patterns are only present for a specific period.

The results show that it is possible to identify behavioral changes using two data-driven techniques. Please notice that this approach does not give a diagnostic tool, it will be just a way to increase the awareness of the caring staff about the well being of the residents. This could serve as a first instance which can be complemented with environmental sensors for physical variables (for example, the temperature), or other wearable sensors used by the residents.

5   Conclusions and Future Work

Behavior analysis for the elderly have been approached with relative success using sensors. However, not all the facilities and institutions have access to the technology. On the other hand, manually annotated logs are widely used in geriatric institutions for legal reasons and to answer queries from relatives. This type of records have larger coverage than sensor data and have received little attention, because manually anotated data is in natural language. In this paper we did follow a different approach, we explored the use of keyword-based, manually annotated activity records of older adults to identify abnormal behaviors using data driven techniques. Six months of real data collected from a geriatric institution were used for the experimentation.

We proposed a representation of the activity records and two types of analysis; one exploiting clustering by time and the other as regarding as sequences of keywords. The clustering analysis have shown that the temporal relationship between the activities are useful to determine deviations which only depend on time. For other type of dependencies pattern analysis can be used by detecting common activity sequences. This type of analysis and techniques could serve as entry points in more sophisticated monitoring systems for older adults. Blending data from sensors and caregivers annotations could lead to better carying and monitoring systems.

Future works include adding more context information by combining the data-driven techniques with knowledge-driven approaches (e.g. using ontologies). We will also explore the incorporation of the proposed techniques into applications used for the staff in the geriatric center.

References

1. Merilahti, J., Pärkkä, J., Korhonen, I.: Estimating older people's physical functioning with automated health monitoring technologies at home: feature correlations and multivariate analysis. In: Rautiainen, M., et al. (eds.) GPC 2011. LNCS, vol. 7096, pp. 94–104. Springer, Heidelberg (2012)

2. Archer, N., Fevrier-Thomas, U., Lokker, C., McKibbon, K.A., Straus, S.E.: Personal health records: a scoping review. J. Am. Med. Inform. Assoc. **18**(4), 515–22 (2011)
3. Kane, R.A., Wilson, K.B.: Improving practice through research in and about assisted living: implications for a research agenda. Gerontologist **47**(suppl 1), 4–7 (2007)
4. Favela, J.: Behavior-aware computing: applications and challenges. IEEE Pervasive Comput. **3**, 14–17 (2013)
5. Barger, T.S., Brown, D.E., Alwan, M.: Health-status monitoring through analysis of behavioral patterns. IEEE Trans. Syst. Man Cybern-Part A Syst. Hum. **35**(1), 22–27 (2005)
6. Fernandez-Llatas, C., Garcia-Gomez, J.M., Vicente, J., Naranjo, J.C., Robles, M., Benedi, J. M., Traver, V.: Behaviour patterns detection for persuasive design in nursing homes to help dementia patients. In: 33rd Annual International Conference of the IEEE EMBS, pp. 6413–6417 (2011)
7. Suryadevara, N.K., Quazi, M.T., Mukhopadhyay, S.C.: Intelligent sensing systems for measuring wellness indices of the daily activities for the elderly. In: 2012 Eighth International Conference on Intelligent Environments, pp. 347–350 (2012)
8. Chernbumroong, S., Cang, S., Atkins, A., Yu, H.: Elderly activities recognition and classification for applications in assisted living. Expert Syst. Appl. **40**(5), 1662–1674 (2013)
9. Zhao, T., Ni, H., Zhou, X., Qiang, L., Zhang, D., Yu, Z.: Detecting abnormal patterns of daily activities for the elderly living alone. In: Zhang, Y., Yao, G., He, J., Wang, L., Smalheiser, N.R., Yin, X. (eds.) HIS 2014. LNCS, vol. 8423, pp. 95–108. Springer, Heidelberg (2014)
10. Loy, C., Xiang, T., Gong, S.: Detecting and discriminating behavioural anomalies. Pattern Recogn. **44**(1), 117–132 (2011)
11. Beltrán, J., Navarro, R., Chávez, E., Favela, J., Soto-Mendoza, V., Ibarra, C.: Detecting disruptive vocalizations for ambient assisted interventions for dementia. In: Pecchia, L., Chen, L.L., Nugent, C., Bravo, J. (eds.) IWAAL 2014. LNCS, vol. 8868, pp. 356–363. Springer, Heidelberg (2014)
12. Suryadevara, N.K., Gaddam, A., Rayudu, R.K., Mukhopadhyay, S.C.: Wireless sensors network based safe home to care elderly people: behaviour detection. Sens. Actuators A Phys. **186**, 277–283 (2012)
13. Rashidi, P., Mihailidis, A.: A survey on ambient-assisted living tools for older adults. IEEE J. Biomed. Health Inf. **17**(3), 579–590 (2013)
14. Soto-Mendoza, V., García-Macías, J.A., Chávez, E., Martínez-García, A.I., Favela, J., Serrano-Alvarado, P., Zúñiga Rojas, M.R.: Design of a predictive scheduling system to improve assisted living services for elders. TIST ACM Transactions on Intelligent Systems and Technology (TIST) Special Issue on Intelligent Healthcare Informatics **6**(4) (2015, to appear). http://dx.doi.org/10.1145/2736700
15. Helaoui, R., Riboni, D., Stuckenschmidt, H.: A probabilistic ontological framework for the recognition of multilevel human activities. In: UbiComp 2013, Zurich, Switzerland, pp. 345–354 (2013)
16. Hoque, E., Stankovic, J.: AALO: activity recognition in smart homes using active learning in the presence of overlapped activities. In: Pervasive Health, pp. 139–146 (2012)
17. Khan, A., Doucette, J.A., Cohen, R., Lizotte, D.J.: Integrating machine learning into a medical decision support system to address the problem of missing patient data. In: 11th International Conference on Machine Learning and Applications, pp. 454–457 (2012)

18. Ohmura, R., Uchida, R.: Exploring combinations of missing data complement for fault tolerant activity recognition. In: Proceedings of UbiComp, pp. 817–826 (2014)
19. Mahmoud, S.M., Lotfi, A., Lane, C., Langensiepen, C.: Abnormal behaviours identification for an elder's life activities using dissimilarity measurements. In: Proceedings of PETRA (2011)
20. Rodriguez, N.D., Cuellar, M.P., Lilius, J., Calvo-Flores, M.D.: A survey on ontologies for human behavior recognition. ACM Comput. Surv. **46**(4), 43 (2014)
21. Lotfi, A., Langensiepen, C., Mahmoud, S.M., Akhlaghinia, M.J.: Smart homes for the elderly dementia sufferers: identification and prediction of abnormal behaviour. J. Ambient Intell. Hum. Comput. **3**(3), 205–218 (2012)
22. Juarez, J. M., Ochotorena, J.M., Campos, M., Combi, C. Multiple temporal axes for visualising the behaviour of elders living alone. In: Healthcare Informatics (ICHI), pp. 387–395 (2013)
23. Chen, L., Nugent, C., Okeyo, G.: An ontology-based hybrid approach to activity modeling for smart homes. IEEE Trans. Hum. Mach. Syst. **44**(1), 92–105 (2014)
24. Katz, S.: Assessing self-maintenance: activities of daily living, mobility, and instrumental activities of daily living. J. Am. Geriatr. Soc. **31**(12), 721–727 (1983). ISO 690
25. Hartigan, J.A.: Clustering algorithms. Wiley, New York (1975)
26. Hartigan, J.A., Wong, M.A.: Algorithm AS 136: a k-means clustering algorithm. Appl. Stat. **28**(1), 100–108 (1979)
27. Bellman, R.: A note on cluster analysis and dynamic programming. Math. Biosci. **18**(3), 311–312 (1973)
28. Wang, H., Song, M.: Ckmeans. 1d. dp: optimal k-means clustering in one dimension by dynamic programming. R J. **3**(2), 29–33 (2011)
29. Agrawal, R., Srikant, R.: Mining sequential patterns. In: Proceedings of the Eleventh International Conference on In Data Engineering, pp. 3–14. IEEE (1995)
30. Lin, Q., Zhang, D., Li, D., Ni, H., Zhou, X.: Extracting intra- and inter-activity association patterns from daily routines of elders. In: Biswas, J., Kobayashi, H., Wong, L., Abdulrazak, B., Mokhtari, M. (eds.) ICOST 2013. LNCS, vol. 7910, pp. 36–44. Springer, Heidelberg (2013)

Contextualized Behavior Patterns for Ambient Assisted Living

Paula Lago[1(✉)], Claudia Jiménez-Guarín[1], and Claudia Roncancio[2]

[1] Systems and Computing Engineering Department, School of Engineering,
Universidad de Los Andes, Bogotá, Colombia
{pa.lago52,cjimenez}@uniandes.edu.co
[2] LIG, University Grenoble, Grenoble, France
claudia.roncancio@imag.fr

Abstract. Human behavior learning plays an important role in ambient assisted living since it enables service personalization. Current work in human behavior learning do not consider the context under which a behavior occurs, which hides some behaviors that are frequent only under certain conditions. In this work, we present the notion of a contextualized behavior pattern, which describes a behavior pattern with the context in which it occurs (i.e. nap when raining) and propose an algorithm for finding these patterns in a data stream. This is our main contribution. These patterns help to better understand the routine of a user in a smart environment, as is evidenced when testing with a public dataset. This algorithm could be used to learn behaviors from users in an ambient assisted living environment in order to send alarms when behavior changes occur.

Keywords: Human behavior learning · Sequential patterns · Context analysis · Personalization · Data streams

1 Introduction

Human behavior learning plays an important role in ambient assisted living since it enables service personalization like sending alerts when changes in behavior are detected. For example, if a user normally takes a walk after lunch but lately she has been napping instead of walking, an alert could be sent to her family to check if everything is fine.

Behavior learning is widely studied and different behavior models have been proposed [1–4]. One such model is sequential patterns in which a behavior is represented as an ordered set of activities. Thus, sequential pattern mining algorithms can be used to learn frequent behaviors of a user. However, most of these algorithms do not consider the context in which a behavior occurs, which can make the applications that use them: (1) miss some behaviors that are frequent only under certain context (i.e. only on weekends) and (2) generate false alarms about behavior changes. To continue with the first example, if it has been raining lately and the user likes to nap when it is raining, then skipping the walk after lunch is normal and should not be notified. A high false alarm rate can cause users to be reluctant to use these systems or to ignore all alarms, so they should be avoided.

© Springer International Publishing Switzerland 2015
A.A. Salah et al. (Eds.): HBU 2015, LNCS 9277, pp. 132–145, 2015.
DOI: 10.1007/978-3-319-24195-1_10

A behavior learning algorithm for ambient assisted living should consider context when learning frequent patterns to find those frequent only under certain conditions. It should also learn behaviors in an online fashion (as data arrive from sensors) and be adaptive, that is, learn new behaviors as they appear.

In this paper, our goal and main contribution is to find sequential patterns of activities that are frequent over a specific day, time or after a specific activity (Sect. 2). We present the definition of a contextualized sequential pattern and propose an algorithm for their extraction. We test the algorithm with a public database and show that considering context yields different patterns than just mining frequent patterns over the entire period of time (Sect. 3). Finally we present related work (Sect. 4) and conclusions and future work (Sect. 5).

2 Proposed Algorithm

In this section we first introduce the notion of a contextualized sequential pattern and then present the data structure and proposed algorithm for mining them from a data stream. We consider day, hour and activity as part of the context but more variables will be included in future work.

2.1 Definitions

Given a data stream of activities S_a, each with a timestamp, a sequence is an ordered (by timestamp) set of activities $a_1, a_2, \ldots a_n$. A sequence s occurs at the day of a_1's timestamp and starts at the hour indicated by it. In this work, a context c is a specific day (i.e. Tuesday), a specific time (i.e. at 9:00 am) or a specific activity (i.e. sleeping) or the combination of any of them. A sequence s is said to support a context if it occurs at the day, hour or starts with the activity specified by c. We denote $occurs(s, c)$ to indicate that sequence s occurs at context c.

A contextualized sequential pattern is a sequence of activities that frequently appear together over a specific context. The pattern describes both the sequence and the context on which it occurs. A sequence is said to be frequent in a context if the number of times it occurs on the specific context over the total number of sequences that support the context is greater than a user-specified minimum threshold (φ). This is expressed by (1).

$$\frac{|occurs(s, c)|}{\sum_j |occurs(s_j, c)|} \geq \varphi \tag{1}$$

2.2 Contextualized Prefix-Tree

For mining the contextualized sequential patterns we use a contextualized prefix tree, which is an extension of the prefix-tree used for prefix span [5]. The root of the tree keeps the total count of sequences that have been seen and also the counts by day and time in a context count matrix (Fig. 1). In this work, we divide time in 15-minute slots (96 timeslots in total for each day), but this could be configured as a parameter for the algorithm. Each cell in the matrix indicates how many sequences have supported both the day and the time represented by the cell.

Each node of the tree represents a sequence, which is the path from the root to the node. A node has a label (indicating an activity label), a total count of the times this sequence has been seen and a context count matrix, which counts how many times the sequence has been seen in each day and hour (Fig. 2).

Days

		Monday	Tuesday	...
...				
7:00am		count	count	
7:15 am		count	Count	
7:30am		count	Count	
7:45am		count	Count	
...				

Hours

Fig. 1. Context count matrix, a 7×96 int matrix that stores the number of times a sequence has been seen on each day and timeslot.

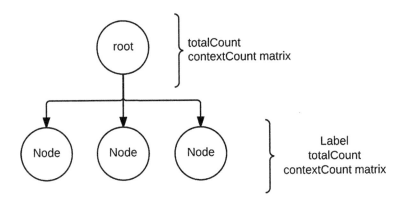

Fig. 2. Contextualized prefix-tree.

2.3   Algorithm

The algorithm for extracting frequent contextualized patterns consists of three steps: segmentation of the stream, insertion in the tree and extraction of frequent sequences. Each step is explained next considering the following stream of activities as example:

$S_a = \{(2010 - 11 - 0715 : 40 : 57.80 \ Meal_{Preparation}),$
$(2010 - 11 - 0715 : 42 : 09.46 \ Eating),$
$(2010 - 11 - 0717 : 19 : 51.47 \ Meal_{Preparation}),$
$(2010 - 11 - 0717 : 30 : 26.96 \ Eating),$
$(2010 - 11 - 0717 : 40 : 51.0 \ Wash_{Dishes}),$
$(2010 - 11 - 0717 : 47 : 05.0 \ Meal_{Preparation})$
$(2010 - 11 - 0719 : 52 : 24.28 \ Work),$
$(2010 - 11 - 0720 : 37 : 41.43 \ Eating),$
$(2010 - 11 - 0720 : 40 : 41.5 \ Meal_{Preparation}),$
$(2010 - 11 - 0723 : 52 : 03.47 \ Sleeping)\}$

Segmentation. First, the stream of activities is segmented to form sequences of equal length (n). From the timestamp of each activity in the sequence, the day of the week and the timeslot are extracted. Each time a sequence of length n is formed (n activities have entered the stream), it is inserted in the tree. The length of the sequences n can be configured as a parameter. Having a very small length results in uninteresting patterns and having a large length could result in many spurious patterns since randomness could make small sequences frequent. Statistical experts advise against large n. Therefore, in this work we use a sequence length of 4.

The stream of the example, would be segmented in the following sequences (the first integer represents the day of the week and the second integer represents the timeslot of the first activity in the sequence, for example the first sequence has time 62 because meal preparation starts at 15:40 which corresponds to the timeslot 62):

$(2, 62, MealPreparation, eating, mealPreparation, eating)$
$(2, 62, eating, mealPreparation, eating, washDishes)$
$(2, 69, mealPreparation, eating, washDishes, mealPreparation)$
$(2, 70, eating, washDishes, mealPreparation, work)$
$(2, 70, washDishes, mealPreparation, work, eating)$
$(2, 71, mealPreparation, work, eating, mealPreparation)$
$(2, 79, work, eating, mealPreparation, sleeping)$

Insertion. To insert a sequence in the tree, the root checks if it has the first activity of the sequence in its children. If it does, then the totalCount and context counts are updated for this node. If it doesn't, then a new node is created with totalCount 1 and the corresponding context count in 1 also. Recursion is used for each element in the sequence.

Following our example, the first sequence is inserted as the first branch of the empty tree with total count = 1 and the corresponding context count = 1 (Tuesday, 62) as shown in Fig. 3. Then, the second sequence is inserted as a second branch like in Fig. 4, updating the root's total counts. Finally, when all sequences have been inserted the tree looks like Fig. 5.

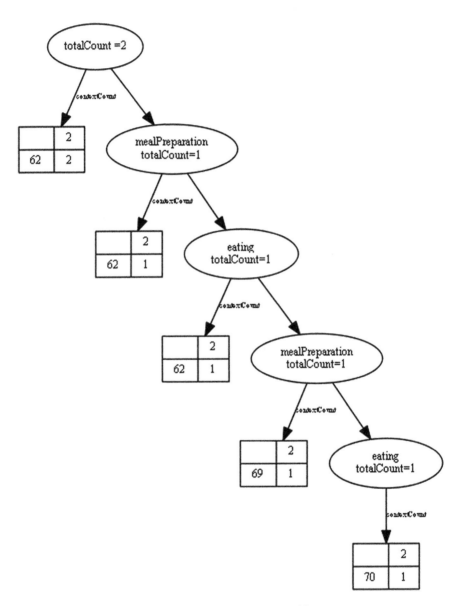

Fig. 3. The prefix tree after the insertion of first sequence.

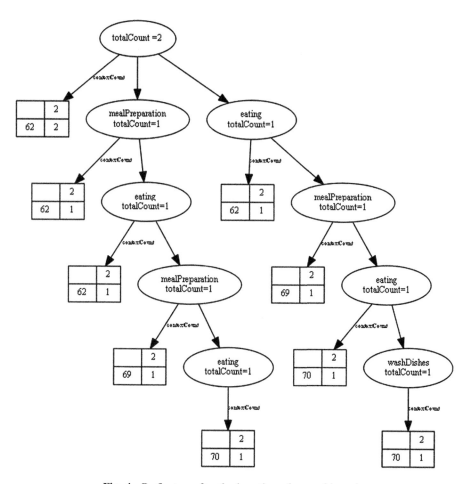

Fig. 4. Prefix tree after the insertion of second branch.

Extraction of Frequent Sequences. To extract frequent sequences by context, the total count of the context t_c is obtained from the root node. If patterns are to be extracted by only day or time then the total count is obtained by summing the corresponding row or column of the root node count matrix. Then, each node checks if its context count is greater than the total count of the context times the minimum support ($t_c * \varphi$). If it is, then the sequence it represents is added to the frequent sequence set.

In the tree of the example, with a minimum support of 0.45, the patterns extracted without considering context would only be meal preparation since it is the only sequence (length 1) that has a support greater than the threshold. Considering context we can obtain some of the following patterns:

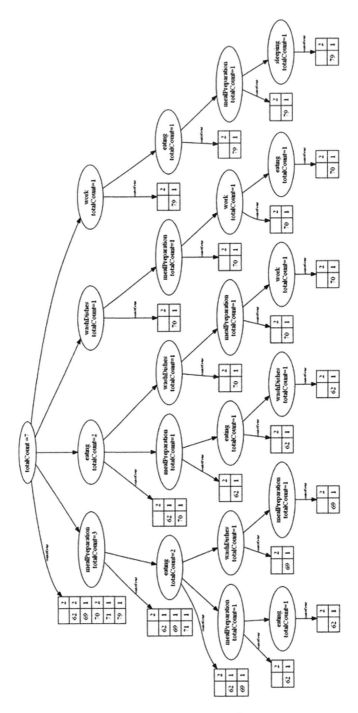

Fig. 5. Prefix tree after the insertion of all sequences.

- At timeslot 62 (around 15:30), it is frequent to prepare meal and then eat.
- At timeslot 70 (around 17:30), it is frequent to eat and then wash dishes.
- It is frequent to eat after work.

Although these toy example has too few data to be really interesting (many sequences have a total count of only 1), it shows that not considering context yields different patterns than considering it and that our algorithm can find patterns that are associated to a time and a day.

3 Results

We tested our algorithm with the Aruba CASAS Dataset, made public by the CASAS project [6] through their repository[1]. The dataset consists of sensor data that was collected in the home of a volunteer adult with annotated activities. We used this dataset because it has data for a long period of time (193 days) and it is collected in real-life settings. The annotated activities in this dataset are: meal preparation, sleeping, relax, wash dishes, work, bed to toilet, enter and leave home, housekeeping and resperate[2].

Each record in the dataset contains a timestamp, a sensor id and a sensor reading. If the event corresponds to the start or end of an activity, then the record also contains the activity label and the word start or end accordingly (see Fig. 6 (a)). Since we are concerned with finding sequential patterns of activities and not of sensor activations, we first transformed the dataset in order to have records that contain the start and end time of the activity, the location and the label (see Fig. 6 (b)). Also, because in the dataset it is common to have the same activity begin and end at very close times, we consider only an occurrence of the activity if no more than fifteen minutes have passed from the end of one occurrence to the beginning of the next.

We first find sequential patterns without considering context using a minimum support of 0.4. On this dataset the patterns found are: relax, meal_preparation. Only these two sequences are found to be frequent, because there are many more occurrences of these two activities than of the others in the dataset. We omit the patterns that only contain these two activities from the following results because of this.

We then find time patterns and patterns based on each of the activities (i.e. what is usually done after eating?). These patterns allow a better understanding of the routine of the person that lived in the smart environment. Some of the patterns found are described below.

- From 21:30 to 1:00 the only frequent activity is Sleeping. This indicates the usual sleeping hour of the person.
- From 1:00 to 4:45, Sleeping is a frequent activity as well as the sequence Sleeping – Bed to toilet – Sleeping. This indicates that the person wakes up at night frequently.

---

[1] http://ailab.wsu.edu/casas/datasets.html.

[2] Resperate is a device used to lower blood pressure.

```
2010-12-07 14:25:27.094846 T001 19.5
2010-12-07 14:25:27.17922 T005 21
2010-12-07 14:35:11.375122 D004 OPEN Enter_Home begin
2010-12-07 14:35:13.05679 M030 ON
2010-12-07 14:35:15.290319 M030 OFF
2010-12-07 14:35:15.371058 M029 ON
2010-12-07 14:35:16.293931 M030 ON
2010-12-07 14:35:16.79131 D004 CLOSE Enter_Home end
2010-12-07 14:35:16.878804 M029 OFF
2010-12-07 14:35:17.921491 M022 ON
```

```
2010-11-04 00:03:50.20 begin Sleeping
2010-11-04 05:40:51.30 begin Bed_to_Toilet
2010-11-04 05:43:45.0 begin Sleeping
2010-11-04 08:11:09.96 begin Meal_Preparation
2010-11-04 09:29:23.22 begin Relax
2010-11-04 09:34:16.85 begin Housekeeping
2010-11-04 09:48:52.34 begin Meal_Preparation
2010-11-04 09:56:41.83 begin Eating
2010-11-04 10:03:21.96 begin Wash_Dishes
2010-11-04 11:29:08.10 begin Housekeeping
2010-11-04 11:41:34.2 begin Leave_Home
```

(a)   (b)

Fig. 6. (a) Original dataset and (b). Transformation done for this paper. We used data that define the start time and label for each activity.

- At 6:00 am Meal Preparation and Relax are frequent activities, which could mean that around this time the user wakes up.
- At 6:45 the sequence Meal_Preparation – Relax - Work is frequent.
- At 20:45 the sequences Relax - Meal_Preparation – Relax - Work and Relax-Meal_Preparation – Relax - Wash_Dishes are frequent.

Patterns by activity include the following:

- Resperate – Relax - Meal_Preparation
- Wash_Dishes - Relax – Sleeping. This sequence can be interpreted as the user usually washing dishes at night, before going to sleep.
- Sleeping – Bed to Toilet – Sleeping. This is an indication of waking up frequently at night.
- Sleeping - Meal_Preparation – Relax - Meal_Preparation – Eating. These sequences indicates that shortly after waking up, the person prepares meal and then eats (breakfast).

These results are consistent with patterns found with prefixspan when data is partitioned to use only activities that occurred in a specific day or time.

3.1 Using the Tree for Activity Prediction

The contextualized prefix tree can be used for activity prediction by obtaining the most probable next activity according to the current context (day, hour and activity). Using the same dataset, we use the tree for activity prediction by predicting the most probable activity as the data arrives. Table 1 shows the precision and recall for all the activities in the dataset and Table 2 shows the confusion matrix obtained.

Some activities show good results such as meal preparation, enter home, bed to toilet, sleeping and relax, but the others have very poor performance. We believe that if the patterns are adapted (removing old patterns) these results could be improved.

Table 1. Precision and Recall for each activity in the dataset using activity prediction

	Precision	Recall
Meal_Preparation	0,54	0,48
Sleeping	0,44	0,98
Wash_Dishes	0,23	0,17
Resperate	0,00	0,00
Work	0,02	0,06
Enter_home	0,96	0,79
Leave_home	0,23	0,28
Bed_to_Toilet	0,50	0,37
Housekeeping	0,00	0,00
Relax	0,69	0,64
Eating	0,31	0,33

Table 2. Confusion matrix for activity prediction

	Meal_ Preparation	Sleeping	Wash_ Dishes	Resperate	Work	Enter_ home	Leave_ home	Bed_to_ Toilet	House keeping	Relax	Eating	Could not predict
Meal_Preparation	545	3	16	1	11	30	138	125	26	94	12	2
Sleeping	187	170	4	0	1	1	4	0	3	9	4	2
Wash_Dishes	19	0	15	0	0	0	4	0	0	25	0	1
Resperate	3	0	0	0	0	0	1	0	0	1	1	0
Work	60	0	3	0	2	7	14	0	9	32	6	0
Enter_home	1	0	0	0	1	317	6	0	0	3	0	1
Leave_home	160	0	12	1	5	21	99	1	8	110	12	2
Bed_to_Toilet	76	0	0	0	0	0	0	78	0	0	0	1
Housekeeping	14	0	1	0	1	0	3	0	0	7	5	2
Relax	67	1	35	1	11	22	75	8	8	742	102	4
Eating	13	0	0	0	3	1	4	0	5	129	70	1

3.2 Discussion and Analysis of Results

Mining contextualized sequential patterns helps to better understand user behavior at home. Using a contextualized prefix tree with a sequence length of 4 we found sensible results, although the parameter could be better configured with further experiments. The contextualized patterns can be used for activity prediction as was tested in this paper, even though the results must be further improved for use in application. The patterns can also be used for measuring behavior drifts, which can be early signs of disease or could be due to new routines. Measuring these deviations and differentiating between alerts and new habits that should be added to the patterns is one of the next steps in our research.

4   Related Work

Learning frequent behaviors of users has been recognized as a crucial aspect for realizing the ambient assisted living as well as the more general smart environments paradigms. Learning frequent behaviors enables service personalization, future behavior prediction, which can be used for the environment to act proactively and to detect abnormalities or behavior shifts, which can be used to generate alerts. Different models have been used for describing and learning human behaviors such as context-free grammars [7, 8], Hidden Markov Models [9, 10], topic models [11, 12] and sequential patterns [13, 14]. Among these models, we select sequential patterns since they are easily understandable by end users and can be used to create readable alerts.

Another key feature in ambient assisted living is context-awareness because it enables the adaptation of services to the circumstances in which they are used [15]. Typical context variables used in smart environments describe both the environment (humidity, noise, lighting levels) and the user (location, physiological variables, posture, activity). In our work, we consider activity, time and weekday as context variables since we believe behavior can change according to these two features. In future work, we will add weather and other typical contextual variables.

Our main objective in this paper is to learn frequent sequential patterns from data streams under different contexts, day and time of day in this work, to better understand the behavior of users. Therefore, we focus on sequential pattern mining with contextual aspects for behavior learning. Surveys of sequential pattern mining can be found in [16, 17] and a survey of algorithms for incremental and progressive sequential pattern mining can be found in [18].

The algorithm Evolving Agent behavior Classification based on Distributions of Relevant events (EVABCD) [3] creates evolving user profiles that are represented by a sequence of events. To solve the problem of unbounded sequences, this algorithm first segments the sequence of events in subsequences of equal length and then stores them in a trie. Each node of the trie stores the number of the times an event (a Linux command in the article) has been seen, so calculating support for each sequence is easy. Each user profile is represented with a probability distribution of the frequent sequences. When a sequence becomes less probable it is eliminated from the profile, thus making it an evolving profile. This method not only mines frequent sequences but it also is adaptive, one of the main features of our proposal. One difference with our problem is that we maintain frequent sequences for each user and that EVABCD only takes into account the events and not the context in which they appear, nor the temporal relations among them.

The SPEDS (Sequential Patterns on Evolving data streams) algorithm [19] obtains the set of sequential patterns over a period of time at any moment. It uses a lexicographic tree in which each node denotes an item and a sequence is represented by a path in the tree. Each node contains a tilted time table that counts the frequency of the item on the corresponding tilted-time window. The tree is incrementally updated after a batch of data is processed with prefixSpan [5] to extract frequent sequences from the batch, and update nodes and counters in the tree. This algorithm allows finding patterns at different time granularities, which is an idea in which we base our proposal. We extend the tilted-time table to consider other contextual variables.

The MobileMiner [14] service discovers personalized frequent co-ocurrence patterns indicating which context events frequently occur together. Since the service runs on mobile phones it is efficient and could be used for mining streams. However, the service does not mine sequences, and thus, does not consider the order in which events occur. We believe that in some cases, the order of activities can be crucial for detecting emergency or must-watch situations. Another difference with our approach is that they use an Apriori-based strategy for mining patterns, while we use the prefix-growth strategy.

Moshtaghi, Zukerman and Russell's model [20] combines the time of day with the region of the house to infer inactivity thresholds that are used to detect abnormal inactivity periods to generate alerts. This approach is similar to ours in that it learns different behaviors according to context (location and time) but it differs from our research in that they are considering inactivity as the only interesting behavior while we would like to learn sequential patterns to describe user behaviors. This is because although there could be activity at home, painting at night could be normal while going out or wandering around could not.

We describe sequential patterns with the context in which they occur, i.e. if a sequence is frequent when it is raining. In this case, context can be seen as a constraint for the sequential patterns. Although some algorithms have been proposed for mining sequential patterns with constraints [21], these constraints must be defined a priori by the user. Our algorithm can discover the context on which the sequences are frequent, as it is done in some other work. For example, in [22], the time period over which a itemset is frequent is automatically discovered. This is done by pattern-growth and by maintaining for each candidate itemset, the period on which it might be frequent. This work has some differences with ours: (1) they are not mining sequential patterns and (2) their algorithm is not online, meaning it is not suitable for data stream processing as is the case in ambient assisted living (mining data coming from sensors).

5 Conclusions

In this work we propose the notion of contextualized sequential patterns, sequential patterns of activities that are associated to the context on which they are frequent, and an algorithm for mining them on data streams. These patterns can describe the behavior of a user in a smart environment and help to better understand the routine of a user. These patterns can be used for service personalization.

Although some algorithms for mining adaptive sequential patterns on streaming data have been proposed, they do not consider context and the algorithms that do consider context do not mine frequent sequences but itemsets. Our algorithm can find patterns that state that a behavior occurs on Mondays but not on other days or at 10 am but not in the afternoon. This, to the best of our knowledge, has not been achieved, as is also stated in [17]. This is the main contribution of this work.

5.1 Future Work

In future work we will add more context variables such as weather and physiological variables to the patterns. Also, merging the context under which the same patterns occurs (i.e. sleeping is frequent from 23:00 to 06:00 on all days) and finding patterns that join different contexts (i.e. patterns occurring on Mondays at 7am) is an important research direction that we will explore. Finally, using these patterns to detect changes in behavior that could signal health deterioration or that an adaptation is needed in the patterns is a crucial step for the application of the patterns in ambient assisted living.

References

1. Monekosso, D.N., Remagnino, P.: Behavior analysis for assisted living. IEEE Trans. Autom. Sci. Eng. **7**, 879–886 (2010)
2. Rodríguez, N.D., Cuéllar, M.P., Lilius, J., Calvo-Flores, M.D.: A fuzzy ontology for semantic modelling and recognition of human behaviour. Knowl. Based Syst. **66**, 46–60 (2014)
3. Iglesias, J.A., Angelov, P., Ledezma, A., Sanchis, A.: Creating evolving user behavior profiles automatically. IEEE Trans. Knowl. Data Eng. **24**, 854–867 (2012)
4. Chua, S., Marsland, S.: Unsupervised learning of human behaviours. In: Twenty-Fifth AAAI Conference, pp. 319–324 (2011)
5. Pei, J.P.J., Han, J.H.J., Mortazavi-Asl, B., Pinto, H., Chen, Q.C.Q., Dayal, U., Hsu, M.-C.H. M.-C.: PrefixSpan,: mining sequential patterns efficiently by prefix-projected pattern growth. In: Proceedings of the 17th International Conference Data Engineering (2001)
6. Cook, D.J., Crandall, A.S., Thomas, B.L., Krishnan, N.C.: CASAS : a smart home in a box. IEEE Comput. **46**, 62–69 (2013)
7. Turaga, P., Member, S., Chellappa, R., Subrahmanian, V.S., Udrea, O.: Mach. Recogn. Hum. Activities Surv. **18**, 1473–1488 (2008)
8. Ryoo, M.S., Aggarwal, J.K.: Recognition of composite human activities through context-free grammar based representation. In: IEEE Computer Society Conference on Computer Vision and Pattern Recognition, vol. 2, pp. 1709–1716 (2006)
9. Ordonez, F.J., Englebienne, G., de Toledo, P., van Kasteren, T., Sanchis, A., Kröse, B.: In-home activity recognition: bayesian inference for hidden markov models. IEEE Pervasive Comput. **13**, 67–75 (2014)
10. Forkan, A.R.M., Khalil, I., Tari, Z., Foufou, S., Bouras, A.: A context-aware approach for long-term behavioural change detection and abnormality prediction in ambient assisted living. Pattern Recognit. **48**, 628–641 (2014)
11. Rieping, K., Englebienne, G., Kröse, B.: Behavior analysis of elderly using topic models. Pervasive Mobile Comput. **15**, 181–199 (2014)
12. Seiter, J., Amft, O., Rossi, M., Tröster, G.: Discovery of activity composites using topic models: An analysis of unsupervised methods. Pervasive Mob. Comput. **15**, 215–227 (2014)
13. Aztiria, A., Augusto, J.C., Basagoiti, R., Izaguirre, A.: Accurate temporal relationships in sequences of user behaviours in intelligent environments. In: Augusto, J.C., Corchado, J.M., Novais, P., Analide, C. (eds.) Ambient Intelligence and Future Trends-International Symposium on Ambient Intelligence (ISAm I 2010), pp. 19–27. Springer, Berlin Heidelberg (2010)

14. Srinivasan, V., Moghaddam, S., Mukherji, A., Rachuri, K.K., Xu, C., Tapia, E.M.: MobileMiner. In: Proceedings of the 2014 ACM International Joint Conference on Pervasive and Ubiquitous Computing (UbiComp 2014 Adjunct), pp. 389–400. ACM Press, New York (2014)
15. Cook, D.J., Augusto, J.C., Jakkula, V.R.: Ambient intelligence: Technologies, applications, and opportunities. Pervasive Mob. Comput. **5**, 277–298 (2009)
16. Mabroukeh, N.R., Ezeife, C.I.: A taxonomy of sequential pattern mining algorithms. ACM Comput. Surv. **43**, 1–41 (2010)
17. Mooney, C.H., Roddick, J.F.: Sequential pattern mining – approaches and algorithms. ACM Comput. Surv. **45**, 19 (2013)
18. Mallick, B., Garg, D., Grover, P.S.: Incremental mining of sequential patterns : Progress and challenges. Intell. Data Anal. **17**, 507–530 (2013)
19. Soliman, A.F., Ebrahim, G.a., Mohammed, H.K.: SPEDS: a framework for mining sequential patterns in evolving data streams. In: Pacific Rim Conference on Communications, Computers Signal Process, pp. 464–469 (2011)
20. Moshtaghi, M., Zukerman, I., Russell, R.A.: Statistical models for unobtrusively detecting abnormal periods of inactivity in older adults. User Model User adapt. Interact. **25**, 231–265 (2015)
21. Pei, J., Han, J., Wang, W.: Constraint-based sequential pattern mining: the pattern-growth methods. J. Intell. Inf. Syst. **28**, 133–160 (2007)
22. Saleh, B., Masseglia, F.: Discovering frequent behaviors: time is an essential element of the context. Knowl. Inf. Syst. **28**, 311–331 (2010)

Activity Patterns in Stroke Patients - Is There a Trend in Behaviour During Rehabilitation?

Adrian Derungs[1]([✉]), Julia Seiter[2], Corina Schuster-Amft[3], and Oliver Amft[1]

[1] ACTLab, Chair of Sensor Technology, University of Passau, Passau, Germany
{adrian.derungs,oliver.amft}@uni-passau.de
http://www.actlab.uni-passau.de
[2] Wearable Computing Laboratory, ETH Zrich, Zürich, Switzerland
julia.seiter@ife.ee.ethz.ch
[3] Research Department, Reha Rheinfelden, Rheinfelden, Switzerland
c.schuster@reha-rhf.ch

Abstract. We describe stroke patients' activity patterns and trends based on motion data acquired during their stay in an ambulatory day-care centre. Our aim was to explore and quantify intensity and development in the patients' activity patterns as these may change during the rehabilitation process. We analyse motion data recordings from wearable inertial measurement units of eleven patients up to eleven days, totally 102 recording days. Using logic rules, we extract activity primitives, including affected arm move, sit, stand, walking, etc. from selected channels of the continuous median-filtered sensor data. Using relative duration of the activity primitives, we examine patient activity patterns regarding independence in mobility, distribution of walking over the days and trends in using the affected body side. Due to the heterogeneity of patients' behaviour, we focused on analysing patient-specific activity patterns. Our exploration showed that the rule-based activity primitive analysis is beneficial to understand individual patient activity.

Keywords: Activity primitives · Trend indication · Exploratory behaviour description · Rule base data extraction

1 Introduction

Wearable motion sensors have great potential for monitoring and continuous interpretation of stroke patient recovery process. In particular, in clinical settings research has shown that data from inertial motion sensors can be used to estimate the outcome of selected scales of standard clinical motor function assessments, such as the Wolf Motor Function Test (WMFT) [22]. Eventually, the interpretation of motion sensor data could complement the information from clinical assessments during times when patients are unsupervised, e.g. at home. However, assessing functional state outside of controlled clinical conditions is still an open challenge. While being successful, most approaches to estimate clinical outcome, focused on sub-scores of clinical assessments only. Thus, the estimation

© Springer International Publishing Switzerland 2015
A.A. Salah et al. (Eds.): HBU 2015, LNCS 9277, pp. 146–159, 2015.
DOI: 10.1007/978-3-319-24195-1_11

requires patients to perform certain exercises, some even require specific accessories. Consequently, there is currently no general solution on how rehabilitation progress could be interpreted remotely when patients have left the clinic.

As any rehabilitation training programmes aim at improving motor function, skills, and patient performance, changes in patient activity patterns are likely. For example, when a hemiparetic stroke patient relearns how to use the affected arm in daily activities, motion balance between affected and non-affected arms may change. Similarly, regaining motor capabilities may have an effect on behaviour and trends in activity patterns. For example, a patient could become more active and involved, thus walk more frequently. Detecting functional changes in patients requires long-term observation, across weeks or months. In contrast, many estimation approaches that focused on clinical assessments investigated momentary patient state, often recording individual exercises only (see related work for details). The heterogeneity of patient capabilities is large, often influenced by personal traits, mood, etc. Previous work of our group on discovering daily routines revealed that patients had widely varying routine patterns and shared only very few routines [18]. Moreover, daily routines, such as eating and socialising are rather abstract and may not reveal trends in activity patterns. Patients will cope differently with their individual limitation in motor capability. Therefore activities may be differently represented in motion sensor data and supervised recognition techniques would require large amounts of annotated motion data to derive statistical models. Due to cost and privacy concerns, annotating continuous day-long recordings across many rehabilitation days seems unfeasible.

In this work, we utilise a rule-based activity primitive detection approach to explore intensity and trends in activity patterns of hemiparetic stroke survivors during their rehabilitation programme. To derive activity primitives, we used conditions on features from individual motion sensor channels. Relative duration and ratios of the activity primitives are subsequently used to describe activity patterns among patients. We analysed motion data recordings of eleven stroke patients up to eleven days in a day-care centre using wearable inertial measurement units (IMUs). As patients attend to the day-care centre on selected days per week only, recording days spread over multiple weeks for each patient.

In particular this paper provides the following contributions:

1. We detail our construction of activity primitives from basic logic conditions and primitive ratios that were subsequently analysed to interpret activity pattern intensity and trends. Our approach utilises domain knowledge to derive the rule set, but remains user-independent.

2. We explore patient activity patterns in a dataset of day-long recordings in a day-care centre, where patients were not constrained in their activities, but had some scheduled training appointments. Study observers followed the patients on selected recording days to annotate and verify their behaviour. Our exploratory analysis considers independent mobility and duration of activity primitives, including sit, stand, walk, moving affected and non-affected arms and legs, as well as to analyse temporal changes in these activity patterns.

2 Related Work

Wearable sensors, in particular IMUs, can continuously record motion data and have been applied in activity and movement analysis, including fall risk detection [7], stroke patient monitoring [4], and upper-body stability analysis during walking [9]. Several approaches exist that use wearable sensor data to evaluate functional ability in patients according to clinical scores. In contrast to therapists, who typically assess patient ability by visual inspection, wearable sensors could provide motion data in much finer resolution. Thus, wearable sensors may be beneficial for patients and therapists to determine and control near-term rehabilitation goals and can be deployed in unsupervised settings (e.g. at home). Wearable sensors have been used in clinical assessments including the Fugl-Meyer-Assessment (FMA) [6] and the Wolf Motor Function Test (WMFT) [22] to assess patient motor ability. To estimate the clinical scores from wearable sensor data, classification and regression techniques were applied to selected tasks of an assessments as described, for example, by Parnandi et al., Patel et al., and Knorr et al. [10,12,13].

Stroke patients often develop compensation strategies (e.g. shoulder and trunk rotations) to cope with functional limitations, thus influencing the original motion behaviour. Compensation strategies and limitations are discussed by Cirste et al., Bourbonnais et al., Di Fabio et al., and Murphy et al. [1,3,5,11]. Behaviour analysis of the elderly in smart homes was investigated to revel trends and changes in health and well-being by Suryadevara et al. and Rashidi et al. [14,20]. Ambient and motion detection sensors (e.g. attached to room heaters, toaster, bed, chair, and similar) were used to detect activities (e.g. sleeping, watching TV, and dining) for subsequent behaviour analysis. A multi modal identification and localisation approach for gesture and pose recognition in smart environments was proposed by Salah et al. [16]. Seiderer et al. explored the utilisation of a digital image frame for lifestyle intervention to improve well-being of older adults [17]. The sensors built into the image frame (e.g. distance sensors, light sensors, microphones, and cameras) were used for information or recommendations (e.g. to drink water, doing exercisers or remind about birthdays) to the user nearby. A sensor and vision based indoor application for elderly care was proposed by Tabar et al. [21]. The system was built from off-the-shelf devices under the constraints of size, cost, and power consumption. Robben et al. considered fall detection, position tracking, and posture classification as useful information for emergency service and a particular benefit of smart homes [15]. Behaviour interpretation of the elderly in the home environment to understand, anticipate, and respond to care needs was also described by Hine et al. [8].

We work focuses on stroke patients in an ambulatory care setting as an essential step towards home monitoring using wearable sensors. With the wearable sensors we can explore motion behaviour and trends in activities independent of the field of view of room-installed sensors, such as cameras or motion detectors.

3   Patient Study

3.1   Participants

Eleven hemiparetic stroke patients (6 males and 5 females) were included in our study. Patients were between 34 and 75 years. Inclusion criteria were: stroke or brain tumour extraction with subsequent upper and/or lower motor function deficits including wheelchair users. Exclusion criteria were: patients with further motor function impairments caused by additional neurological diseases other than stroke or brain tumour. Participants visited the ambulatory day-care centre of the Rehabilitation clinic Reha Rheinfelden, Switzerland. All included patients signed a consent form to participate in the study. This study was approved by the Swiss cantonal Ethics committee Aargau. Patient details are summarised in Table 1. The study dataset was previously used to investigate daily routine discovery as described by Seiter et al. [18].

Table 1. Overview of included patients. "Type" refers to type of locomotion (Wheelchair or Walker). "Duration" refers to total rehab duration in days. "Rec" refers to the number of recorded study days.

ID	Type	Gender	Age [a]	Duration [days]	Rec [days]	ID	Type	Gender	Age [a]	Duration [days]	Rec [days]
1	W'chair	m	57	79	11	7	W'chair	m	64	28	9
2	Walk	m	47	18	8	8	Walk	m	34	28	11
3	W'chair	m	53	77	10	9	Walk	f	72	30	7
4	Walk	f	52	16	7	10	W'chair	f	68	30	9
5	Walk	f	74	35	10	11	Walk	f	55	28	9
6	Walk	m	38	66	11						

3.2   Design

Patients received varying scheduled therapies and followed their individual routines for the remaining time at the ambulatory day-care centre. Visit frequency was two to three times per week. On selected recording days and in agreement with therapists and patients, patients were accompanied and observed by the study observer, up to eight hours per day. The study observer annotated patient activities using an Android based open-source smartphone framework CRNTC+ [19]. We defined a catalogue with activity primitives including, walking, walking stairs, sitting, etc. In addition, six activity routines (eating/leisure, cognitive training, medical fitness, kitchen work, motor training, and resting) were defined as reference for subsequent behaviour and trend description.

Fig. 1. Patient at the day-care centre marking his drinking glass with a clothes peg. The wearable sensors positions at the wrist and the upper legs that were considered in out analysis are highlighted (S1,...,S4).

3.3 Recording

Shimmer3 sensors [2] were used, providing three axial information from accelerometers, gyroscopes, and magnetometers. The sensors were configured to log acceleration (range $\pm 4\,g$) with a sampling frequency of 50 Hz to an SD card integrated into Shimmer3 sensors. Participants were greeted in the morning and got sensors attached on both wrists, upper arms, and upper legs. During special therapy sessions, e.g. lymph drainage, massages, or water therapy, sensors were temporary detached. Figure 1 shows the wrist and upper leg sensor positions considered in our analysis. At the end of each therapy day, the study observer detached all sensors and said goodbye to patients. In total, we recorded 102 days including 738 h of motion data.

4   Motion Data Analysis Procedure

For our exploratory behaviour and trend analysis, we extracted activity primitives from the wearable sensor data. In this section, we detail our rule-based approach to derive activity primitives and the comparison with ground truth.

4.1 Activity Primitive Extraction

We considered activity primitives for sit, stand, walk, and motions of the affected and non-affected arms and legs. Table 2 provides an overview on all activity primitives extracted.

Activity primitives were extracted from the accelerometer sensor data (wrist and upper leg sensors) by applying logic rules. Initially, time-domain features *mean* and *variance* were calculated from acceleration data, using 1 s windows. Subsequently, we applied a median filter to remove signal outliers. We derived the duration of each activity primitive to explore the motion behaviour and trends.

Table 2. Activity primitives considered for our analysis. For each activity primitive, logic operations (NOT (!), AND (&), Or (|)) were applied to acceleration sensor features (*mean* and *variance*). Sensor positions: RA (right arm), LA (left arm), RL (right leg), LL (left leg). Sensor axes: x,y, and z. Body sides: A = affected side, NA = non-affected side. Here AP1, AP2, and AP3 describe rules applied to RL.

Activity primitive	Description of AP	Rules applied to extracted sensor data features
AP1	Sit	$RLacc_y - RLacc_z <= 0$
AP2	Stand	$RLacc_y - RLacc_z > 0$
AP3	Walk	$RLacc_y - RLacc_z > 0 \ \& \ RLacc_{y_{var}} > threshold$
AP4	Arm (A)	$!RA \ \& \ LA \ or \ RA \ \& \ !LA$ on acc_{xyz}
AP5	Arm (NA)	$!RA \ \& \ LA \ or \ RL \ \& \ !LL$ on acc_{xyz}
AP6	Leg (A)	$!RL \ \& LL \ or \ RL \ \& \ !LL$ on acc_{xyz}
AP7	Leg (NA)	$!RL \ \& \ LL \ or \ RL \ \& \ !LL$ on acc_{xyz}

4.2 Ground Truth Overlay

During the study at the day-care centre, study observers accompanied the patient on selected days to annotate activities. The annotation was not always possible, e.g., when only one observer was present while two or even three patients were recorded at the same day. Annotations were reviewed and revised where necessary after completion of the recording day to derive a ground truth for further analyses.

While our rule-based approach required setting thresholds, the threshold values were kept unchanged across all patients. Thus, the logic rules could be used independently of a patient and provide a basis for repeatable experiments. Thresholds were determined by visual inspection of motion acceleration data representations at each body part.

To inspect the extracted activity primitives, we divided the recording day into an hourly scale and compared primitives detection to the available ground truth. Figure 2 shows an example plot for the "Walk" activity primitive of one participant across eight recording days. Where available, we illustrated the ground truth and plotted the acceleration sensor variance for a leg.

5   Exploratory Results

5.1 Daily Analysis

Figure 2 shows the activity primitive "Walk" over the course of a day for Patient 2. Besides the ground truth, the walking moments detected using the logic rules, and the motion signals variance are shown. The illustration reveals the patient's mobility across the day regarding daytime and duration. Moreover, we concluded from the analysed data that the walking detection resembles well with the leg motion variance.

5.2 Difference Analysis

Differences between patients' motion duration are shown in Fig. 3 for all activity primitives. The activity primitives durations were normalised by deriving the ratio of the activity primitive duration per day divided by the corresponding recording time the day ($t_{norm} = \frac{t_{activity}}{t_{recduration}}$).

The boxplots represent then a comparison of the activity primitives for affected and non-affected body sides, sit to stand, and sit to walk. As Fig. 3 shows, the movement duration of the non-affected arm was longer than the duration of the affected arm, for all patients except for Patient 4. The "Leg" comparison plot shows the duration of the affected and the non-affected activity primitives. Similar to the comparison of the arm motion, we observed a lower activity duration of the affected leg compared with the non-affected leg.

Figure 3 furthermore shows "Sit" and "Stand" durations. The differences in the sit and stand durations could be an indication of the patients' ability to move. The duration varies more for Patient 1, 3, 4, 5, 7, and 10, than for Patients 2, 6, 8, and 9. Patient 11 is the only one, where the duration for standing was higher then the duration of sit.

We moreover compared the average motion duration of "Sit" and "Walk" of each patient during the rehabilitation at the day-care centre. "Sit" and "Walk" were highly correlated activity primitives ($r_{Pearson} = -0.806$), however the average duration of "Sit" is significantly higher than the average duration of "Walk" ($\rho = 0.0027$).

5.3 Trend Analysis

To further describe patient behaviour and analyse its relation to the recovery process, we investigated trends in in activity primitives. In Fig. 4 the normalised durations of the activity primitives describing motion of the affected and non-affected arms are illustrated. In addition to trend lines of the affected and non-affected arms, we calculated the ratio of the arm motion durations $R = \frac{affected}{non-affected}$. Figure 4 shows the computed ratio too. From the arm motion example, we observed a positive trend of the motion ratio of affected to non-affected body side for Patients 1, 2, 5, 6, 9, and 10. Negative ratio trends were observed for Patient 3, 4, 7, 8, and 11.

We calculated the first order polynomial fit coefficients (slope and offset of the trend line) of the activity primitive duration ratios for each patient. In Fig. 5 the calculated slope coefficients are illustrated as bars, indicating trends of the individual patient. For the trends of the arm motion (top left), sit/stand (bottom left), we observed a balanced between patients. Positive and negative trends occur almost evenly distributed among the patients. However, the leg movement ratio (eight positive and three negative) and the sit/walk ratio (two positive and seven negative) indicate clearer trend separability.

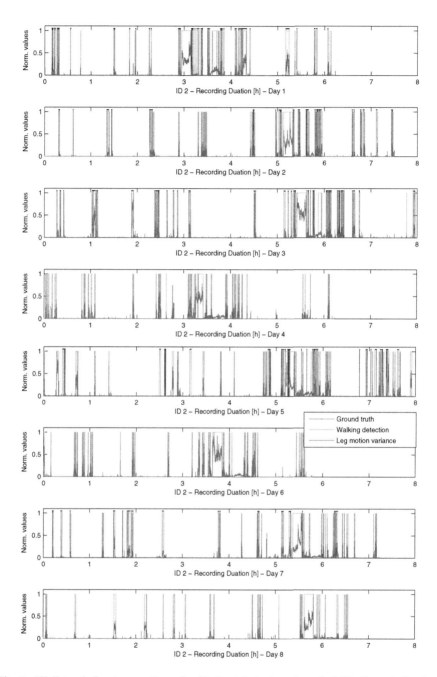

Fig. 2. Walking behaviour pattern for Patient 2 during the rehabilitation at the day-care centre. The ground truth was available at days 1, 2, 3, 5, and 7. Variance of the affected leg acceleration signal is illustrated. Variance over a thresholds was considered to be walking.

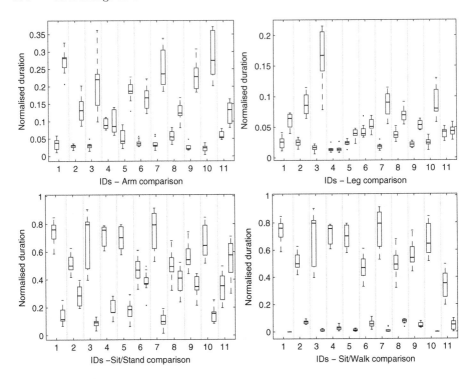

Fig. 3. Activity primitives "Sit", "Stand", "Walk", as well as arm and leg motion of the affected and non-affected side for each patient. The boxplots indicate the normalised durations of each activity primitive detection during the rehabilitation at the day-care centre. The activity primitives are considered here to describe the patients' motion behaviour.

6   Discussion

Combining context information (e.g. therapy schedule, therapy type, and expert knowledge) with wearable sensor data could provide information beyond the possible observation by therapists, thus applicable in unsupervised environments (e.g. at home). The present work is a step towards unsupervised monitoring, where the emphasis is on generic activity representation, instead of abstract daily routines. We investigated the motion patterns under the hypothesis that a patient's motor development should be observable in basic motion and trends across a rehabilitation stay. Our analysis results partially confirm the assumed positive trends, however do show negative trends too.

It is clear that the motion variability between stroke survivors is large due to various confounding factors that could not be completely assessed in the presented study. It is nevertheless interesting to observe that the generic rules to extract activity primitives and the duration analysis confirm clear trends, either positive or negative. The implementation of linear regression models for trend exploration was motivated by the limited amount of observations available.

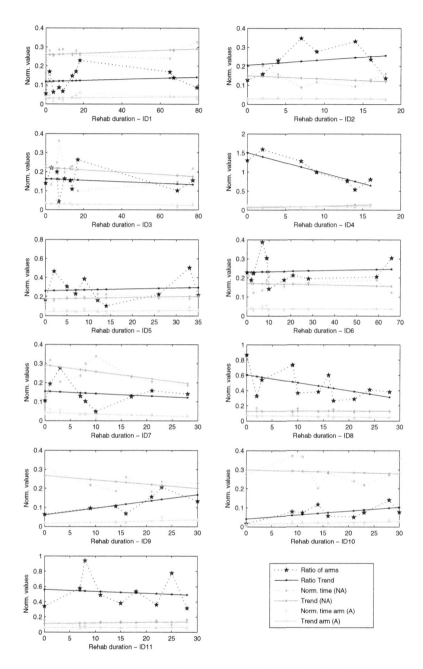

Fig. 4. Arm motion duration of the affected (A) and non-affected arm (NA) of each patient. In addition, a ratio of the arm motion duration and trends are plotted against the rehabilitation stay at day-care centre. The used marker indicate recording days. The vertical axis represent the normalised arm motion duration. Normalisation was done again by total daily recording duration.

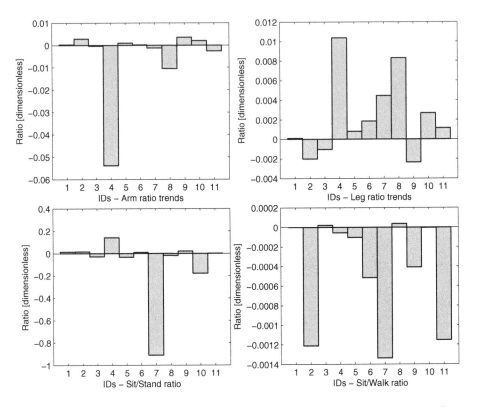

Fig. 5. Slope coefficients of the activity primitive duration ratios. The bar charts illustrate trends of each patient. Wide variations can be observed between patients and considered activity primitives. For the arm ratio trends, 6 out of 11 patients showed an upward trend. For the leg ratio, 8 show an upward trend. For sit to stand ratio, 6 patient show an upward trend and for sit to walk ratio, 2 patients show an upward trend. Both patients showing the upward trend in the sit to walk analysis were wheelchair users. For Patient 1 (w'chair user) no walking was indicated by the detection rules.

Although a big dataset including 102 days was recorded, the patient variability is large and prohibitive to pooling patient data.

Context information could add beneficial information to interpret individual behaviour. By extending the inertial sensor set with light, temperature, vital signs, or acoustic sensors, a patient's situation could be better interpreted. Light and temperature sensors provide information about location (e.g. in the house or outside), microphones could indicate leisure behaviour (e.g. watching TV or listening to music), and optical wrist worn sensor could monitor heart rate variability. The fusion of different modalities might also decrease the amount of sensors required to extract relevant context information.

We received positive feedback from the participants of the clinical study in the day-care centre. In informal conversations, patients did not complain regarding the wearing comfort of the sensors. Thus we assume that a similar sensor set-up could be successfully applied in fully unsupervised monitoring too. Our experience in the day-care centre and from conversations with patients suggest that an easy and quickly attachable, waterproofed, and unobtrusive set of sensors are important requirements for long-term, power optimised, recordings.

7   Conclusion

In this work, we explored patient behaviour represented as motion patterns. We modelled motion patterns in activity primitives and analysed trends and variation of the activity primitives among study participants. Our rule based data extraction is beneficial to understand individual patients, thus provide information to evaluate the patients' motion behaviour.

We conclude that our generic rule-based activity primitive extraction from wearable sensor data has the potential to interpret stroke patients' behaviour and recovery trends. Our approach is also applicable for the elderly, thus an alternative to ambient sensors or vision systems used in home environments. Our activity primitive detection rules were implemented to derive basic motion patterns including sit, stand, and walk, thus apply in the same way to fully unsupervised monitoring applications with a low number of wearable sensors.

8   Further Work

In further work we aim to describe patients' behaviour in even more detail by using postures and orientations calculated from IMUs. Orientation and posture information of extremities could permit us a description of range of motions (e.g. to assess reaching tasks) or to estimate angles between extremities (e.g. lower and upper arm). Quantified information are required to compare the affected and non-affected body side, to identify compensation strategies, and could be used to tailor rehabilitation exercises to individual patients. In further research, we furthermore aim to reduce the amount of sensors or integrate them, e.g. in garments, which decreases the burden on wearers.

Acknowledgements. We are thankful to the study participants and the therapists at the Reha Rheinfelden. This work was supported by the EU Marie Curie Network iCareNet, grant number 264738 and the Dutch Technology Foundation STW grant number 12184.

References

1. Bourbonnais, D., Noven, S.V.: Weakness in patients with hemiparesis. Am. J. Occup. Ther. **43**(5), 313–319 (1989). http://dx.doi.org/10.5014/ajot.43.5.313
2. Burns, A., Greene, B.R., McGrath, M.J., OShea, T.J., Kuris, B., Ayer, S.M., Stroiescu, F., Cionca, V.: Shimmer ^TM- a wireless sensor platform for noninvasive biomedical research. IEEE Sens. J. **10**(9), 1527–1534 (2010). http://dx.doi.org/10.1109/JSEN.2010.2045498

3. Cirstea, M.C.: Compensatory strategies for reaching in stroke. Brain **123**(5), 940–953 (2000). http://dx.doi.org/10.1093/brain/123.5.940
4. Del Din, S., Patel, S., Cobelli, C., Bonato, P.: Estimating fugl-meyer clinical scores in stroke survivors using wearable sensors. In: 2011 Annual International Conference of the IEEE Engineering in Medicine and Biology Society, August 2011. http://dx.doi.org/10.1109/IEMBS.2011.6091444
5. Di Fabio, R.P., Badke, M.B., Duncan, P.W.: Adapting human postural reflexes following localized cerebrovascular lesion: analysis of bilateral long latency responses. Brain Res. **363**(2), 257–264 (1986)
6. Fugl-Meyer, A.R., Jääskö, L., Leyman, I., Olsson, S., Steglind, S.: The post-stroke hemiplegic patient. 1. a method for evaluation of physical performance. Scand. J. Rehabil. Med. **7**(1), 13–31 (1974). http://www.neurophys.gu.se/digitalAssets/1328/1328802_the_post-stroke-hemiplegic_patient.pdf
7. Gietzelt, M., Wolf, K., Kohlmann, M., Marschollek, M., Haux, R., et al.: Measurement of accelerometry-based gait parameters in people with and without dementia in the field. Meth. Inf. Med. **52**(4), 319–325 (2013)
8. Hine, N., Judson, A., Ashraf, S.N., Arnott, J., Sixsmith, A., Brown, S., Garner, P.: Modelling the behaviour of elderly people as a means of monitoring well being. In: Ardissono, L., Brna, P., Mitrović, A. (eds.) UM 2005. LNCS (LNAI), vol. 3538, pp. 241–250. Springer, Heidelberg (2005). http://dx.doi.org/10.1007/11527886_32
9. Iosa, M., Fusco, A., Morone, G., Pratesi, L., Coiro, P., Venturiero, V., De Angelis, D., Bragoni, M., Paolucci, S.: Assessment of upper-body dynamic stability during walking in patients with subacute stroke. J. Rehabil. Res. Dev. **49**(3), 439–450 (2012)
10. Knorr, B., Hughes, R., Sherrill, D., Stein, J., Akay, M., Bonato, P.: Quantitative measures of functional upper limb movement in persons after stroke. In: Conference Proceedings of the 2nd International IEEE EMBS Conference on Neural Engineering (2005). http://dx.doi.org/10.1109/CNE.2005.1419604
11. Murphy, T.H., Corbett, D.: Plasticity during stroke recovery: from synapse to behaviour. Nat. Rev. Neurosci. **10**(12), 861–872 (2009). http://www.nature.com/nrn/journal/v10/n12/pdf/nrn2735.pdf
12. Parnandi, Wade, E., Mataric, M.: Motor function assessment using wearable inertial sensors. In: 2010 Annual International Conference of the IEEE on Engineering in Medicine and Biology Society (EMBC), pp. 86–89 (2010). http://ieeexplore.ieee.org/stamp/stamp.jsp?arnumber=5626156
13. Patel, S., Hughes, R., Hester, T., Stein, J., Akay, M., Dy, J., Bonato, P.: A novel approach to monitor rehabilitation outcomes in stroke survivors using wearable technology. Proc. IEEE **98**(3), 450–461 (2010). http://dx.doi.org/10.1109/JPROC.2009.2038727
14. Rashidi, P., Cook, D.J., Holder, L.B., Schmitter-Edgecombe, M.: Discovering activities to recognize and track in a smart environment. IEEE Trans. Knowl. Data Eng. **23**(4), 527–539 (2011). http://dx.doi.org/10.1109/TKDE.2010.148
15. Robben, S., Pol, M., Kröse, B.: Longitudinal ambient sensor monitoring for functional health assessments: a case study. In: Proceedings of the 2014 ACM International Joint Conference on Pervasive and Ubiquitous Computing: Adjunct Publication, UbiComp 2014 Adjunct, pp. 1209–1216. ACM, New York (2014). http://doi.acm.org/10.1145/2638728.2638812
16. Salah, A.A., Morros, R., Luque, J., Segura, C., Hernando, J., Ambekar, O., Schouten, B., Pauwels, E.: Multimodal identification and localization of users in a smart environment. J. Multimodal User Interfaces **2**(2), 75–91 (2008). http://dx.doi.org/10.1007/s12193-008-0008-y

17. Seiderer, A., Hammer, S., Andre, E., Mayr, M., Rist, T.: Exploring digital image frames for lifestyle intervention to improve well-being of older adults. In: Proceedings of the 5th International Conference on Digital Health 2015 - DH 15 (2015). http://dx.doi.org/10.1145/2750511.2750514

18. Seiter, J., Derungs, A., Schuster-Amft, C., Amft, O., Troester, G.: Daily life activity routine discovery in hemiparetic rehabilitation patients using topic models. Meth. Inf. Med. **54**(2), 248–255 (2015). http://dx.doi.org/10.3414/ME14-01-0082

19. Spina, G., Roberts, F., Weppner, J., Lukowicz, P., Amft, O.: Crntc+: a smartphone-based sensor processing framework for prototyping personal healthcare applications. In: 2013 7th International Conference on Pervasive Computing Technologies for Healthcare (PervasiveHealth), pp. 252–255, May 2013

20. Suryadevara, N., Mukhopadhyay, S.C., Wang, R., Rayudu, R.: Forecasting the behavior of an elderly using wireless sensors data in a smart home. Eng. Appl. Artif. Intell. **26**(10), 2641–2652 (2013)

21. Tabar, A.M., Keshavarz, A., Aghajan, H.: Smart home care network using sensor fusion and distributed vision-based reasoning. In: Proceedings of the 4th ACM international workshop on Video surveillance and sensor networks - VSSN 06 (2006). http://dx.doi.org/10.1145/1178782.1178804

22. Wolf, S.L., Catlin, P.A., Ellis, M., Archer, A.L., Morgan, B., Piacentino, A.: Assessing wolf motor function test as outcome measure for research in patients after stroke. Stroke **32**(7), 1635–1639 (2001)

Identification of Basic Behavioral Activities by Heterogeneous Sensors of In-Home Monitoring System

Vasily Moshnyaga$^{(\boxtimes)}$, Tanaka Osamu, Toshin Ryu,
and Koji Hashimoto

Department of Electronics Engineering and Computer Science,
Fukuoka University, 8-19-1 Nanakuma, Jonan-ku, Fukuoka 814-0180, Japan
vasily@fukuoka-u.ac.jp

Abstract. Caregivers of people with cognitive impairment need assistive technologies capable of reducing stress of constant monitoring of patient. In this paper we discuss information technologies employed for sensing and identification of basic behavioral activities of a patient in a low-cost caregiver assisting system. By analyzing readings from heterogeneous sensors, the system automatically detects the activities, assesses risks which they may have for the patient's health, evaluates emergency of assistance and alerts the caregiver in a case of emergency. We present algorithms for activity identification, emergency computation and show results of empirical evaluation in a prototype in-home caregiver assisting system. As experiments revealed, the system has identification rate for basic activities higher than 94 %.

1 Introduction

Dementia is a syndrome which deteriorates memory, thinking, behavior, language and the ability to perform everyday activities. Nowadays, over 4.6 Million people (15 % of population over 65) are suffering from dementia in Japan and the number is predicted to reach 7.3 M in 2025 [1].

Caring for a person having dementia is very difficult. The work requires constant (24/7) monitoring as person with cognitive and perceptual deficits can make wrong judgment or be lost if left alone. It takes time, disrupts sleep, putting enormous stress on caregivers, who frequently are relatives of the sick person, live in same home or flat and do the caregiving voluntarily. Even if family caregivers live close to the carried person, they have their jobs, own families, and obviously cannot supervise around the clock.

Due to overwhelming stress, anxiety, irritability and a tall the task puts on caregiver's health and job [2], almost 70 % of families suffering from dementia in Japan [3] are forced to opt for nursing homes though neither people with dementia nor their spouses and families want to do so. However, majority of the families cannot afford this option due to the enormously high cost of nursing facilities and long span of the decease. More than 60 % of people with dementia in Japan now stay at home [2], placing a major burden on their relatives. Hiring a personal caregiver is also expensive

© Springer International Publishing Switzerland 2015
A.A. Salah et al. (Eds.): HBU 2015, LNCS 9277, pp. 160–174, 2015.
DOI: 10.1007/978-3-319-24195-1_12

and going to be much harder with the fast aging of population. Therefore, many families do not have any way but suffer. Clearly, new information and communication technologies, capable of reducing the burden and strain of caregiving at home are increasingly important.

Numerous technologies have been developed to assist people with dementia (PD). The technologies can be active, enforcing a PD to wear a sensor, to pull a cord, or to push an alarm, or be passive, i.e. embedded into environment to detect potential problems [4]. Examples range from active technologies that directly interact with the user to support daily living activities such as wheelchairs and large-button cellphones, to systems, such as computer controlled "smart homes" that provide support for persons with cognitive impairment. Majority of existing systems target internet-based reminiscent therapy for seniors and telecommunication between the patient and the physician [5]. The most advanced systems support remote collection of patient data, whether physiological or emotional, send alerts to patients on changes in health status, medication, reminders, upcoming appointments, or motivational statements, sends alerts to caregivers and providers on changes in health status and/or warning signs [6]. Some systems can help PD at work or at home by memorizing and delivering necessary data [7, 8]. The others aim to assist old people at group homes and hospitals [9–11]. A good survey of assistive technologies and systems can be found in [12].

Several ICT systems [13–19] have been proposed to assist family caregivers at home. They can detect whether the PD is up and moving around the home; receive phone/text/email alerts if medications are missed; receive alerts if the person fell down or left the premises; chat "face-to-face" with the person via live video calls; sending the person an email without the need of computer; and creating a socialization and networking environment for the patient. However, these systems either cost up to several thousand dollars or require the PD to wear devices or enforce the caregiver stay in close proximity of the PD, limiting his or her functionality.

In our work, we developed a new intelligent system for assisting family caregivers. Unlike existing solutions, our system is made from conventional off-the-shelf-components; inexpensive, yet effective. The system provides unobtrusive, around-the-clock, automatic monitoring of PD, assessing possible health risks (e.g. fall-down, exit from home, immobility, etc.), which may exist to the PD's health in the current situation, alerting the caregiver attention is necessary, enabling the caregiver to watch and talk with the PD, as well as access the monitoring data in real-time via smartphone or PC. In our prior work [19] we discussed system organization, sensing network and user interface. This work focuses on issues related to detection and recognition of basic PD's activities by the heterogeneous sensors, employed by the system, assessing risks which the activities may have for the PD's health, evaluating emergency of assistance and alerting the caregiver in a case of emergency.

The paper is organized as follows. In the next section we briefly outline system organization and sensing technologies employed for unobtrusive patient monitoring at home. Section 3 describes the task of PD monitoring and algorithm employed for assessing the PD's behavior and risks, which may occur to his/her health. Section 4 shows experimental results. Section 5 presents conclusion and outlines work for the future.

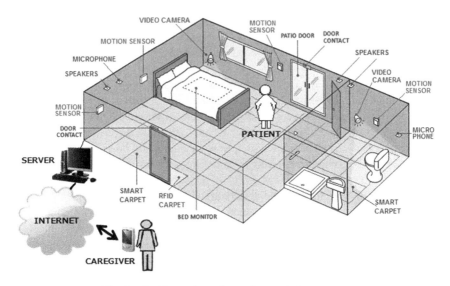

Fig. 1. An illustration of caregiver assisting system.

2   The System

2.1   An Overview

The proposed caregiver assisting system is dedicated to:

1. Identify and monitor the person's movement.
2. Determine the current status of the dementia person (e.g. lying in bed/sofa/floor, sitting on the chair/sofa/bed/floor, walking, exiting her room, vising toilet, bath, corridor, attempting to open home doors, etc.);
3. Assess risks that a cognitively impaired person may have in the current situation;
4. Alert the caregiver in emergency for assistance in form of customizable alarm, text, and voice;
5. Record the patient's movement, status, assessed risks, generated alarms, as well as data introduced by the caregiver (e.g. schedule of medical treatment, etc.)
6. Display the results of patient's monitoring on caregiver's device (phone or PC)
7. Deliver a real-time view of the patient' location as well as audio communication with the patient.
8. Provide graphic interface to display history of patient's movement, status, frequency of visiting facilities and frequency of alertness.

The system performs automatically functions 1–5, while functions 6–8 are done on the caregiver's demands. Structurally, it consists of a network of heterogeneous sensors, microphones and speakers placed in the flat of dementia person and a server, implemented in software on ordinary personal computer, as shown in Fig. 1.

The sensor network includes Smart Carpet (SC), Posture Sensor, Bed Sensor (BS), Door Sensors (DS), Motion Sensors (MS), and video cameras (or video sensors) equipped with speakers and microphones. The data from the sensors are wirelessly sent to the server that fuses the data and applies artificial intelligence to assess position of the person and need for assistance and generate alerts to caregiver. The results of monitoring and assessment are stored in data base and can be viewed online from the caregiver's personal device or PC. The caregiver can also watch the monitored person in real time and communicate with him or her if necessary. The system frees the caregiver from the need to be at home and monitor the patient all the time. It provides the caregiver with ambient intelligence, which enhances the caregiver's monitoring ability, memory and mobility.

Below we discuss the system components in more detail.

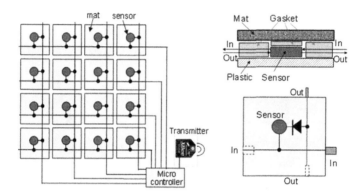

Fig. 2. Organization of the smart carpet having 4 × 4 mats (left); cross-sectional view of a mat (right-top); mat wiring (right-bottom).

2.2 Sensing Technologies

Smart Carpet. The smart carpet (SC) consists of an array of mats, each having a pressure sensor FSR406 [20] placed under an expanse of carpeting. Figure 2 shows the SC organization on example of 4 × 4 mats (left image), cross-sectional view of a mat (right-top) and the mat electronics (right-bottom). As one can see, the mat electronics is very simple. It has only one small sensor and one diode. If no pressure is put over the mat, the sensor idles. Otherwise, the sensor outputs a signal to horizontal and vertical lines. The coordinates of the active mats are detected by the microcontroller and sent wirelessly (via XBee transmitter) to the server. Because each mat has a fixed position in the carpet, the location of a person over the SC is easily defined through the reading of mat sensors. Walking, staying, sitting or lying down over the SC is reflected by a proper signal pattern.

Figure 3 exemplifies the patterns displayed on the server PC and the smartphone, when a person was walking and lying over the SC (of 4 × 7 mats, 40 cm x 40 cm in size each). The mats that sensed the pressure are shown in red. The tests [21] revealed that the SC detects person's motion and fall accurately. The pressure sensors successfully detect gait characteristics and are not perceptible to the people as they walked across

Fig. 3. The smart-carpet test snapshots: walking (right image), fall down (left image).

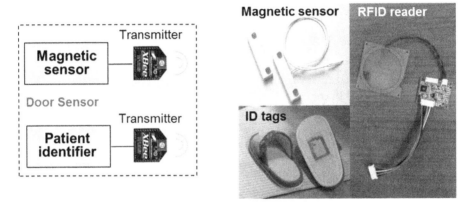

Fig. 4. An illustration of door sensor and its implementation components.

the SC. Similarly to the mats, the pressure sensors can be embedded in chairs, sofas, etc. to determine the patient's position and trace his/her activity. The total cost of a single mat is around US8$.

Door Sensor. Door sensors (DS) are employed to alert a caregiver when a monitored person exits his room and/or opens an entrance door. Unlike existing DS that just sense the door opening and closing, our sensor detects who opens/closes the door and alerts the caregiver when it is done by person with cognitive impairment (PCI). The device combines a magnetic sensor with a radio-frequency identifier of the patient, as shown in Fig. 4 (a). To identify the PD, we embed a RFID passive tag in his/her slippers, as shown in Fig. 4 (b) bottom-left, and place antenna of active RF-reader (Fig. 4 (b), right image) under the carpet mat in front of a door, similarly as in [22]. However, unlike [22], our RFID readers are wireless. Both the magnetic sensor and the RF-reader are connected to the Xbee transmitters, which signal the server whether the door is open or close and whether the person at the door is the PD or not, respectively. Based on this pair of signals, the server (see Fig. 4) assesses if the door is opened by the PD. The tests confirmed that both tag and the RFID antenna are not perceptible as they walked. Also, using slippers as RFID-tag is an acceptable solution, since elderly people usually wear slippers at home all the time. The passive RFID tags do not require charging batteries minimizing the maintenance tasks. The overall cost of the sensor is US30$.

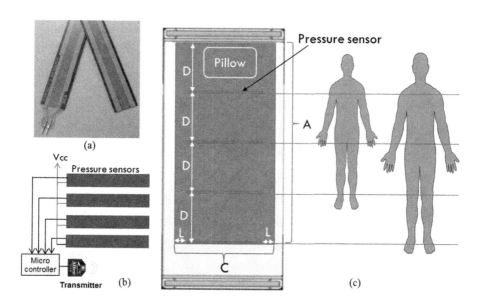

Fig. 5. Bed sensor design: (a) A photo of FSR408, (b) bed sensor circuit; positioning of the pressure sensors over the bed.

Bed Sensor. The bed sensor (BS) detects the presence of a person in bed. The sensor utilizes for 10 mm × 622 mm pressure sensing strips FSR 408 (Fig. 5a) each of each connected to a microcontroller and a power source, as shown in Fig. 5 (b). The sensors are positioned at distance D from each other and fixed over a pad of 160 × 80 cm2 in size, as shown in Fig. 5 (c). The pad (shown by the dark pattern in the figure) is placed over the mattress and under the sheet. When a person sits or lies on the bed, he or she presses the sensor strips and thus forcing them to generate signals to the microcontroller. Because each sensing strip has a fixed position at the pad, the location of a PD over the BS is easily defined through the reading of the pressure sensors. As our tests revealed, to distinguish correctly the in-bed event from the out-of-bed event for patients of different height (see Fig. 5c) and shape, the strips have to be placed at distance D = 40 cm. The patient is considered in bed if more than 2 pressure sensors are activated. If none of the sensing strips is active, the patient is assumed to be out of bed. The total cost of BS is US70$ including the 8bit ATMEGA 328 microcontroller.

Posture Sensor. The posture sensor (PS) is dedicated for areas (e.g. toilet, bathroom, hallways, etc.) where the smart carpet cannot be allocated. The PS detects the person's fall, or a situation when a monitored person cannot stand up or is motionless longer then a pre-defined time. The design consists of two motion sensors (S1, S2) placed one over another on a distance (D) in between and connected via microcontroller to wireless XBee transmitter, as shown in Fig. 6 (a). Each sensor is implemented by pyro-electric infrared motion sensing module SE-10 PIR, capable of detecting motion up to 5 m (Fig. 6b). The sensors have to be positioned to distinguish a standing posture from a posture of a sitting person, or a person lying on the floor. Figure 6 (c) illustrates the posture detection algorithm. Namely, when both sensors sense motion, the standing posture is detected. When sensor S2 reports motion but S1 does not, the sitting or lying posture is detected. When both sensors idle not sensing motion, no activity is detected.

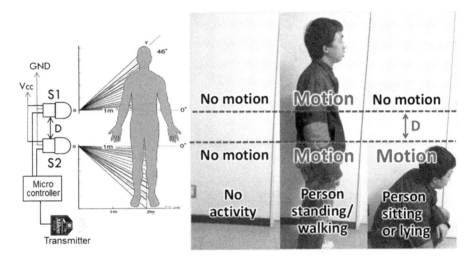

Fig. 6. Illustration of (a) the posture sensor and (b) human activity detection.

Empirically we found that placing the sensor S2 at the height of 40 cm from the floor and sensor S1 at the 24 cm distance (D) from S2 provides good differentiation of postures for a person 170 cm tall. The tests also reveal that the best results (100 % of correct detection of staying and sitting postures) are at up to 140 cm distance from the sensors, though each sensor is able to sense the person up to 2 m distance. The total cost of the PS consisting of two sensors, the Arduino Uno microcontroller, XBee transmitter, 2 resistances and breadboard is less than US50$.

Other Sensors. In addition to abovementioned sensing technologies, we use simple motion sensors installed over the bed, rooms, hallways, etc. to detect patient motion. Also in order to provide visual and audio communication with the patient in a case of emergency, network-based video cameras (such as AXIS M1033-W) equipped with speakers and microphones are used. We assume at least one video camera (with embedded microphone and speakers) is installed in each room of the home.

3 Human Activity Assessment

The human activity analysis and risk assessment is performed by the system server based on information received from the sensors. If the results indicate the risk to the PD health, the system alerts the caregiver by sending him or her messages via the internet. We use two types of messages to caregiver: alert and alarm. An alarm requires immediate action from caregiver and is accompanied by an audio signal. Alert is information only. The caregiver can change type of message depending on the health condition of the monitored person, the time (day or night), etc. For example, individuals with cognitive impairment, who are frail or unsteady, require rapid response from a caregiver as they exit the bed. Consequently, the out of bed activity of such a person may generate an alarm. From the other hand, caregivers of a more physically stable individual do not want notification of Out of bed activity at nighttime until this individual had actually left the bedroom areas. So in this case, the Out of bed activity may be indicated by alert.

Furthermore, we categorize the PD's activities by emergency for assistance they demand from a caregiver. For people with mild dementia, the following levels of emergency are used:

- **Low.** The person is stable and in familiar environment. No assistance is required.
- **Medium.** The person is stable but in unfamiliar condition. There is a risk that he or she will make a judgmental error if left unsupervised. Attention is needed. The caregiver is alerted by proper information.
- **High.** A rapid help is required. The person might be unstable or have difficulty to stand or walk. The caregiver is alarmed.
- **Urgent.** The person cannot stand or walk and needs an immediate assistance due to a high risk to his/her health. The alarm has the highest level.

Table 1. Recognizable Events and Emergency for Assistance

No	Activity	Sensors/Timers	Emergency
1	In bed	BS, MS(bed), T1	Low to high[a]
2	Out of bed	BS, SC	Low/medium
3	Walking/stand/sitting	SC, PS	Low
4	Room exit	DS(room), MS(room)	Medium
5	In bathroom	DS(bath), MS(bath)	Medium
6	In bathroom too long	DS(bath), MS(bath), T2	Medium
7	Floor fall (Room)	SC, T0, T3	High/urgent
8	Floor fall (Bathroom)	PS,T0, T3	High/urgent
9	Entrance door	DS(entrance)	High
10	Exit from home	DS(entrance)	Urgent
11	No motion	No activity from MS, T4	Urgent

[a]The level is changed as the programmable timer passes a pre-defined threshold value.

Legend: BS: bed sensor, SC: smart carpet, PS: posture sensor, MS: motion sensor, DS: door sensor

Table 1 lists the PD's activities (or events), which our system can recognize, the sensors employed in assessing the events and the level of emergency associated with each event. The events are defined as follows:

In Bed. This event occurs when the monitored person is in bed. It is recognized by active signals from BS and the motion sensor (MS), monitoring the bed, inactivity of the smart carpet. Usually, the event has low emergency level. However, when the patient has been 'in bed' motionlessly longer than the pre-defined time limit T1, the emergency level is elevated to medium or even 'high'.

Out Of Bed. It is detected by inactive BS signals and active signals from the SC. While this event usually has low emergency, it may have elevated to medium level when the patient is required to stay in bed.

Walking/staying/sitting. These activities are detected either by SC (in PD's room or hallway) when less than four mats are active simultaneously or by PS (in toilet, bathroom). The emergency level of the activities is low.

Room Exit. This activity is detected when the active signals generated by DS in the patient's room are followed by inactivity of the motion sensors inside that room.

In Bathroom. When an active signal from the door sensor of the bathroom is followed by active signal from the motion sensor within the bathroom.

In Bathroom Too Long. When the system detects that patient is inside the bathroom, it starts timer T2. If the timer goes OFF, a "Bathroom Occupied Too Long" event is detected. An input from the bathroom door contact resets the timer.

Floor Fall. In the PD's room or places in which SC can be allocated, this event is detected when more than 4 mats of the SC become active and the pattern change is abrupt i.e. the duration of the change is less than T0. In bathroom or toilet, the event is detected by the PS. If a PD fails to get up within a pre-defined time interval (T3), the emergency level becomes 'Urgent'.

Entrance Door. This situation occurs when the monitored person gets close to the entrance door and is detected by the entrance door sensor. Any attempt to open the entrance door by a person with cognitive impairment is alarming.

Exit From Home. The system identifies this event based on the exit door sensor, when the monitored person actually opens the entrance door. It has the 'Urgent' emergency level.

No Activity. When monitored area is known to be occupied but there has been no motion for the given time (T4).

Figure 7 shows the flowchart of the activities assessment algorithm. Here, parentheses determine location of the corresponding door sensor: patient's room, bathroom or home entrance; T1 ~ T3 are programmable timers. The initial values of T1 ~ T3 as well as emergency levels, associated with activities, can be changed by the caregiver based on the PD's condition. With new message received, the activity assessment module determines its source, assesses the PD's activity, and generates a corresponding alert or alarm to caregiver. After logging the activity in data base, it re-assesses its criticality in a timing loop or waits for a new message from sensors. For example, 'in-bed' event usually has low emergency level. However, when the patient has been 'in bed' motionlessly longer than the time limit T1, the emergency level is elevated to

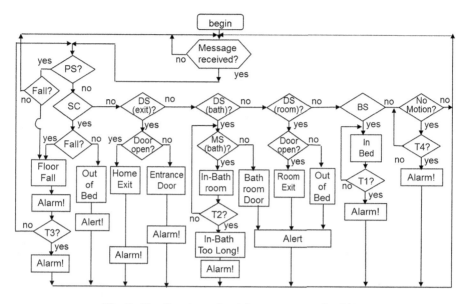

Fig. 7. The flowchart of activity assessment algorithm.

alarm. Any reading from the MS or SC resets the timer. Similarly, when the system detects that the PD is inside the bathroom, it starts timer T2. If the timer goes off, a 'Bathroom Occupied Too Long' event is detected. An input from the bathroom door sensor resets the timer T2.

4   Implementation and Evaluation

We built a prototype caregiver assisting system using a Toshiba PC (2 GHz Intel Core Duo CPU, 2 GB RAM) as server and 2012 Asus Nexus 7 as mobile (caregiver's) device. The mobile device has Android™ 4.3 OS, Tegra3 T30L 1.3 GHz CPU, 1 GB RAM, 7-inch display. The server software, the client software and the user interface were developed in Java using Java-script interpreter. The internet based communication was implemented through the Internet Socket API (ws2_32.lib), WiFi Local Area Network and TCP/IP transport protocol. To support the OS-based control of the communication, a dedicated programming interface was also created. The sensor-server communication was implemented based on Xbee Wifi communication protocol using the I2C master-slave based bus interface.

The prototype system has three operation modes, Setting, Monitoring, and Review, which are activated through simple selections from the touch panel. In the Setting mode, the caregiver sets parameters for timers, assigns emergency levels for PD activities, selects camera (if several) for visual monitoring, sets reminders for medication, services, consultations, etc. The "Monitoring" mode provides monitoring of the PD in his room or flat, textual information about alerts, reminders and the real-time visual and audio communication with the PD. In the "Review" mode, the user can view the previous PD activities for the specified time interval (hour, day, month, and year) in the forms of graphic or row data (time, place, activity, generated message) or see frequency or duration of selected activities (e.g. leaving the room, approaching the entrance door, visiting toilet, etc.) over the given period of time (day, month, year).

Figure 8 shows screenshots of PC and smartphone in the Monitoring mode. The window at the left of PC's screen is the real-time visual of the event. The central window displays statistics of the monitored activities. The window at the right shows the flat's floor-plan with location of the monitored person. The text over the window (in yellow) describes the detected activity: in bed (in Japanese).

Fig. 8. A screenshot of the system interface at the PC and smartphone.

To evaluate quality of behavioral activity recognition and real-time monitoring, we performed a number of tests in a mock-up "flat" setting, shown in Fig. 9. Here, SC denotes the smart carpet; MS the motion sensor; DS the door sensor; BS the bed sensor; VC1-VC4 video cameras. Each test involved six participants (faculty and students ages 20 to 60 without health concerns). The participants had different heights and shape. During the experiment, each participant was asked to perform a series of postures, namely sitting/lying down in bed, walking/standing/sitting, lying down at the room floor in a "stretched" position, and a "tucked" position, standing, imitating a fall down, laying at the floor after the fall for a period of time (longer than T3), standing-up, walking to the bathroom-door, opening the door, entering the bathroom, walking, siting at the chair for a period (longer than T2), sitting at the floor, standing, imitating a fall down, standing up, exiting the room, walking to the room door, opening it, entering the

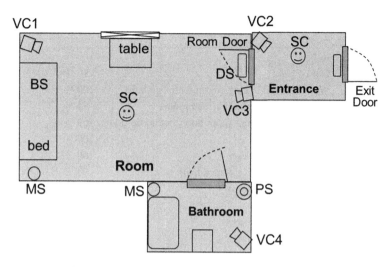

Fig. 9. A floor-plan of the experimental mock-up flat.

entrance hall, sitting/lying on the carpet, standing up, approaching the entrance door, opening the door, exiting the "flat". These scenarios were repeated three times by each subject in a random order. In between the tests, the system was for the "no motion" activities within the "flat".

The tests totaled 90 fall-simulated activities and 486 non-fall–simulated activities. The true positive rate for the fall detection by the smart carpet installed in the room and in the entrance hall was 98 % with the false positive rate of 0.03 %. The true positive rate for the fall detection in the rest-room was 94 %. The posture sensor was able to effectively distinguish a person standing, walking or sitting on a chair, from a person, lying or sitting on a floor. However, we observed, that the quality of detection strongly varies with the person's height. For example, the sensors, which are preset for a tall person, may not correctly detect postures of a small person, and vs. versa. The bed sensor displayed perfect (96 %) accuracy in differentiating the patient in-bed and out-of-bed, respectively. The false positives events here were observed when bags were put over the bed. The door sensor was confirmed to correctly identify the events, related to room exit; entrance door, exit from home. Motion sensors, PS, and timers also were very effective in identifying "no motion" and "Too long" events as well as for changing the assistance emergency.

Table 2 summarizes the detection rates for the basic activities performed in the test. The average activity detection rate was 98 %. The delay of displaying the results on Nexus 7 device was 0.6 s.

Overall, the conducted tests have suggested high efficacy of the proposed system in person monitoring, assessment of person's activity, and alerting the caregiver on emergency. The work is under way to evaluate the proposed system in homes of people with dementia.

Table 2. Activity Recognition Ratios

No	Activity	Accuracy
1	In bed	100 %
2	Out of bed	96 %
3	Walking/stand./sitting (room, entrance hall)	100 %
	Walking/standing/sitting (bathroom)	94 %
4	Room exit (opening room door, bathroom door)	100 %
5	In bathroom	100 %
6	In bathroom too long	100 %
7	Floor fall (Room, entrance hall)	98 %
8	Floor fall (Bathroom)	94 %
9	Entrance door	100 %
10	Exit from flat (Home)	100 %
11	No motion	100 %
Overall:		98 %

5   Conclusion

As the population continues to age and the number of people suffering from dementia grows, the need for information and communication technologies and systems capable of remote monitoring of PD will grow. In this paper, we presented several technologies for sensing and identification of basic behavioral activities of a patient in a home environment by a low-cost caregiver assisting system. As tests revealed, the proposed system provides effective activity monitoring of a single person, assessing the events, evaluating the assistance emergency related to events and alerting the caregiver online in real time. By using the system, the caregiver does not need to supervise the PD all the time as the system does it. At the same time, the caregiver can access the monitored activities from PC or smartphone anytime and communicate with the patient remotely. As the system does not produce alerts or alarms, the caregiver can do any other work, go shopping, or relax. The ambient intelligence of the technologies and the system enhances the caregiver's monitoring ability and mobility.

In the current work we restricted ourselves to identification of basic behavioral activities. Also, we acknowledge that the work is limited to flats or households used by a single person. Though many old persons live alone in Japan, a general case of multiple users of the flat/home must be considered. Extending the study to cover multiple users and identification of many other activities will be performed in the future. Although much work remains to perfect the system, we plan to install it in real residential settings of dementia people to conduct methodologically rigorous trials.

References

1. Number of dementia patients to reach around 7 million in Japan in 2025, The Japan Times, 8 January 2015, Accessed on www.japantimes.co.jp/news/2015/01/08/national/number-dementia-patients-reach-around-7-million-japan-2025/

2. Hara, K.: Dementia Policy in Japan, Accessed on www.igakuken.or.jp/english/e_research/ …/list00.pd (in Japanese)
3. Pollak, C.P., Perlick, D., Alexopoulos, G., Gonzales, A.: Disruptive nighttime behaviors in elder caregiver pairs. Sleep Res. **23**, 305 (1994)
4. Raintz, M.J., Skubic, F.M., Alexander, G., Aud, M.A., et al.: Improving nurse care coordination with technology. Comput. Inform. Nurs. **28**(6), 325–332 (2010)
5. Yasuda, K., Kuwahara, N., Morimoto, K.: Remote reminiscence talking and scheduling prompter for individuals with dementia using video phone. In: Stephanidis, C. (ed.) Universal Access in HCI, Part I, HCII 2009. LNCS, vol. 5614, pp. 429–438. Springer, Heidelberg (2009)
6. Technologies to Help Older Adults Maintain Independence: Advancing Technology Adoption, Center for Technology and Aging, July 2009. Accessed on www.techandaging.org
7. Davenport, T.H.: Thinking for a Living: How to Get Better Performances and Results from Knowledge Workers. Harvard Business School Press, Boston (2005)
8. Mihailidis, A., Barbenel, J.C., Fernie, G.R.: The efficacy of an intelligent othosis to facilitate handwashing by persons with moderate to severe dementia. Neuropsychol. Rehabil. **14**, 135–171 (2004)
9. Nakagawa, K., Sugihara, T., Koshiba, H., Takatsuka, R., Kato, N., Kunifuji, S.: Development of a mimamori-care system for persons with dementia based on the real world-oriented approach. In: Apolloni, B., Howlett, R.J., Jain, L. (eds.) KES 2007, Part II. LNCS (LNAI), vol. 4693, pp. 1261–1268. Springer, Heidelberg (2007)
10. Miskelly, F.: A novel system of electronic tagging in patients with dementia and wandering. Age Ageing **33**, 304–306 (2004)
11. Informedia Caremedia: Automated video and sensor analysis for geriatric care. Accessed on www.informedia.cs.cmu.edu/caremedia/
12. Bharucha, A.J., Anand, V., Forizzi, J., Dew, M.A., Reynolds, C.F., Stevens, S., Wactlar, H.: Intelligent assistive technology applications to dementia care; Current capabilities, limitations and future challenges. Am. J. Geriatric Psychiatry **17**(2), 88–104 (2009)
13. Just Checking, Helping people to stay at home. Accessed on http://www.justchecking.com.au/
14. Williams, K., Arhur, A., Niedens, M., et al.: In-home monitoring support for dementia caregivers: a feasibility study. Clin. Nurs. Res. **22**(2), 139–150 (2013)
15. Intille, S., Larson, K., Tapia, E.M., et al: Using a live-in laboratory for ubiquitous computing research, in Proc. Pervasive06, pp. 359–365 (2006)
16. Klingbeil, L., Wark, T.: A wireless sensor network for real time indoor localization and motion monitoring. In: Proceedings of the 7th International Conference on Information Processing in Sensor Networks, pp. 39–50 (2008)
17. D'Souza, M., Ros, M., Karunanithi, M.: An indoor localisation and motion monitoring system to determine behavioural activity in dementia afflicted patients in aged care. Electron. J. Health Inform. **7**(2), 1–8 (2012)
18. Rowe, M., Lane, S., Phipps, C.: CareWatch: a home monitoring system for use in homes of persons with cognitive impairment. Top. Geriatr. Rehabil. **23**, 3–8 (2007)
19. Moshnyaga, V.G., Tanaka, O., Ryu, T., Hashimoto, K.: An intelligent system for assisting family caregivers of dementia people, IEEE Symposium on Computational Intelligence in Healthcare and e-Health (2014)
20. FSR 406 Data Sheet, FSR 400 Square Force Sensing Resistor, Interlink Electronics. Accessed on www.interlinkelectronics.com

21. Tanaka, O., Ryu, T., Hayashida, A., Moshnyaga, V.G., Hashimoto, K.: A smart carpet design for monitoring people with dementia. In: Selvaraj, H., Zydek, D., Chmaj, G. (eds.) Progress in Systems Engineering. Advances in Intelligent Systems and Computing, pp. 653–659. Springer, Switzerland (2014)
22. Miura, M., Ito, S., Takatsuka, R., Sugihara, T., Kunifuji, S.: An empirical study of an RFID mat sensor system in a group home. J. Netw. 4(2), 133–139 (2009)

Author Index

Printed in the United States
By Bookmasters